AT RISK

Social Justice in Child Welfare
and Other Human Services

In *At Risk*, Karen J. Swift and Marilyn Callahan examine risk and risk assessment in the context of professional practice in child protection, social work, and other human services. They argue that the tools, technologies, and practices used to measure risk to the individual have gone unquestioned and unstudied, and that current methods of risk assessment may be distorting the principles of social justice.

Central to this study is an examination of the everyday experiences of workers and parents engaged in risk assessment processes in Canadian child welfare investigations. Swift and Callahan go beyond theory to highlight how risk evaluations play out in actual interactions with vulnerable people. In pointing out the ways in which standardized risk assessment tools do not take factors such as class, race, gender, and culture into account, *At Risk* raises important questions about the viability of risk management plans that are not tailored to individual situations.

KAREN J. SWIFT is a professor in the School of Social Work at York University.

MARILYN CALLAHAN is professor emeritus in the School of Social Work at the University of Victoria.

KAREN J. SWIFT AND MARILYN CALLAHAN

At Risk

Social Justice in Child Welfare and Other Human Services

UNIVERSITY OF TORONTO PRESS
Toronto   Buffalo   London

© University of Toronto Press Incorporated 2009
Toronto Buffalo London
www.utppublishing.com
Printed in Canada

ISBN 978-0-8020-9331-8 (cloth)
ISBN 978-0-8020-9499-5 (paper)

Printed on acid-free, 100% post-consumer recycled paper with vegetable-based inks.

Library and Archives Canada Cataloguing in Publication

Swift, Karen
At risk : social justice in child welfare and other human services /
Karen J. Swift and Marilyn Callahan.

Includes bibliographical references and index.
ISBN 978-0-8020-9331-8 (bound)   ISBN 978-0-8020-9499-5 (pbk.)

1. Child welfare – Canada – Case studies.   2. Risk assessment – Canada –
Case studies.   3. Social justice – Canada.   4. Human services – Canada.
I. Callahan, Marilyn, 1942–   II. Title

HV715.S88 2009   362.70971   C2009-902851-4

University of Toronto Press acknowledges the financial assistance to its
publishing program of the Canada Council for the Arts and the Ontario Arts
Council.

University of Toronto Press acknowledges the financial support for its
publishing activities of the Government of Canada through the
Book Publishing Industry Development Program (BPIDP).

You know more than you think you know, just as you know less than you want to know.

Oscar Wilde

Contents

Acknowledgments

We acknowledge first of all the generous funding of our research project by the Social Sciences and Humanities Research Council of Canada. Supported by this funding, we were able to contact and interview many people knowledgeable about risk assessment. We were also able to bridge the many miles between the two authors through meetings and innumerable telephone conversations, finding a process for analysing and writing that eventually worked for us.

We are also most thankful to our editors at University of Toronto Press, particularly Virgil Duff whose expertise and support brought the book to fruition. We commend him for helping not only us but many researchers in the social sciences and especially social work to produce published work in Canada. Thanks also to Anne Laughlin for her valuable assistance in the final stages of editing and to Noeline Bridge, who created the index.

Dr Henry Parada, research associate on the project, made major contributions to this research, bringing not only his experience in the practice of child protection but his expertise in institutional ethnography and his clear thinking to bear on our investigations. His wit and willingness were priceless contributions.

Many, many research assistants have worked with us over the years on this project. We are especially grateful to Debra Brown, Yvette Daniel, and May Freidman for their outstanding work.

Our partners, Peter Holland and Brian Wharf, reviewed countless drafts and articles, listened to our quibbles and concerns and provided helpful ongoing advice. For their wisdom and good cheer throughout a project that went on much longer than they (or we) expected, we are immensely grateful.

Finally, but with the greatest of enthusiasm, we thank those mothers, fathers, workers, supervisors, and students whose experiences, life stories, thoughtful commentaries, and critiques have breathed life into the book.

AT RISK

Social Justice in Child Welfare
and Other Human Services

Introduction

Lila

Early in our study, we interviewed Lila, a woman of Metis background who was living in a run-down social housing complex. We sat together in her living room next to a large window that faced into the courtyard of the complex. From this window we could see the various comings and goings of other residents and visitors. Lila told us about her experience with risk assessment. A social worker had come to her door because an anonymous person, presumably a neighbour, reported that she was not caring adequately for her young daughter, an accusation she denied. She mentioned that she is a much better mother than her neighbour, the one she suspects had reported her. Lila told us that the social worker asked her a lot of questions, filled out some kind of forms, but never returned. Although this happened many months ago, Lila is still very upset about the incident. When she sees someone new coming in the gate of the complex, she wonders if 'they are coming for me.'

This vignette could be viewed as just another child welfare investigation, one of the many thousands taking place every year in Canada. As reported in the *Canadian Incidence Study of Reported Child Abuse and Neglect* (Trocmé et al., 2005), a total of 130,594 such investigations took place in 2003, many of which would have resembled this one. On the other hand, this story can be treated in a way that makes visible a considerable amount of information about ruling and the power relations related to risk – the subjects of our book. Since we were fortunate enough to meet and speak with Lila, we can make some of the invisible underpinnings of this story visible to readers.

As we, the co-authors of this book, sat looking out of Lila's window, we were acutely aware that although all three of us were mothers, our paths through life and motherhood had been significantly different from Lila's. As white, middle-class academics, we arrived in Lila's home with what we hoped were good intentions to learn more about risk assessment. Our life histories reflected our good fortune and privilege based on the accidents of birth, as well as the many opportunities offered to and taken up in various ways by each of us. As mothers, we two had never been viewed as potential risks to our children, and we recalled the neighbourhoods in which we had raised our children as being places of rich experience and support. Lila's situation reflected the marginalized location of Metis people in Canada. Her economic position is one shared by many women of her social and cultural background. Since Lila lives in social housing, it is certain that she is poor. Her neighbourhood, utterly unlike the ones we researchers grew up in, is very short on resources for parents and children. It is a site frequently visited by inquisitors searching out instances of failure to follow rules and norms established by the state. These comparisons of researchers and researched provide information about some of the relations and circumstances of class, race, and gender in contemporary Canada. There certainly is no level playing field, and the concept of *risk* as applied to this picture therefore cannot be either neutral or objective. The role of caring for children remains one assigned primarily to mothers; women without resources for this job will generally be the ones investigated for slippage.

The positioning of people in relation not only to material resources but to knowledge and information is similarly unequal. As we realized in speaking with Lila, we knew more about what had happened to her than she did. We knew that the idea of *risk* had instigated and organized the presence of the social worker in Lila's living room and that texts dealing with risk and its assessment governed the tenor and content of the discussion there. We had studied the risk assessment documents and work processes and recognized immediately that the questions posed by the social worker were guided by the specific items on the risk assessment instrument itself – these formed part of the 'ruling relations' coordinating the activities of the worker in relation to Lila . We knew that a complex set of power relations associated with risk assessment allowed the social worker to enter Lila's home, to ask questions, and to fill out forms in ways unrevealed to Lila.

Lila's frustration and concern about the social worker's visit reflect her powerless position in relation to the institutions that affect her life. She has been told little or nothing about the status of her 'case,' and she is in no position to ask, since she fears that asking might trigger more investigation. Lila's description of her defence of her mothering behaviour reflects her particular life circumstances. She compares herself favourably with her imagined accuser, who lives in circumstances similar to her own but whom she views as an enemy rather than a friend and ally who might come to her defence. Lila is alone with her questioner and must fight her battles unaided.

As experienced social workers ourselves, another thing we knew was that Lila's case was very probably closed by now, if it had even been opened in the first place. At the same time, we understood that having been questioned once meant that Lila's risk rating would be higher should she come to the attention of child welfare authorities again. We recognized that she had reason to be apprehensive in such circumstances. She had been reported; she was 'in the files.' While Lila might be seen by some people to be overly suspicious, we saw her sense of being under unending surveillance to be an understandable, if ineffective, measure of self-protection.

Lila is now part of the apparatus of risk that has entered into the work practices of many, perhaps most, human service professions. Lila's story mirrors the themes that we have discovered and followed in our investigations of risk in human service work. In the following pages we explore this relatively new terrain.

Introducing Risk and Risk Assessment

Risk and the management of risk are so much a part of everyday life that we may not even notice that we often think in these terms. A quick scan of any newspaper or television program will reveal frequent references to risks facing individuals or populations and likely suggest measures that people should be taking to avoid those risks. Risks to health, national security, or of being victimized by violence are common examples. But what is a *risk*? Dictionary definitions of risk note associations with threats, uncertainty, hazards, and danger. In fact, risk in everyday talk about it is most closely associated with fear and with the efforts that people make to increase their security and safety.

In the human services, this attempt to ensure safe conditions has evolved into specific strategies for the assessment of risk. Tools known as *risk assessment instruments* have been developed for this purpose for use in a wide range of fields employing helping professionals. A substantial literature exists detailing the benefits of such instruments. In this book, we examine both risk and risk assessment in the human services, and especially as they have been used in the profession of social work and practised in the specialized field of child protection.

The introduction of formal risk assessment was greeted in the 1990s by many Canadian child welfare workers with both joy and relief. At the time, we (the authors) had not given much thought to the idea of risk as an organizing concept in professional life or of the actual work involved in assessing risk. As details of the new risk assessment tools and the labour involved in completing them began to emerge, we increasingly took notice. Eventually, we developed a research project designed to explore the phenomenon of understanding and measuring risk.

In the course of our explorations, we examined a wealth of academic literature on the subject of risk, and we became increasingly aware of the role of risk thinking in everyday life. We deconstructed arguments, talked to many different people, and had lengthy debates and discussions with each other. This book is the culmination of these investigations.

Setting the Stage:
Modernity, Postmodernism, and Neoliberal Politics

Modernity is the name now often given the historical period following from the Enlightenment, a period that resulted in an explosion of new knowledge. This 'scientific' knowledge offered the potential of freedom from myths and blind faith, thus weakening the hold of religion on the general population. The modern era opened up possibilities for the emancipation of ordinary people from miserable living conditions, and it appeared to create the conditions for ongoing progress. Science brought with it promises of the discovery of objective, neutral truths about not only the physical world but the social world as well. Such discoveries, it was thought, could lead to more orderly social relations based on the certainty of the knowledge created by science. These truths would apply to everyone; consequently, high value came to be placed on the 'rational' individual, someone who learns and abides by the 'truths' created through scientific research.

With science, however, has come a downside. The categorizing, objectifying, and homogenizing practices of science in its search for knowledge of essential 'truths' have been challenged and resisted. Critical theorists, including those loosely cast as *postmodern*, have disputed the idea that universal truth actually exists, and they have discarded the notion that scientists can achieve neutral objectivity. Postmodern theorists see the fixed, bounded, and often binary categories of modernist science as misleading at best and often damaging. In their place, diversity and difference are offered. For postmodernists, scientific 'guarantees' of truth are seen to be false promises; uncertainty is viewed as the actual condition of life.

Although both modernity and postmodernity are at one level abstract constructs, their characteristics are reflected in social relations and in the actual practices of daily life. Capitalism, the welfare state, class politics, and much of the theory and practice expertise followed by human service professionals were produced by the social relations of modernity. On the other hand, challenges to truth and authority, attention to the importance of differences among individual human beings and groups, and the fracturing of states, communities, and population groups reflect a postmodern condition. The expertise of scientists and professionals is questioned, and the welfare state – with its 'one size fits all' programs – begins to disintegrate. Class loyalties are diminished. Mass social action against oppression becomes fragmented and begins to dissipate.

Into this scenario has come neoliberalism with its focus on the market as the answer to most human striving. Neoliberalism, according to Leonard (1997), is now a cultural form affecting virtually everyone. Neoliberal politics reflect one kind of resolution of the contradictory modern and postmodern tendencies at large in the world. The success of the neoliberal project depends in significant ways on belief in scientific certainty and the control and order that can be imposed through such convictions. Nevertheless, neoliberalism has benefited from and perhaps is made possible by postmodern challenges to modernist forms of authority, challenges to the welfare state, and challenges to professional expertise. As Leonard says, the global market is the new One: that to which we must all attend. The marketplace, according to neoliberals, will give us progress based on 'scientific rationality and order' (1997: 25). The 'Others,' now fragmented and isolated, cannot form a significant challenge to the politics of the market.

The state, far from retreating as neoliberal politicians like to claim it is doing, has changed its form and focus in support of furthering corporate and market interests. The major apparatuses of domination in the neoliberal period are the state, the world capitalist market, and according to Leonard, mass culture, which too, is made possible by the science of modernity. Mass culture supports the expansion of world markets through the 'manufacture of desire' (1997: 76). Mass culture and mass media perform not only a function of selling commodities, but they also exercise control functions through the shaping of self-image, images of Others, and patterns of consumption. The homogenizing effects of mass culture stand in contradiction to the postmodern impulse towards diversity, but seem to have appeal for people struggling to find some sense of certainty in an uncertain world.

Our book focuses on one element in this picture, the idea of risk, which we investigate as it is embedded in this shifting social context. Risk and its technologies reflect both the science of modernity and the challenges to authority and expertise represented in postmodernism. We examine some of the ways in which the scope and reach of risk discourses have developed in the neoliberal era and especially how the idea of risk is taken up and applied in the everyday world of work. We particularly examine how power relations are embedded in and facilitated by the concept and apparatuses of risk, and we identify some of the purposes they serve and their beneficiaries. We explore how the notion of risk is made concrete through discourse, social practices, and especially through the activities of human service professionals engaged in the assessment and reduction of risk. We also explore apparatuses of domination in relation to risk. An important purpose of this book is to examine how people in everyday life experience these apparatuses of domination, what they internalize, what they challenge, and what emerges from this process.

We make no pretense of neutrality in this project. Our interests relate to practices of domination and subordination and the effects of these practices. Our goal is to make a small contribution to the emancipation of human beings and their potential. Along with Leonard (1997), we also hope to contribute to the reconstruction of those elements of both modernity and postmodernism that have the potential to further the projects of welfare, well-being, and social justice.

The Context: Risk and the Changing Welfare State

When we first began the study, our thoughts were mostly confined to the arena of child welfare, which would be our primary study site. However, we soon became aware that risk plays a growing role in understandings of the welfare state and the social and economic context in which welfare states now operate. Since our research topic involved services funded by and embedded in the welfare state, it clearly was important to try and understand the larger picture within which risk assessment has been developed and deployed. In so doing, we were introduced to literature examining processes of governance and social control in contemporary capitalist societies. Most of the writings that develop the connections between risk and the changing shape of the 'Keynesian' welfare state (see Mulvale, 2001) have been produced in Europe, and they have yet to make a substantial impact on the thinking of welfare policy scholars and researchers in North America. Also, most of this literature owes a debt of some sort to the work of the German social scientist, Ulrich Beck.

Beck's book *The Risk Society* was first published in German in 1986, and an English translation came out in 1992. This book appeared at a time when substantial shifts in the welfare states in both Europe and North America were already well under way. Beck's thesis clearly struck a nerve, especially in Europe, and it is significantly different from other explanations for the changes that have been occurring. In North America, we have been hearing for some years that the shape and cost of social welfare programs in the West requires change. A frequent explanation for this requirement provided by politicians and the media has been that debt levels and budget deficits were too high to be supported by revenues. A related explanation is that entitlements of programs offered through the welfare state far exceed the contributions of citizens. Critiques of this explanation have come primarily from the political left, and they have focused on the damage done to vulnerable and marginalized groups as a result of closing some social programs and reducing the benefits of others. Critics also say that the neoliberal prescription of individual responsibility as the solution to the 'crisis' of the welfare state unfairly punishes the poor and that it will not in any case solve the problems of debt and deficits.

Beck comes at these issues from a different perspective, which we explore in more depth in Chapters 1 and 2. His idea is that welfare states, understood to be those states in the West that formed on the basis of capitalist and industrial production, are waning 'because of [their] very success' (1992: 185). The welfare state, Beck says, has done its job of creating and distributing wealth, at least to the extent that 'genuine material need' is reduced and isolated (1992: 19). The role of the state in this new 'risk' era, according to Beck, must change from the traditional role of the welfare state in redistributing 'goods' to one of limiting and distributing the 'bads' resulting from this form of productivity.

The recent discourse of risk and the welfare state has extended Beck's ideas of power shifts in governing. The publication of *The Foucault Effect* (Burchell et al., 1991) brought attention to the relationship between risk and governing, especially through the work of Robert Castel (1991) on dangerousness and risk. The academic discourse on risk has expanded substantially during the past two decades. Important theorists of risk include among others Anthony Giddens (1990), who is generally seen as similar to Beck in his views; Nikolas Rose (1999, 1996), who expands on Beck's ideas of the role of risk in governing; and Patrick O'Malley (2004, 1999), who explores risk and uncertainty in relation to liberalism and the project of 'freedom.' These theorists draw primarily on Foucault rather than from the tradition of Marx and leftist politics, and they focus on issues of 'governmentality' and 'managerialism' in exploring the meanings and mechanics of risk.

Critics of Beck are numerous, and he himself has responded to and elaborated his arguments (Adam et al., 2000). Not the least of these criticisms is Beck's apparent rejection of class as a feature of the 'risk society' (Rigakos, 2002, 1999), a critique we examine in Chapters 1 and 2. However, part of Beck's legacy will no doubt be the introduction of risk into academic and policy circles as an idea that should be taken into account in analysing the contemporary welfare state, the political context in which it operates, and perhaps declines, and its future.

In this book, both the critiques of neoliberalism and the discourses of risk and risk society are examined. Our primary focus is on Canadian experience. However, our analysis is not by any means confined to what we see in Canada or in the specific site of child protection. What we are seeing across the globe is shrinking welfare states in the West and new welfare structures in developing and formerly communist countries, created as they adjust themselves to capitalism on a global scale, with the attendant consequences of large population sectors losing out in the competition for jobs and goods. Universities in the West are frequent partners in exporting welfare state knowledge and expertise to developing countries. Since risk has become a feature of this knowledge base, we can expect that what we are learning about risk in the West will become 'globalized.'

Helping Professions and the Welfare State

The helping professions we refer to are located generally in non-profit, but sometimes profit-making, organizations, supported in part or wholly by the state. In contemporary times, these organizations may be supported through contract arrangements. Whatever form the funding arrangements take, the helping professions are enmeshed in the dynamics and politics of the welfare state and its 'sub-politics' (Beck, 1992: 186), a term used to describe an unseen inversion of power relations between elected officials and bureaucrats. In this scenario, explored in more depth in Chapter 2, elected officials essentially answer to the unelected staff and technocrats who hold the power of knowledge in their hands, in this case the power to define and make judgments about risk.

Fields in which risk has become directly relevant to the helping professionals include health, mental health (including psychiatry), criminal and juvenile justice, gerontology, women's services, community services, child welfare, addictions, and various kinds of family support services. People working in these arenas may be trained as nurses, doctors, community workers, child development specialists, social workers, psychologists, and other kinds of workers whose central tasks involve helping people to solve problems. Throughout this book, we use the term *workers* synonymously with *professionals*. Although some of these workers do not have professional credentials, we consider them to be human service professionals because they operate in contexts governed by professional guidelines, supervision, and ethics.

We speak primarily from the perspective of social work. However, the analyses of risk and risk practices presented in this book go well beyond social work because the issues and technologies of risk have clearly extended to work in the human services more generally – an arena that Parsloe (1999) calls 'social care.' Two relatively well-known edited volumes (Lupton, 1999; Parsloe, 1999) have explored some of the terrain of risk and the helping professions. However, no major work to date has examined the issues of risk primarily from the perspective of those who do the front-line work of assessing risk and those who are assessed for risk. Our book takes up that perspective.

The case study of child protection presented in Part II maps the introduction and consequences of risk technologies in a specific field of practice. In the first and last parts of this book, however, we will discuss risk as it appears in other fields and professions of practice and, indeed, in the everyday lives of all of us.

Description of the Study

The research project from which this book arose is based on a study of risk assessment in child protection organizations in two Canadian provinces, British Columbia and Ontario. We examined documents related to risk assessment and conducted numerous (forty-six) interviews with managers and planners, social workers, and parents to explore the everyday world of doing the work of assessing risk.

Our interest in this particular study was stimulated by the introduction of complex risk assessment instruments into child protection practice, an initiative that seemed likely to change work practices in significant ways. As we explored the literature on this topic, we became interested in Beck's proposition that risk is now displacing class as an organizing concept for state welfare policy, a shift that would mean social goals of minimizing danger rather than of redistributing wealth on the basis of need. Through this insight we broadened our interest to issues of the welfare state and a study of risk on a more conceptual level. We began to read about risk as a topic of concern in physical and environmental sciences and in the insurance industry, sites in which risk perhaps has the potential to be calculated with some precision and usefulness. We questioned whether it made sense to export this kind of risk thinking into the social sciences and especially into human service practice with individuals, given that the science of human behaviour is far less exact than that of the physical sciences. We wondered whether risk and its technologies of measurement might exacerbate or even create power shifts and social injustices that could produce serious effects for those involved in these practices.

In the course of our study we did, in fact, observe many examples of the way the work of 'helping' has been reorganized under the banner of risk. As two experienced, long-time social work practitioners and academics, we became concerned not only about the way social work in this context is carried out but about ethical contradictions faced by contemporary social workers and other human service professionals asked to assess for risk.

Broadly, this research is informed and shaped by 'critical theory,' which posits that knowledge cannot be objective but rather begins from the interested position of the researcher (Neumann, 1991). Critical theory is premised on a particular view of the nature of reality. From a critical perspective, reality involves a fusion of surface appearances and those more or less hidden realities that are not immediately apparent but nevertheless are shaping and reproducing appearances, an ontology challenging the traditional positivist view that reality is evident, fixed, predictable, inevitable, and universal. Critical theorists, therefore, do not seek universal truths but rather try to understand how appearances are created and sustained. An important focus of critical theory is on the relations of power, and advocates of this approach generally seek knowledge for explicit purposes of social change.

We draw on the methodologies of case study and social policy research to explore our topic. Our primary methodology, however, is institutional ethnography (IE), an approach related to a lengthy tradition of field work in the social sciences (DeVault, 1999) and developed within a framework of critical theory. Ethnography relies on close observation of selected settings and reliable description of what actually happens in those settings. Institutional ethnography involves a further commitment to explicate how a social setting is embedded in and articulated to larger social processes. It is a way of discovering and understanding 'the social as it extends beyond experience' (Smith, 2005: 10). This form of enquiry draws heavily on the work of Dorothy Smith and, as Smith explains, is useful in examining social organization and ruling relations in an era of corporate organization and control. By ruling relations, Smith does not refer to actual people in power nor does she imply necessarily oppressive forms of ruling. Rather, the term *ruling relations* refers to the textually mediated 'complex of relations' that connect us across space and time and organize our everyday lives (2005:10).

From Smith's perspective, the idea of power is quite different from Foucault's notion of power/knowledge (Foucault, 1980), which she describes as ideological. For Smith, power arises in the form of people's actual activities coordinated to 'give the multiplied effects of cooperation' (1990: 70). Power relations are not necessarily the same as ruling relations, although they often overlap in significant ways. We examine this idea of power, especially in Part II, showing how everyday activities of working up cases of child abuse and neglect express and reproduce relations of power that can be oppressive, not only to service users but to the professionals who carry out these institutionally prescribed activities.

An important feature of this methodology is the treatment of abstractions. Marx and Engels argued more than a century and a half ago that science begins with real life, with the actual activities of human beings, and not in the mind. 'Life,' they said, 'is not determined by consciousness.' Rather, 'life determines consciousness' (1947 [1846]). This view of what they considered to be proper science is taken up in institutional ethnography. In this approach, abstractions are viewed as problematics to be studied rather than as already fixed, bounded, and determined entities into which aspects of human life are to be fitted. Thus, a concept is something to be explored as an expression of social relations, meaning the ways in which actual people in specific locations intend and coordinate their activities in the interests of some accomplishment. In our study, we view *risk* as an abstraction from this perspective, showing that although risk is often seen as having obvious meanings of chance and danger, it is actually expressive of various kinds of social relations, and especially risk is expressive of power relations. We also examine risk as it is taken up and accomplished by actors in a specific site, a strategy that allows us to explicate how everyday activities help to realize relations of ruling.

Following major tenets of institutional ethnography, we have entered the terrain of risk assessment in child protection at points of actual activity, examining the engagement of those people who are most involved in accomplishing the work of assessment: child protection workers and the parents who are assessed for risk. In this research these individuals are viewed as 'experts' in navigating the everyday work of producing risk assessments. In addition, we have examined the texts and discourses, including legislation and major policy documents, which guide risk assessment. As researchers, we approach the field of study as knowledgeable observers, having worked in and studied child protection systems and practice over many years. (For a more complete description of our use of institutional ethnography as a guiding methodology for this study, see Appendix A.)

Institutional ethnography is a method of enquiry that helps us understand how the relations of ruling are produced and reproduced. This is accomplished through detailed examination of the ways in which local and particular sites of activity are coordinated through generalizing discourses and ideological forms of thought. Ideology, here, refers to processes and procedures that mask the actual activities and social relations of real people as they are grounded in material conditions (Smith, 1990). Institutional ethnography does not prescribe or necessarily suggest a course of action that should be taken in response to the analysis. Helping professionals, on the other hand, must find courses of action to pursue in their everyday working lives. For this, we draw on ideas of social justice, literature exploring professional challenges in contemporary society (Harlow, 2004), and on our own experience of processes of social change.

In the following chapters, we introduce readers to the sometimes mystifying world of risk and risk assessment and its accompanying technologies. Part I of the book addresses the social context of risk. Part II provides analysis from the research study itself. In the final chapter, we develop the analysis further and make some observations and proposals concerning the future of the helping professions in light of recent developments related to risk and its attendant values and processes. We have been advised by most of the people whom we interviewed and spoke to *not* to recommend the elimination of risk assessment. The reasons given range from the investment of resources already committed to this approach to a fondness for the guidance that risk assessment provides. We take this advice seriously, but propose instead some different uses for the idea and application of risk rationalities from those that are currently in use.

PART I

Part I of this book addresses the social context of risk. Institutional ethnography requires that the 'problematic,' in this case the concept of risk, be placed in its historical, social, economic, and political contexts, since these are the social terrains that play out in people's everyday lives.

We begin with an examination of the concept of risk itself, exploring how it is used in everyday life and work, how it has been theorized, and what kinds of social relations are built into and expressed by it. We also comment on some of the ways in which risk has become relevant to the helping professions.

In the following chapter, we explore in more depth the relationship between risk and the welfare state, showing how risk has become an important concept for human services and for examining the implications of this relationship.

Chapter 3 shows the effects of the restructured welfare state in Canadian social policy and in the way policies are administered. This examination helps to set the stage for Part II of this book, since the state and its programs help to produce the climate and conditions which Canadians must navigate in their efforts to avoid or minimize their 'risks.' Most risk assessments carried out by human service professionals will focus on people, usually mothers, who are poor, often members of racialized minorities, and especially vulnerable in some way. This chapter explores the increasingly difficult social and economic circumstances in Canada that have been produced by the shift away from an ethic based on socially shared risks.

Chapter 4 examines risk and risk work in the human services more generally, exploring the links between risk and managerial forms of governing and the organization of work processes and practices.

1 The Social Relations of Risk

I have been through some terrible things in my life, some of which actually happened.

Mark Twain

Risk invites us to worry, to think ahead, to create detailed pictures in our minds of things that *might* happen, to experience in imagination the gamut of possible outcomes, to 'go through' some terrible things on our way to deciding what to do about a possible given situation. We calculate risks on a regular if informal basis in our everyday lives. The simple acts of driving, eating, walking, and allowing our children to surf the web involve estimations of risks that might be involved. Often, we will have been exposed to information through the media or from 'experts' about the potential risks of these kinds of activities, based on the assumed characteristics of different age groups, genders, races, or income groups.

Scientists, meanwhile, are constantly discovering and announcing new risks to our health and safety. Whole industries devote their efforts to identifying, containing, and compensating risks, including not only insurance companies but a raft of initiatives devoted to safety and health (O'Malley, 2004). Perhaps because so many risks are legitimized through 'scientific research,' the existence of risk and the need to limit risk are ideas that we take for granted and seldom challenge publicly. On the contrary, most of us make some efforts, however grudgingly, to reduce the risks made known to us through the mass media and experts. We gauge our health risks and resolve to change 'risky' habits. We save money if we can to avoid the risk of poverty, and we buy insurance to cover the costs of unforeseen risks like fire damage or natural disasters. Life becomes to some extent a 'planning project' involving self-governance in the interests of managing risks (Beck-Gernsheim, 2000; Webb, 2006). Risk is not only about individual self-management, though. In the social sciences, there are ongoing debates about whether risk is, in fact, the 'mobilizing dynamic' of contemporary societies (Giddens, 1999b). For human service professionals, the concept of risk has many practical applications. Human service professionals try to gauge risks posed to and by those with whom we interact. With increasing frequency, professionals are also asked to engage in processes of formal risk assessment, involving pre-established markers of risk and forms of documentation.

In this chapter, we explore the idea of risk, and we identify some common aspects of how risk is thought about and deployed in contemporary Western societies. We also explore various academic literatures and discourses of risk, along with some critiques of these, and we suggest the relevance of these discourses for human service professionals. An important feature of these explorations is a focus on the social relations of risk, risk thinking, and risk technologies. As Smith points out, 'concepts and categories reflect social relations' (1990: 56). Concepts such as risk are constructed through the activities of identifying, selecting, and organizing aspects of life experience, history, and events, activities that are themselves governed by concepts and categories. Close examination of a concept such as risk can, therefore, reveal considerable information about the kinds of relations that have, over time, come to 'inhabit' the idea and that, in turn, produce its use and meanings. In the conclusion of the chapter, we focus especially on relations of power 'held' in the idea of risk, as these have significant relevance for everyday practice in the human services.

Theorizing Risk

Risk, as defined by Ulrich Beck in his influential book *The Risk Society* is 'a systematic way of dealing with hazards and insecurities induced and introduced by modernization itself' (1992: 21). Risk is often defined simply as 'a probability statement' (Ericson and Doyle, 2004: 4) focused on both the frequency of a possible occurrence and the likely severity of losses should it occur. Risk is widely cited as a concept that makes the 'incalculable, calculable.' For some people, these calculations are real and useful, enabling the 'taming of chance' (Hacking,

1990). For others, calculations of risk are 'quantified expressions of ignorance' (Adams, 2003: 90). All conceptions of risk incorporate past, present, and future. Probabilities of a particular future occurrence are calculated on the basis of what has happened in the past. Action taken in the present, based on these probabilities, can presumably increase the likelihood of a positive outcome in the future. Of course, as Bernstein (1996b: 50) points out, data taken from the past are not entirely trustworthy because salient variables in the future will never be exactly the same as they were in the past.

Although Beck associates risk with the contemporary era, risk itself is certainly not a new idea. Bernstein (1996a, 1996b) traces the beginnings of risk calculation to the Renaissance and the discovery of probability laws, which he claims have underpinned all major improvements in the quality of life since then. Of considerable importance, according to Bernstein, is the challenge that the idea of risk calculation has posed to superstition and faith. Before methods of calculating risk were invented, human beings had simply to accept their life circumstances as fate. For millennia, human beings at best could try to anticipate the future and mitigate the worst circumstances through resort to myth, ritual, and appeals to various higher powers. The discovery of probability theory, according to Bernstein, marked 'the boundary between modern times and the rest of history' (1996b: 47) in its challenge to the faith-and-fate approach to managing life chances.

Contemporary theories of risk assume a secular world. Lupton (1999) has summarized three of the most important sociological theories of risk. One prominent theory is the cultural and anthropological approach to risk epitomized by Mary Douglas (Douglas and Wildavsky, 1982; Douglas, 1992). Her published work on risk, beginning in the 1980s, focuses on the role of risk in creating and maintaining cultural boundaries. She is especially interested in examining the selection of individuals and groups culturally identified as *risky* and the social purposes served through such public association. Risk, according to Douglas, serves as a 'forensic resource' (1990) allowing examination of and providing explanations for things that have 'gone wrong.'

The second theory identified by Lupton is the 'risk society' thesis produced by Beck (1992) and also explored by Giddens (1994). This approach concentrates on theorizing a shift in late modernity from the welfare state society, with its attention to distribution of 'goods,' to a risk society that distributes and attempts to limit the 'bads' that are produced by contemporary pressures for constant economic growth. This growth, according to risk theorists, generates not only global threats to the environment but also to familiar social bonds such as family and social class. Giddens (1999a: 3), for instance, argues that contemporary ideas of risk are associated with two essential transformations, which he refers to as the end of nature and the end of tradition. By 'end of nature' Giddens means that there is now human intervention in nearly all parts of nature, leaving almost no aspect of the natural world pristine. The 'end of tradition' signals that societies in general rely less on fate and more on planning to cope with uncertainty. As we focus on planning for the future, we begin to abandon rituals, habits, and relationships that formerly sustained us. The solidarity of the labour union, for example, may be left behind as we use personal financial gains acquired through collective bargaining to invest in companies that exploit labour.

Both Beck and Giddens also see the era of risk in terms of its threats to and demands on the individual. Beck speaks of 'reflexive modernization.' He imagines that with intensified modernization, and the decline of industrial social organization, the individual not only has fewer traditional supports but also fewer structural constraints, including the constraints of class. This situation forces individuals to become more active in shaping social processes and in planning their own biographies (1992: 87), a process facilitated by education, increasing mobility, and intensified competition. Looked at in the most positive way, people will increasingly think of themselves as having control over the levels of danger to which they expose themselves. Giddens (1994) concurs that in the contemporary era individuals must take a more active role in decision making. He does not mean individualism in the sense of neoliberal views of downloading responsibilities onto individuals, a theme that will be taken up in Chapter 2. Rather Giddens suggests that the politics of left and right have essentially exhausted themselves. Freed from ideological constraints, individuals will attain more autonomy in a risk society, which in turn will require a more active and reflexive stance.

Lupton's third theoretical position is summarized as 'governmentality,' built on the ideas of Foucault. Sociologists such as O'Malley (2004) and Dean (1999) examine contemporary strategies of discipline used for the surveillance and management of both individuals and populations, ideas that echo Foucault's notion of exploring the 'conduct of conduct.' In relation to risk, governmentality authors are interested in the neoliberal focus on individual responsibility and in the 'prudentialism' now required of individuals. This work explores norms and the social processes through which norms are determined and maintained. One way norms are sustained, these theorists suggest, is through professional activity. Designated professionals engage in work processes that slot people identified as deviating from established norms into 'risk' categories. These 'risky' people may then be subjected to retraining and/or to ongoing management and scrutiny.

These three perspectives overlap to some extent. All are concerned with the 'social, cultural and political nature of risk' (Lupton, 1999: 5). Each attends to somewhat different aspects of risk, its meanings and effects, and each sheds some light on the importance of risk for human services. Each also provides some insight into what we might begin to see as the social relations of risk. Risk is theorized here as both produced by and producing practices through which traditions and institutions of the past are challenged by present circumstances, social norms are established, and boundaries are established between cultural groups.

Lupton identifies a substantial gap in all this theorizing, however, which is that virtually no attention has been paid to risk as it plays out in actual experience. We do not see much in the literature about how risk is understood by those who carry out the monitoring and managing of risky populations, we do not see the practical activities associated with risk, and we know little about the experiences of those deemed to be risky. These are topics that we help to address in Part II.

An exception to this analysis is the work of Rigakos on policing (2002). Taking a Marxist perspective, Rigakos examines risk from the perspective of the 'counter-project' of security (Beck, 1992: 49). Rigakos is interested in the commodification of security: how security is sold, how surplus value is extracted, how control of the workforce is maintained, and how security is symbolically produced and reproduced (2001: 13). He maintains that the provision of security is now 'characterized by the selling of commodified social control to risk markets that have been created by fear' (2001: 25). This process, he maintains, is closely related to processes through which citizens are increasingly transformed into consumers. His study examines policing, especially private policing, in its everyday aspect. Front-line security staff and their daily activities are explored and described in considerable detail (see also Rigakos, 1999). From a theoretical perspective, Rigakos critiques much of the governmentality literature for ignoring the 'real life' of risk management and also for concentrating on 'micro-histories' while ignoring the 'durable' and long-term social and economic histories that form the backdrop for risk and its management in contemporary times. Risk management, according to Rigakos, is not a relatively new phenomenon, as some governmentality scholars claim, but rather, risk has been part and parcel of the capitalist project since the seventeenth century. This author, in other words, takes up the 'real life' of risk and its production, showing the mediating effects of the concept of 'security' and making clear the power relations that the idea of risk has the potential to invoke and enforce.

It is not the purpose of this book to prove, disprove, or approve any of these theories. Theorizing about risk from these various perspectives both reflects and constructs some current thinking about risk and is useful to us in exploring the social relations of risk. In the following discussions, several familiar issues and ideas associated with risk are explored, associations that provide us with material for further understanding social and power relations contained in and expressed by this concept.

Risk and Insurance

Giddens describes insurance as 'the basis of security where fate has been ousted by an active engagement with the future' (1999b: 3). Capitalist economies, as Giddens says, thrive on taking risks against the future and would, in fact, be 'unthinkable' without institutionalized means of providing insurance. Insurance comes in many forms, covers a wide variety of potential risks, and is housed in different types of institutions. Ewald suggests that what is common to various forms of insurance is the 'art of combining various elements of economic and social reality according to a set of specific rules' (1991: 197). This 'art' is generally referred to as actuarialism, involving the statistical calculation of risk. The concept of risk in popular thought is perhaps most often associated with insurance and specifically with the large and profitable private insurance industry, in which sophisticated actuarial methods are employed to establish probabilities of risk and the costs of insuring against risks. Ewald, in fact, defines insurance as 'the technology of risk.' Risk itself, he says, has no real meaning except as 'a category of this technology' (1991: 198).

Insurance is essentially the pooling of risk; that is, the calculated risks do not disappear because they are insured, but actual harms can be compensated to some extent by sharing the costs of harm and loss. In the context of insurance, according to Ewald's well-known account, risk is not so much associated with danger as with probabilities of events that can and do occur within a population. Insurance captures the notion of recurring events and spreads the potential for compensation across the whole, thus creating a form of justice. Many losses cannot be fully compensated, but there can be collective recognition of the unfairness of one's suffering a loss that could have happened to 'anyone.' Although risk defines conditions confronting the whole population, risks to individuals can be differentiated by specific probabilities depending on particular characteristics of sub-populations. Insurance schemes identify these specific groups, but make no attempt to predict which individuals within a group will suffer harm. Compensation involves consideration of both the particular and the social characteristics of the situation to arrive at a 'just' response. This aspect of insurance is especially meaningful in the context of the social insurance programs developed in Western welfare states beginning in the late nineteenth century, and it is discussed in detail in Chapter 2.

Ewald goes on to explore the basic rationality of insurance in relation to a rationality of morality (1991: 203), arguing that the insurance concept has the capacity to contain both justice and morality. Rationalities of morality assume negligence, carelessness, or wrongdoing as the fundamental causes of events and imply punishment as an appropriate response. Although constructed as a response to probabilities, insurance does not eliminate the possibility of fault or 'liability,' in the language of insurance and law. Thus, smokers and accident-prone drivers may pay higher premiums to be insured – a form of punishment for behaviours 'chosen' by the individual. This perspective calls on individuals to be future oriented, to contemplate not just the risks on the current horizon but also those that may result from an accumulation of 'misjudgments' or from a lack of foresight.

According to Ewald (1991), then, there is no such thing as objective or real risk. Rather, it is the task of insurers to create a believable 'schema of rationality' through which familiar and ordinary events become associated with calculations of risk. Risk, in this view, does not actually exist but is produced through processes of rearranging and analysing elements of reality with the objective of creating an insurable category. In doing so, however, risk comes to appear objective and real. Actuarial computations produce mathematical probabilities that suggest or even demand action.

Although often not recognized, the historic association between risk and actuarial practice is significant for those practising in the helping professions. The programs that support many of our professional activities and functions are embedded in the welfare state, which itself is an organized system of social insurance against the risks of capitalist forms of production. Also, the technologies and actuarial practices associated with insurance have influenced the development of the sciences of risk and probabilistic thinking (Hacking, 1975) that now permeate human service planning and delivery. These ideas and practices form the basis for the various forms of risk analysis and management of particular social groups examined in Chapter 4. Through such practices, aggregates of people who have no subjective experience of membership in the group are created (Simon, 1988). People generally do not define or identify themselves as members of a risk group, but rather, they are grouped together through statistical procedures. Insurance thinking thus assumes and produces an 'average, sociological individuality' (Ewald, 1991: 203) based on actuarial practices. Further, as Austin has noted, 'insurance companies do not view any insured as a whole person. Rather, every insured is compartmentalized ... an adult, a female, a divorcee, a parent' (1983: 547). Through similar kinds of actuarial computations, many recipients of helping services may now be assigned to one or more aggregates, with or without the knowledge of the individual. Such groupings, as Simon (1988) points out, have little possibility of resistance or political action because their assignment does not represent their own subjective experience or identity and because it is a fractured representation of the self. In fact, people themselves may not even know they have been cast as members of such groups. Part II of this book explores how this occurs in the context of human service delivery and with what effects.

Finally, insurance technologies have demonstrated how risks can be made 'objective' through calculation. What formerly did not exist, even in imagination, suddenly appears as objective reality. What we simply thought of as fantasy, as an imagined future bad experience, is transformed through calculation into a concrete possibility (Ewald, 1991: 200). Whereas we as professionals might previously have *hoped* that bad things would not happen in the future, actuarial forms of risk analysis ask us to *predict* bad outcomes and circumvent them with interventions. Without prediction, people would be perceived as subject to fate and, therefore, less responsible; once we accept that the risk of harm is predictable, we are under some obligation to factor that information into our plans.

Calculations designed to identify 'risky' individuals depart in some particulars from the way insurance rates are usually calculated. Insurance technologies calculate the probability of some specific occurrence within a given population, and they may identify sub-populations at greater risk, but they do not purport to discover which individuals will be affected. The 'science' of risk analysis in the human services very often aims to isolate, identify, and act on a particular individual before any harm is done. In so doing, boundaries are drawn between the assessors of risk and the people who are deemed risky.

Risk and Science

Risk as we understand it now is completely imbricated with science. For Beck, science is part of the apparatus that has created new and unmanageable risks. For others, science is what will save us from frightening global risks like climate change. Both of these perspectives, of course, reflect reality. But these different perspectives remind us that science is not uncontested in either its content or its outcomes.

Science, scientific methods, and knowledge based on science, of course, are central to the character of modernity. The Enlightenment ushered in an era in which it was supposed that truth could, through science, be discovered and known. When we knew the underlying truths of nature, including human nature, we could build a safer, more comfortable world. Increased security and greater control of our lives were at the centre of this happy view. This era, now often referred to as 'modernity,' is characterized by the notion that we are on a trajectory of 'progress,' that things are always getting better. Scientists in this scenario are generally seen to be a breed apart from the rest of us – they are the 'knowers' and the experts. They have access to the mysteries of the universe that we, mere laypeople, could not hope to understand and generally do not dare to challenge.

Science, in this way of thinking, represents objective reality and truth. This perspective, referred to as positivism, remains the dominant idea held by most people of what constitutes 'real science.' It is characterized by adherence to specific methodologies that rely on clear evidence to reveal laws of nature. Once these laws of physics, chemistry, biology, and so on are demonstrated through careful experiments and observations, they can be used to predict outcomes based on relationships among specified variables. Drawing on probability theory, mathematical computations are applied to generalize findings and arrive at satisfactory levels of reliability and validity so that predictions can be relied on. Because of these methodological safeguards, findings cast as 'scientific' have considerable legitimacy, not only among members of the scientific community but among laypeople as well. Although originating in the so-called hard or physical sciences, many social scientists have adopted this approach in their studies of human behaviour.

There are, of course, significant challenges to the belief that we can discover the laws of nature, or even that such immutable laws exist. The 'critical' approach to science challenges the view that reality is readily apparent and that it is fixed, stable, predictable, inevitable, and universal. The general view of critical social science is that *things are not what they seem* (Heap, 1995). A fundamental task of critical science involves showing how appearances are built or put together. Critical theorists try to show how knowledge is used in the exercise of power, with the liberation of people from oppressive conditions as an explicit goal. Social scientists working from these ideas might ask, as Marx did, how ideology arises and how it is maintained in ruling relations (Heap, 1995). Of course, there are wide variations of belief and commitment among scientists following these two paradigms, positivist and critical, but they roughly describe two primary positions taken by scientists engaging in the study of risk.

Statistics, O'Malley (2004) notes, came into use in the first half of the nineteenth century as a feature of governing. Statistical information could be used to know and understand the population and its enduring problems, such as illness and poverty. The study of statistics quickly came to have political implications. It was seen as a 'science [that could] bring a measure of expertise to social questions ... by the certainty of careful empirical observation' (Eghigian, 2000: 43–4, quoted in O'Malley, 2004: 39). This marriage of science and mathematics had positive outcomes leading, for instance, to the realization that social rather than individual interventions could be the most effective way to solve widespread health and other problems. The introduction of clean water and fluoridation of water are examples. However, there are some other, less positive, implications of the use of statistics in the social sciences. Attempting to follow the physical sciences, social science has a tradition of using statistics as a form of control of particular populations, such as the mentally ill, criminals, and even women of reproductive age (O'Malley, 2004; Swift, 1995b). If 'deviant' behaviour could be scientifically predicted, it was reasoned, prevention through the control and monitoring of potentially deviant people would be possible. Further, the use of supposedly neutral and objective scientific methods in these operations seemed to ensure that moral and political influences could be kept to a minimum. Not widely recognized until the mid-twentieth century was the idea that morality and politics were themselves embedded in science (Popper, 1969). Even now, in spite of significant questioning of the supposed neutrality of science, many people have considerable faith in the objectivity of scientific findings.

Giddens argues that this faith is crumbling. Risk society does not necessarily present us with more hazards than in previous eras, but it is a 'highly technological frontier which ... generates a diversity of possible futures' (Giddens 1999a: 3). This presumably means that in an age of risk we will become more acquainted and engaged with scientific reasoning and methods, and also more critical in our judgment, as we attempt to enhance the outcomes of the decisions we make about our own lives. With the intensification of scientific research into almost all areas of life experience, the truth claims of science will come into question, according to Giddens. In daily life, we are constantly exposed to opposing findings and recommendations with apparently equal claims to 'science.' We cannot simply accept the findings and pronouncements of scientists, because they not only disagree regularly with one another but because scientific findings are continually found to be wrong. Science, according to Giddens, is and should be an 'inherently skeptical endeavour' (1999a: 1), subject to constant challenge and change. This scepticism is supported by critical theorists from Marx onward, who challenge the existence of fixed laws that govern human experience. Since reality is constantly changing, they argue, so too, must the knowledge we develop about reality change.

However, the appeal of positivist science, especially as expressed in the language of numbers, is far from dead. In fact, in this era of risk, it probably has been given new life. Human service professions have regularly sought out and applied various kinds of science and technology in order to 'improve' practice and increase professional standing (Swift, 1995c). Generally speaking, the science incorporated into professional practice has been drawn from positivist science, which retains its reputation in this context as reliable and respectable. The medical profession, which remains at the top of the hierarchy of professions, legitimizes positivist science for other professions. The most recent trend in many professions appears to be 'evidence-based' practice, which claims that professional practice must be supported by research evidence and by 'hard' data, numbers and statistical computations rather than by professional theory and knowledge, intuition, or subjective experience. This approach is supported by most funders and policy makers, who maintain the view that numbers are more reliable than words and that sensory evidence trumps the 'hidden realities' (Marx and Engels, 1947 [1846]) that critical science explores. In many professions, as examined in Chapter 4, risk analysis is among the currently favoured topics for positivist science to address and legitimize.

Is Risk Real?

The positivist view of risk is currently dominant in the human services. In concrete form, and contrary to the claim by Douglas and Wildavsky (1982) that risk has little to do with technical computation, calculations of risk increasingly materialize in the form of risk assessment tools and management techniques. These technological devices are often advertised as being derived from scientific methods and are used to determine the activities and decision making of professionals. In the bureaucratic setting, the measurement of risk is often considered unproblematic, based on assumptions that risks are real and that they can be measured and controlled by experts in the interests of safety and security (Fox, 1999).

Tierney (1999) and many others challenge the positivist view, proposing that the study of risk cannot proceed from a view that risk is an 'object' to be identified, analysed, and managed. Rather, an understanding of risk must include the roles of power, institutional interests, and the state in the construction and allocation of risk. A related view (Douglas and Wildavsky, 1982; Casteneda, 2000) is that risk must be viewed from a cultural perspective. That is, risk highlights a society's values related to what is negative and unwanted among the group. This idea picks up on Ewald's (1991) notion that the researcher's task is not to discover objective risks but is to explore why particular institutions shape risk in certain ways and not in others – in other words, to explore the ideological purposes of calculating and objectifying particular risks.

This debate is closely related to another debate about risk, touched on earlier, which is the question of whether or not risks are 'real.' Is risk a 'thing' that actually can be identified, measured, studied, and altered? Or is risk simply a social construction, a questionable artefact of science itself (Douglas, 1992), made up of actuarial computations based on past experience? Some commentators see these positions as a dichotomy – risk is either objective or subjective (Wilkinson, 2001) – while others (Lupton, 1999) recommend viewing perspectives on the reality of risk as a continuum, with theorists themselves sometimes moving from one point on the continuum to another.

Discussions of the reality of risk expose the close association between risk and danger. Ericson and Doyle (2004), for instance, suggest that Beck should have called his book 'Uncertainty Society' because he deals with the uncertain effects of actual dangers rather than with risks. Douglas castigates 'intelligent reviewers' who seem to suggest that risk is a figment of our imagination, a mere construct without basis in actual dangers, which she views as 'only too horribly real' (1992: 29). Castel (1991) argues that calculations of risk have come to replace the concepts of danger and dangerousness in the practice of social administration. Danger itself is a problematic concept, since the proof that danger exists can only be demonstrated convincingly after the fact. The helping professions, of course, regularly struggle with this problem, which is closely tied, as Castel points out, to the concept of prevention. How, professionals ask, can we predict danger before harm occurs? The calculation of risk appears to solve this problem. In this sense, risk does not reflect actual danger but is 'the effect of a combination of abstract *factors* that render more or less probable the occurrence of undesirable modes of behaviour' (1991: 287). In this view, risk is constructed rather than real and serves the purpose of mediating the relation of danger to prevention.

A series of discussions in the United Kingdom and the United States about the reality of risk (Doern and Reed, 2000: 10–11) occurred in the early 1980s. These deliberations were concerned with both 'objective' risk and also the idea of 'perceived' risk, a derivation of the notion that risk is culturally determined. Physical scientists were reportedly much less likely than social scientists to accept the cultural view. Britain's Royal Society tried to bring some closure to the debate, coming down more or less on the subjective side: 'assessments of risk ... necessarily depend upon human judgment' (Royal Society, 1992: 89–90). However, the discussion continues, with both physical and social scientists actively engaged in processes of measuring and predicting risk (Lupton, 1999) and in processes of challenging the reality of risk.

Debates about the reality of risk have very practical implications. Giddens (1999a, 1999b) describes a push and pull in the contemporary politics of risk between fear mongering and covering up. If politicians publicly ignore a risk, claiming it has no basis in reality, and subsequent harm occurs, they will be accused of a cover-up. If politicians deploy substantial resources in actively trying to reduce a risk that is not seen to have any substance, they will be accused of fear mongering, of 'inventing' risks to justify the use of public money or to give themselves unwarranted power. This is where science enters the picture. If 'risks' can either be substantiated or refuted through socially acceptable scientific tests and tools, then actions taken or not taken appear justified. If the sense of science as reliable can be widely maintained, then public questioning of political decisions will likely be reduced and neutralized; in this scenario, risk becomes 'real':

Idea of risk>>>Risk assessment>>>No risks found>>>No liability>>>No action required

Idea of risk>>>Risk assessment>>>'Real' risks established>>>Liability>>> Action>>>Reduced liability

In either case, the question of the reality of risk is apparent. Is there a risk or isn't there? Put more politically, can people be convinced there is or is not a risk?

It seems that, in general, people are convinced that a great many risks do exist. Certainly, a healthy industry involving the assessment of risks of all kinds has sprung up over the past few decades. Entering 'risk assessment' into a Google search produces millions of entries. These cover risk assessments to safeguard business, all manner of environmental threats and dangers, health risks too numerous to mention, and risks posed *by* particular populations such as dangerous offenders as well as risks *to* specific groups such as refugees. Readers may be interested to know there is even a Risk Assessment Centre, sponsored by the Government of Canada, which deals with border issues and interfaces with local, national, and international intelligence agencies. Possibly our current reliance on risk assessment can be explained by our long history in the West of 'robust faith in sciences' (O'Malley, 2004) and by the later connection of science to risk. In any case, 'scientific' risk assessment is a technology that is well entrenched in the practices of practically every sector of organized endeavour. It seems that in our zeal to know the future, we are willing to rely on the past and trust statistics to tell us what we can expect.

Risk, Anxiety, and Fear

How do I protect my child after 9/11?

Ontario mother (Crawford, 2007)

A sense of imminent danger in Western nations has escalated in the new century and is often thought to pervade virtually all areas of everyday life, as implied by this mother. Risk analysts may sometimes try to reduce fear by advertising probability statements, but fear, anxiety, and worry persist anyway, and they often form the basis for action. Perversely, anxiety may even serve the purpose of soothing our minds. Soros (1998), speaking personally, says worrying makes him feel safer, presumably because it provides a sense of doing something about the source of fear. There are, of course, still 'good risks' – those that lead to new experiences and especially those that lead to financial gain. In the business world, 'risk' generally retains positive connotations of the entrepreneurial spirit. However, most people try to avoid and minimize risk in everyday life, motivated by 'risk anxiety' (Giddens, 1991; Beck, 1992). In the helping professions, risk is usually seen as a 'bad.' The tension between positive and negative emotions about risk reflects a prevalent social tension in North America between a desire to move cautiously in the interests of safety and a desire to pursue new and profitable experiences through 'rugged individualism.'

As Wilkinson (2001) notes, many major theorists have commented on anxiety and fear of the future as features of industrialized society. He cites Marx, Weber, and Durkheim, who all allude to anxiety, anomie, and a sense of meaninglessness experienced by people as features of our forms of social organization. In *Civilization and Its Discontents*, Freud (1946) suggested that perhaps all of us become more neurotic and fearful as we 'civilize' ourselves. C. Wright Mills (1959) identified urbanization, economic uncertainties, and the breakdown of intimate relationships as sources of widespread anxiety, poetically described by W.H. Auden in his Pulitzer Prize–winning epic, *The Age of Anxiety* (1948).

Even before 9/11, security had become big business in the West. Private police (Rigakos, 1999, 2001), guard dogs, and alarm services are all offered to help us guard against the risks of everyday life. In the United States, especially, firearms are considered necessary forms of security by many. Some say that security is the fastest growing industry in the world (Bunting, 2004). The media appear to fuel fears that life is a risky business. Lupton's (1999) content analysis of Western news media shows ever-increasing appearance of the word 'risk' in the 1990s, used as a synonym for threat, danger, hazards, and disaster. There are many ways that perceptions of risk can be amplified (Wolfe, 2006; Kasperson and Kasperson, 2006, 1996). Intense mass media coverage of disasters, published reports, political speeches, and the imposition of more security measures, for instance, all lend the impression that there is more to be feared than before. Of course, 9/11 helped to ratchet up levels of fear in almost everyone on the North American continent and in many other places around the world. Terrorists, we are frequently told, could be lurking anywhere. It has become commonplace for politicians to boost their ratings in the polls by promising improved security (Bunting, 2004). According to McNally (2006), fear and anxiety about all-encompassing phenomena like terrorism serve an ideological purpose. The abdication of Western governments from providing protections against market insecurity is successfully covered over by first advertising and then proposing to minimize other threats and risks. Wood (2003) essentially supports this argument, saying that the strategy of American capital is to wage endless war. One component of that strategy is its element of never-ending fear of what might happen next.

Glassner argues that even when the sense of threat is ill-defined, individuals are increasingly expected to know what are the 'right' things to fear (1999: 11). As this expectation becomes entrenched, people are held to a standard of 'calculative rationality' and increasingly expected to mitigate these 'right risks.' Fear and anxiety about the future certainly help to produce public support for the use of risk assessment and risk management measures to be taken. There is virtually no public challenge to airport searches of luggage and pat-downs of passengers, for instance, even though the public has been presented with no actual evidence that these activities reduce our chances of attack. In the United States, phone taps and other efforts to identify terrorist activities have also gone largely unchallenged, even when they appear to violate legal privacy protections. Many intrusive initiatives go unnoticed, as we become used to the 'need' for protection. An example is the U.S. policy called the Automated Targeting System, which calls for a risk assessment to be carried out on all passengers flying to or over the United States. This policy requires collection from private airlines of specific information about individual passengers without their permission or knowledge (U.S. Department of Homeland Security, 2006).

The common sense conclusion we might come to is that consciousness of risks increases our fear and anxiety levels. As fear increases, we tolerate more incursions into our private space in the name of security. Wilkinson challenges and complicates this impression, pointing out that we actually have very little knowledge of how people process and react to media portrayals of risk. He argues that the language and technologies of risk (2001a: 132) are just a few of the many ways to address the tension we feel about the unknown future. From a psychological perspective, LeDoux (1998) explores the question of whether people actually react to possibilities rather than to probabilities. Examining fear pathways in laboratory animals, LeDoux concluded that the first fear response is located in the primitive part of the brain and that shutting down this response takes time and effort. From this, he hypothesizes that we likely tend to focus fear responses on possibilities rather than on probabilities, which would be calculated some time later by higher regions of the brain. The mother who does not know how to protect her child in the 9/11 era likely has no probability data to base her fears on. According to LeDoux's theory, she is reacting instead to possibilities frequently reiterated and amplified in news stories and everyday conversation.

Whether we live in a time of increasing risks is open to question. That we are exposed to a context of proliferating stories and information about potential risks, threats, dangers, and hazards seems clear. This 'culture of fear' seeps into our everyday professional lives in the form of specific fears that we don't know the 'right risks' to look for or that we will inadvertently overlook some recognized risk that we should have seen. Organizations increasingly include the administration and interpretation of risk assessment in their expectations of professional workers. With fear comes the politically charged expectation that we can see risk coming and prevent harm somehow.

Risk, Blame, and Morality

How shall we live?

Weber (1919; and others)

Furedi (2006) has said that we live in a world of blame, of finger pointing, and of finding ways to avoid our own responsibility for what goes
wrong. Malpractice suits, court and legal action, 'special interest'
groups, protestations of corporate and government fault for our own
dilemmas characterize a wide swath of social relations. We expect
authorities not only to take responsibility and accept liability for what
has happened, but also to predict and prevent bad things that *might*
happen. In the industrialized countries we also live in a state of more
or less constant want – not need, but want. We are exposed to a phe-
nomenal amount of material goods that are supposed to make our
lives easier, safer, and happier. Religion and other organized systems
of morality play a decreasing role for many in the West, as we focus on
our material world and its benefits. Modernity, as Webb has said,
brings the possibility of 'moral impoverishment' (2006: 33).

Yet we have not abandoned morality. We retain ideas of good and
bad, right and wrong, acceptable and unacceptable. Some people are
labelled as 'evildoers' and some as 'good guys.' Webb argues that there
is, however, decreasing social agreement concerning acceptable ethics
and moral codes. He asks how a society can maintain a coherent
ethical stance in the face of decreasing social solidarity. There are, in
fact, socially organized systems and practices that help us sort out who
is who, what is better, and what to do with the evildoers. Among these
practices are those related to conceptions and technologies of risk.

Mary Douglas (Douglas and Wildavsky, 1982; Douglas, 1992) is the
best known theorist connecting risk with morality, although numerous
others have taken up this theme as well (e.g., Webb, 2006). She maintains that the risks we choose to focus on are socially selected, based
on the strength and direction of social criticism (Douglas and Wildavsky, 1982: 7). In other words, the risks we select to pursue depend
on the identification of a person or group that it is *socially acceptable to
blame*. When we make these choices, we implicitly invoke a moral
code, and a sense of valuing some things over others. 'Blameworthi-
ness,' according to Douglas and Wildavsky, 'takes over at the point
where the line of normality is drawn' (1982: 35). Thus, when we identify risks and evaluate their effects, we expose social norms and iden-

tify those who are in violation of them. Often these are people at the margins of society, the 'unworthy' poor and others who resist, challenge, or are rejected by 'mainstream' society. We further reinforce those norms through practices that blame someone for their violation of them:

Risks identified>>>> Norms revealed/reinforced>>>> Blame apportioned

New technologies continually produce new norms and produce cultural reassessment of currently acceptable norms. For instance, knowledge of the effects of alcohol on unborn babies has resulted in new norms of how pregnant women should behave. Considerable social condemnation of pregnant women who drink alcohol is not uncommon, and institutional responses have also been devised to discourage this practice:

New technologies >>>New risks identified >>> New/revised norms>>> Blame apportioned

Because risk is an expression of social organization, changing the selection and perceptions of risk requires changing the ways in which we are organized (Douglas and Wildavsky, 1982).

An important difference between scientists who study risk and laypeople who deal with risks in everyday life is that laypeople do not attempt to conceal their moral choices, while experts frequently take cover behind the supposed neutrality of the 'facts' of risk. Laypeople talk about what ought to be, while scientists purport to talk about what *is* (Douglas and Wildavsky, 1982: 73). However, many people writing about risk argue that science itself expresses values and moral codes. The 'science' of risk assessment is a case in point. Professionals in the human services who administer risk assessment tools are generally told that the instruments they are using have some scientific validity. The implication is that they are value free, that the findings from assessments represent 'truth' and can be relied on to predict aspects of the future with some accuracy. From a cultural point of view, however, these professionals are actually reinforcing cultural norms by identifying and blaming 'deviants' from those norms. They do this, of course, in a context of contested morality and ethics and also in an ever-changing context of what is to be considered 'normal.' In Marxist terms, we might say that risk assessment, therefore, helps to accomplish the

processes of reproducing social divisions. Technologies of risk assessment encode norms of acceptable behaviour and experience, and
simultaneously mark out for attention sub-populations related to
class, race, and gender. Populations and individuals identified as
'risky' to the social whole can then be targeted through risk practices
for special management by the state, thus legitimizing and reifying
existing social relations. Described in Chapter 4 are some of the groups
of people currently identified for this kind of management by human
service professionals.

Conclusion

In several ways, risk has been a significant factor in changing social
beliefs and practices, beginning with its challenge to fate and faith. In
its very origins, we can see a set of power relations inscribed in the
idea of risk. The faith-based approach to dealing with the future has
not disappeared with the discovery of risk or for that matter with other
discoveries of the modern era. Many people continue to put their fate
into the hands of a higher power and perhaps appeal through prayer
for divine intervention and guidance. Risk, posed as statements of
probability, suggests we can and perhaps even should, instead, rely on
ourselves to control the future. As a challenge to faith, risk implies
an ongoing power struggle between the notion of a modern, secular
society and one steeped in faith and religion.

As one modernist solution to facing the future through calculations
of risk, insurance technologies provide a basis for the creation of risk
groups and for the fragmenting of individual identities through
processes that establish social groupings not chosen by individuals for
purposes of their own. The very idea of insurance embeds the notion
of liability firmly in the public mind, helping to create social divisions
between those who are 'good risks' and those who are not.

Risk and its attendant technologies mark a shift in the way we think
about our lives and perhaps reduce our capacity to make collective
change. Our increasing preoccupation with security and the proliferation and commodification of security technologies frequently supersede attention to what used to be seen as demonstrated need. Preoccupation with risk brings with it an emphasis on the importance of
planning for the future as opposed to focusing on the present and on
traditional ways of living. However, predictions about the future are
based on the past, so, ironically, risk also produces an intense focus on

selected elements of the past. This insight suggests that attention to risk reduces the potential for social change, as decision makers concentrate on reproducing what has 'worked' in the past rather than on risking untried possibilities. Recognized 'dangers' are repeatedly identified. Past forms of safety and security are reified, and these become the goals for the future.

Also, 'risk society' is now being posed as a shift away from class politics and the welfare state. The current emphasis on risks and liability directs attention away from the redistribution of social 'goods' and towards the allocation of the 'bads' produced and overproduced through capitalism and the welfare provisions of the twentieth century. While we may not completely accept Beck's thesis of an emerging risk society, there is no question that risk, often conflated with danger, dominates our thinking and many of our social practices, including those engaged in by human service professionals.

In its contemporary forms, risk and its technologies reflect social relations of producing and reproducing 'normal' people and groups and the socially sanctioned processes of identifying deviants. As Douglas has suggested, risk creates boundaries between cultural groups, between the mainstream and those whom it is considered socially acceptable to blame, and between 'regular' citizens and those who are 'different.' In the current context, risky groups and 'evildoers' are identified, their culpability described, and actions to contain them prescribed. Further, risk technologies discover particular individuals among us who can, through socially sanctioned processes, be named as 'risky' and whose activities can be curtailed as a result. In this process, politicians, professionals, and others who fail to notice the 'right risks' will be marked off from those who have made no such mistakes, or whose mistakes have not yet been discovered. Court actions, liability suits, voter dissatisfaction, firing, and other job actions single these people out from others, sometimes very publicly and painfully.

Fears, both specific and general, meanwhile, act to loosen our insistence on privacy. Very intrusive actions and investigations by people in positions of authority, from national leaders to security staff, can be launched in the service of alleviating or at least reducing our sense of anxiety about the future.

These observations return us to the issues of the social and power relations expressed by risk. To better understand these relations, it is helpful to notice the actors involved in the production of risk and their positioning in the risk enterprise. We need to ask who can speak authoritatively about risk, and who cannot, who can effectively lay blame, and who can act on blame laid through the invocation of risk. The exploration in this chapter shows that scientists, especially those doing positivist forms of science, have become prominent speakers in discourses of risk relevant to human services. Government officials who set policy, bureaucrats who manage risk systems, and professionals who administer risk assessments are also powerful players on the terrain of risk. On the other hand, people marked as deviant, bad, risky, or different in some socially selected way make their contribution to the discourses of risk through other channels, especially through being assessed via organized systems of risk assessment.

Thus, risk is shown to be a concept carrying considerable freight from the past, to be pervaded with meanings that are not necessarily obvious, and to carry into everyday risk practices both established and developing sets of power relations. These relations can intensify the power positions of already powerful social elites. As we will see, they also help to shift the positions of various actors in relation to each other, for as Beck notes (1992: 186), bureaucrats and managers who administer systems of risk can replace government officials as the actual decision makers in this scenario, taking on a patina of moral purpose in the process. Professionals who administer risk assessments that are widely accepted and seen as scientific can improve their power positions. Of course, they can also lose status in the wake of disaster. And as we will see in the following chapter, even well-established and widely accepted notions of risk can be discredited and superseded by new ideas with implications that shift the relationship of the individual to society.

Of considerable importance to us is the capacity of risk and the power relations it reflects to create conditions facilitating social critique, debate, and challenge. Our analysis suggests that the emphasis on past practice in risk systems, the potential for powerful players to increase their authority through risk practices, and a general climate of fear mitigate against social change efforts aimed at reducing oppressive conditions for vulnerable people. It is our intention to explore these conditions in the interests of locating spaces for change. We will see risk 'from the ground up' (Rankin and Campbell, 2006: 41) and explore its potential for social justice goals.

2 From Social to Individual Risk

Human service professionals in many Western democracies are acutely aware of changes that have taken place in our 'social safety net' over the past two or three decades. These changes, generally associated with neoliberal government, have been marked by substantial cutbacks in funding, the eradication of many social programs, long waiting lists for services, the delisting of previously accessible publicly funded services, and the 'outsourcing' of programs and tasks to private organizations, both non-profit and for profit. There is widespread awareness that this trend has taken hold not only in Canada but also in the welfare states of Europe and the United States. Staff employed in government-sponsored programs spend more of their time providing gatekeeping and referral services than they used to, while staff in private sector organizations spend much of their time preparing funding proposals to keep their programs alive. In both sectors, staff find themselves responsible for much more detailed accounting of their time and resources than in previous eras. In both the public and private arenas, risk and risk assessment play a much larger role than they did in past years. In this chapter, we explore the debates and discourses associated with the shift from a relatively well-developed and widely accepted welfare state to a state shaped by neoliberal ideas and designed to encourage individual responsibility. We examine some features of the way 'risk' is placed in this altering landscape, with a view to better understanding the social policy context within which human service professionals now labour.

Foundations of the Welfare State

What we now think of as 'the social,' according to Rose, has a history beginning in the nineteenth century and extending into the first half of the twentieth century. The 'social' here refers to complex social relations and loyalties within a 'bounded territory governed by its own laws' (Rose, 1996b: 328). Our understanding of the social was made possible and shaped by the evolution of social statistics, the development of sociology, the creation of institutions serving populations which could be known through information and statistics collected about them (O'Malley, 2004: 38–9), and the acceptance by political rulers in Europe and North America that nations must and should govern from the point of view of social interests. With the shift to neoliberal forms of governing, the existence of the social comes into question. The contemporary neoliberal position is that society is actually the product of government and its intervention, through the welfare state, into private life (Burchell, 1996: 27). As the welfare state weakens, 'society' is diminished. Margaret Thatcher, former British prime minister, went even further to declare that society does not actually exist (Keay, 1987).

The beginnings and deepest roots of the contemporary welfare state are found in the provisions of the Elizabethan Poor Law of 1601 (Splane, 1965). The transformation of these charity-based schemes into the state-sponsored programs associated with the welfare state occurred primarily in the twentieth century, although some social security arrangements in Europe had actually begun to develop in the late 1800s. William Beveridge (1942) is credited with developing a comprehensive series of programs to fight the five 'giant evils' – want, disease, ignorance, squalor, and idleness. His plans were based on an ideal of full employment, supplemented by a national health service and national insurance contributions paid by all people of working age. In Western Europe, North America, Australia, and New Zealand, variations of programs based on these principles were adopted in the post–Second World War era.

The welfare state is associated with nations defining themselves as liberal democracies. In its modern form, liberal democracy based itself on economic principles of full employment and broadly accessible rights of citizenship. This form of government is firmly grounded in capitalism, but certainly a version of capitalism that detaches some aspects of life from the demands of the market. These 'social' areas are usually identified as health, education, retirement, and protection of the most vulnerable groups of people. Through this 'historic class compromise' (Broadbent, 1999: 24), members of the working class accepted income inequality through capitalist mechanisms in exchange for equality of social rights – capitalism softened somewhat by a shared sense of social responsibility. Since the contemporary welfare state is founded on this compromise, an important task of governing has been to promote morality and order while simultaneously restricting the boundaries of government in the interests of both liberty and the autonomy of society and its members (Rose, 1996a).

Social Rights, Social Insurance, and Risk

The concept of social rights was a development of the twentieth century, according to T.H. Marshall (1992 [1950]). His view, first presented in a series of lectures published in 1950, connected the modern era with struggles for civil, political, and finally, social rights, culminating in a 'citizenship package' (Broad and Antony, 1999: 9) suited to the development of the welfare state. Social rights, in this conceptualization, involve those mechanisms that offer some protection to workers in a capitalist society from the vicissitudes of the marketplace, including trade union rights and government-sponsored social insurance programs (Teeple, 2004: 14).

Social rights are made possible largely through the provision of insurance against the common and predictable risks of living in a particular society. Insurance mechanisms do not guarantee safety and security, but rather offer ways to mitigate expectable losses and costs. Since social insurance covers groups of people rather than individuals, it can be characterized as a collective form of activity, which also individualizes through technologies ascribing probability for risk to particular individuals. Insurance as a social form fits very well with liberal government, as Ewald notes, because it combines a 'maximum of socialization with a maximum of individualization' (1991: 204).

Insurance could also be seen as the commodification of risk. Almost anything can be socially selected as a risk to be insured against. Giddens (1999a: 4) points out that there are two main kinds of insurance sponsorship associated with industrial society. One is private insurance, created and sold by profit-making companies. The other is public insurance, which is the concern of the welfare state, and it involves a set of mechanisms designed to spread risk through the social whole. Of course, the state and private sectors sometimes work together to 'spread the costs of risk and provide security' (Ericson and Doyle, 2004: 4). Heimer (2002: 117–18) has argued that both social and private insurers are becoming less willing to ensure a broad range of risks and that both kinds of insurers have the capacity to differentiate the worthy from the unworthy recipient. To be rejected by either a public or a private insurer, she points out, can substantially affect an individual's financial and social standing. Rejection implies that an individual is 'high risk' in some way that could be costly to the insurer. These identified risks can be used as eligibility criteria that lead to the denial of other benefits, and they can even be used as criteria in hiring decisions (Stone, 1989).

Many of the programs associated with the welfare state are clearly insurance based. That is, potential recipients pay premiums directly into the program. These include employment insurance and retirement pensions (Canada Pension Plan). There are elements of the welfare state, of course, that are supported through general revenues, for instance, Old Age Assistance and welfare. Even these programs, which are guaranteed to citizens with particular attributes regardless of tax or other contributions, share some features of insurance. They are based on the underlying assumption that risks related to growing old or falling on hard times apply throughout the population. They are also based on a shared sense of social responsibility to ensure against the most grievous forms of injury to social members, and on a belief that risks of living can and should be identified, compensated, and perhaps even mitigated. For the past half-century, Canadians along with people in other Western capitalist countries have enjoyed a wide range of benefits resulting from welfare state programs, and to some extent we all have viewed social insurance as an integral and permanent part of liberal democracy. Everyone directly benefits from welfare state programs, some of which, like Old Age Assistance in Canada, are still universal; however, it is the 'targeted' programs, especially income support programs, with which the welfare state has come to be identified.

Numerous critiques of the welfare state have been submitted, from all parts of the political spectrum. The welfare state, with its emphasis on social insurance, was after all founded on an uneasy compromise. Classical liberals embraced the welfare state as a method of averting socialism, and it was at the same time viewed by socialists as a first step in the direction of their goal of socialized government (Rosanvallon, 2000: 16). Welfare state programs address the problem of social reproduction, meaning the resources required for the workforce to reliably supply its labour when required by capital. Social insurance as represented by the welfare state at first appeared to reconcile the tensions between labour and capital, allowing workers and their families the support they needed to be productive without undue costs to capital. The welfare state also offered an apparent resolution to the contradictory relations between society and the individual, allowing individuals to benefit from the social whole while living autonomously (Ewald, 1991, quoted in Rosanvallon, 2000: 16).

The often uneasy tensions between labour and capital and between society and the individual, however, have never been fully resolved. The notion of social insurance against life risks has always been tainted with fears that it will induce indolence and reduce the foresight required to avoid risks. A related concern has been the potential that a fully developed welfare state, one that assists people from 'cradle to grave,' will produce passive rather than active and participating subjects and will encourage people to withdraw from the labour market. These fault lines have allowed business interests a space for critique. Corporations and their various allies and lobbyists were the first to launch an attack on the welfare state. These critics gained a substantial political advantage in the 1980s with the election of Margaret Thatcher in Britain, Ronald Reagan in the United States, and Brian Mulroney in Canada, all of whom initiated vigorous strategies aimed at reducing or even dismantling the welfare state (Mulvale, 2001).

However, not only critics from the political right have gone on the attack. The welfare state itself helped to produce a strong and growing rights movement constituted of specific groups claiming discrimination by the homogenizing policies and programs presumably designed to produce equality. Critiques of the welfare state made by a growing number of its supposed beneficiaries also appeared during the 1980s. Feminists pointed out that the design of the welfare state was based from the beginning on assumptions of a 'normal' family with a male breadwinner and female homemaker (Swift, 1995a), and on an attempt to impose this model on all families. Related to this, feminists note that the 'full employment' idea of the modern welfare state has always referred almost exclusively to paid employment and has, at the expense of women, ignored the largely unpaid labour involved in social reproduction and caring labour (Cossman and Fudge, 2002: 8; Neysmith, 2000). People who are members of minority groups based on race, citizenship status, sexual preference, and/or disability have complained of harassment by program staff, attempts to regulate their behaviour and morals, impersonal bureaucracies, systemic discrimination, and various reasons for unequal access to services (Mulvale, 2001). Because of means testing and other practices designed to ensure that only eligible applicants receive benefits, bureaucrats representing the welfare state have frequently been accused of overly intrusive surveillance of recipients. Clearly, the taint of stigma has become attached to many programs, particularly those benefiting 'target' populations, and to the individuals and groups who benefit from them.

A critique coming from less obvious beneficiaries of the welfare state – the middle and upper classes – is that citizens can be beneficiaries without having to take any responsibility for their own troubles. These critics likely support such plans as the development of 'workfare,' which requires recipients of benefits to train for and seek employment. The allegedly high cost of welfare programs, accompanied by some unpopular taxation policies, have served as primary justifications not only for recent cuts in welfare programs but also for increased accountability for expenditures. An often-cited explanation for budget deficits is that program benefits offered through the welfare state far exceed the contributions of citizens and keep taxes high. Budget deficits have, from the 1970s on, provided political justification to call for significant reductions in both the scope and eligibility of programs, which in turn, can justify tax cuts. The trend to reducing costs and services is observed in virtually all of the Western welfare states, although less so in most European countries than here in Canada.

Neoliberal critics have identified some genuine problems of welfare states in adjusting to structural changes in both the domestic labour market and in national and global economies (Culpitt, 1999; Rose, 1996b). The welfare state model relies on a concept of national identity, reciprocity among national citizens, and established boundaries supported by law. With intensifying economic globalization, new economic relationships replace previous agreements and national loyalties. Trade agreements, rulings by international bodies like the World Bank, and independent business transactions carried out between corporate interests can supersede national practices and laws. Large corporations, holding assets greater than those of some countries, can easily bypass national governments to do business (Culpitt, 1999). As business interests try to improve their competitive position in global markets, jobs are outsourced to cheaper labour in other countries. The flow of people from one country to others is increased, partly as a result of the way opportunities shift across national borders and partly as a result of the upheaval related to struggles for resources and power. Capital is detached from national governments and consequently answers almost exclusively to the market. In this economic context, as Cossman and Fudge (2002) point out, capital becomes increasingly removed from the costs and organization of social reproduction.

National governments try to adapt to these global circumstances, including the adjustment of their social welfare schemes, to line up with global requirements and markets (Taylor-Gooby et al., 1999). In these circumstances, a sense of social and national coherence may begin to dissipate, as individuals and groups try to compete in the changing economic context. Further, the revolution in communications means that people all over the world can access current information and competing explanations for events. As Taylor-Gooby et al. (1999: 178) point out, this rapid change in how we come to know our world has 'profoundly corrosive' effects on the kind of centralized authority that the welfare state had come to represent.

Another issue that has been identified to be a problem of the welfare state involves the question of inclusion. In the context of unemployment, underemployment, and the export of jobs that globalizing economies tend to produce in specific economic sectors, compensatory social insurance schemes can become semi-permanent income for a proportion of the population; this has actually been the case in Britain for several decades. According to Rosanvallon (2000), compensation intended to produce social inclusion has in these circumstances become a source of labelling and social exclusion, leading to yet other forms of risk. He offers the American Aid to Families with Dependent Children (AFDC) and French Revenu Minimum d'Insertion (RMI) programs as evidence of this argument. These programs have produced strong and lasting effects of stigma and marginalization for recipients. Rosanvallon claims these exclusionary practices have led to the first thorough revisioning of rights since the advent of liberal individualism in the seventeenth century. In this new vision social rights are increasingly seen as conditional; they are linked directly to the state of the economy and tied to certain kinds of individual activity and behaviour.

These critiques have encouraged and allowed politicians and other policy makers to change the nature and scope of welfare states. Some argue that public support for welfare state programs remains high, although with a new understanding that citizens will be required to take more personal responsibility for addressing their own needs and risks (Taylor-Gooby et al., 1999). However, there is certainly an appearance of public support for change, encouraged no doubt by the mass media, and buttressed by the election to public office of political parties that support tax cuts and a reduced welfare state. This support is largely based on beliefs that 'welfarism' (Baker and Simon, 2002) cannot be sustained financially, that programs and benefits have produced a lazy and sometimes corrupt class of 'takers,' and that countries supporting expensive welfare programs cannot be competitive in today's global markets.

Of course, this perspective has not gone unchallenged. Critiques of these explanations have come primarily from the political left, and they have focused on the damage done to vulnerable and marginalized population groups as a result of closing some social programs and reducing the benefits of others. Critics (e.g., Teeple, 2004) also say that the neoliberal prescription of individual responsibility as the solution to the 'crisis' of the welfare state unfairly punishes the poor and will not in any case solve the problems of debt and deficits. Nevertheless, the idea that risks are social and should be socially insured has gradually given way to different ideas of the nature of risk and how risks should be addressed.

'Risk Society' and the Welfare State

The idea of prudent planning for the future is hardly new; it is a feature of classical liberalism. However, there is undoubtedly a new and contemporary focus on risk, on bringing the future into the present to be acted on based on actuarial computations. Most theorists hypothesizing the existence of 'risk society' see its inception as closely related to changes in the welfare state, which in turn, is connected to an industrial society that 'has come up against its own limitations' (Giddens, 1999a: 6).

Ulrich Beck's publication of *The Risk Society* (1992) arrived at a time when substantial shifts in the welfare states in both Europe and North America were already well under way. As noted in the Introduction, Beck analyses the problems of the welfare state from a unique perspective. His idea is that welfare states are waning not because they have failed but 'because of [their] very success' (1992: 185). The 'goods' produced in the modern industrial era of science and technology, according to Beck, are so plentiful that they have become threats to the well-being of all societies. He cites, for example, pollution of the air, water, and soil as a result of industrial production and overproduction. The welfare state, Beck says, has succeeded in creating and distributing wealth (1992:19). Now, as societies, we must turn our attention to containing the damage we have wrought through our own inventiveness.

The previous era in Beck's model, which overlaps risk society, he refers to as 'the society of scarcity.' The scarcity model draws on the conceptualizations of Marx and Weber, who concerned themselves with questions of how socially produced wealth could be redistributed in the interests of greater equality. These ideas are compared with the evolving risk society, which Beck poses as preoccupied with the distribution of 'bads' and the management of risk – 'discovering, administering, acknowledging, avoiding or concealing hazards' (1992: 20).

Like Rosanvallon (2000), Beck examines how risks and their effects have changed since the development of 'insurance society.' For one thing, risks themselves become available for economic exploitation. The very corporate entities that create risks offer costly antidotes to them: the escalating power of weapons of warfare provide an example. The profit motive, in other words, creates a powerful disincentive to contain and diminish risk. This flexibility and the willingness to profit from destruction are, of course, among the great ironies of capitalism.

Risks in late modernity are created within society, and their magnitude is substantial, in fact, incalculable, according to Beck. Numerous risks now affect the population of the entire world. This means in some instances a new levelling of the playing field: if weapons of mass destruction are unleashed, both the wealthy and the poor will be similarly affected. However, this levelling does not allow us to ignore analyses of different social and economic positions among the population, because the distribution of risks overall will usually be uneven. While 'smog is democratic' (Beck, 1992: 36), its effects on people will differ according to their age, gender, habits, health, occupation, and so on. The diffusion of risks, therefore, does not break completely with the logic of capitalism, Beck argues, but raises class analysis to a new level. Wealth continues to accumulate at the top, while risks accumulate at the bottom, a topic explored further in Chapter 3.

Among the very important points Beck makes about his notion of risk society is that it is characterized by a 'loss of social thinking' (1992: 25). We become accustomed to frightening and endless risks, but survive through relief when the risk 'only' affects someone else.

Threats of the 'end of the world' become a matter of indifference, since there is no escape anyway. Concerns with threats to the social whole have become the preserve of 'tree huggers,' ironically disparaged as narrow thinkers. Despite the primacy of science, there is no expert on risk, Beck claims. There are always competing claims, and social norms and values in the end must be accounted for along with actuarial calculations in determining the line between acceptable and unacceptable risks.

Another proponent of 'risk society' is Mary Douglas (1990, 1992), although her view of the current era stands in significant contrast to Beck's theory. Rather than suggesting that we are in the midst of a radical change from previous eras, Douglas emphasizes continuities between the current era and previous ones. The contemporary view of risk, she maintains, couples it with dangerousness, both individual and social. She points out that lapses in social solidarity are frequently countered and contained by widespread suggestion of impending disasters; the American 'war on terror' is a case in point. The threat of disaster has the benefit of reproaching the group for any potential discord or disunity and also of providing a common enemy that works to bring dissenting elements of the group together. Thus, representations of risk provide an integrative function. Douglas even compares risk debates to religious discourses, suggesting that we have merely substituted risk for sin in an effort to single out someone to blame.

While Beck argues that we must question and challenge experts and authorities who produce and promote catastrophic risks, Douglas proposes that scientific experts and legitimate government authorities are the best judges of risk and that the general population would be pragmatic to entrust them with the management of real disasters. These two opposing opinions of the nature of contemporary society, its risks, and responses to risk seem to mirror very well the public ambivalence about risk. On the one hand, we are inundated with statistics predicting future harm and daily stories of disasters befalling the imprudent. On the other hand, we frequently see accounts of apparently successful humanitarian responses to adversity – 9/11, of course, stands as the exemplar of the new century.

There are numerous criticisms of both Beck and Douglas (Scott, 2000). One critique (Wilkinson, 2001) is that Beck's analysis is a 'partial' view of risk, based more on his political ambitions to create a credible perspective than on empirical evidence. He is seen as 'inspirational but sociologically dubious' (O'Malley, 1999: 142). Another, perhaps more serious issue, is the question of whether we are actually in a new era. O'Malley (1999), a governmentality theorist, questions whether 'risk consciousness' pervades society and is the guiding force for the state and virtually all social and organizational structures. Such a view, according to O'Malley, appears totalizing in a way that precludes alteration and cannot be empirically supported. Governance, in such a circumstance, must necessarily be negative, focused on the distribution of the 'bads' and seeking harm reduction. Beck is often accused of a sort of 'darkness' in his analysis and of a scientific determinism that would appear to preclude a brighter future.

Beck does allow a solid place for social location in his analysis, noting that 'bads' are not evenly distributed. However, he is often accused of minimizing the ongoing role and importance of class in his analysis. Beck (1992: 87) asserts that risk individualizes social inequality, forcing people to manage their own risks and, in fact, their own 'political economy' (Ericson and Hagerty, 1997, as quoted in Rigakos, 2001: 62). Rigakos and Hadden (2001) argue, in contrast, that risk has had a class basis from its very inception and that this remains firmly in place. They suggest that we view risk not as the triumph of risk over class, as some scholars have claimed, but rather as a method by which 'class is ideologically and structurally recast and reorganized' (2001: 65) through actuarial practices that support capitalism.

Douglas' views of risk as a continuation of the past may appear to respond to some of these critiques. However, as scepticism grows about the management of the risks in the post-9/11 world, her prescriptions may seem suspect. Wilkinson (2001) claims both Beck and Douglas wish to cast risk as a social construction rather than as a reality, but at the same time wish to have their preferred view taken as an objective reality. Perhaps the most useful part of Wilkinson's critique from our perspective is the question of whether any of this theorizing reflects the everyday experiences of people as they encounter 'risks' or notions of risk in their everyday lives. He cites research (2001: 10) showing that people hold a variety of contradictory, partial, and ambiguous views about the findings of science. As Kasperson and Kasperson (2005, 1996), point out, our knowledge of risk, after all, is thoroughly embedded in processes of social discourse that shape how we see the potential severity of hazards. These more empirical views would seem to challenge the totalizing views of some theorists.

While Beck, Douglas, and other influential authors call attention to the pervasiveness of concern about risk, they do not speak very well to the everyday concerns of professionals who are asked to deal with risk in the context of their work. The importance of risk theorists from this perspective lies, first, in the attention they bring to the role of risk in the development of science and scientific expertise. Risk is a site of dispute about the reality of risk, the science of risk, the experts who produce predictions, and social responses to risk. Whether we see risk as displacing class or as an ideological attempt to disguise class, it is crucial that theorists of risk debate this issue and that they examine the legitimacy of scientific claims about risk. Theorists also help us to place risk in the social policy arena. Practitioners, as we will see in Chapter 4, are called on not to theorize the relationship between risk and policy but to identify and ameliorate risk. Functions and practices of risk in the contested terrain of social policy are often invisible to those who do this work; theorists help to bring attention to the effects of positioning risk in the context of contemporary social policy.

'Ask Not': Risk and Neoliberalism

Social and economic developments over the past several decades do suggest a loosening of social bonds, sometimes described as the 'death of the social' (Rose, 1996b), and a new reliance on individuals to manage their own welfare and risks. The nature, scale, and our perceptions of risk in the current era have altered the relation of the individual to the state. Through the last half of the twentieth century, social solidarity was based on a sharing of social risks more or less evenly distributed across a population through insurance mechanisms and guaranteed income programs created by the welfare state. This model relies heavily on the idea that social rights should be equally distributed among the population of a nation-state. The increasing visibility of different 'gains and losses' resulting from these mechanisms has reduced public confidence in this approach (Rosanvallon, 2000) and legitimated a newly energetic focus on individual responsibility for anticipating and managing risks. This recent emphasis in both government and civil society on individual risk is generally associated with a trend towards neoliberal thinking in social policy: a minimal state, critiqued regularly and with vigilance; the market as the primary mechanism of wealth distribution; economic risk-taking and an entrepreneurial spirit; individual responsibility for risk; and the inevitability of social inequality. In 1960, when the welfare state was approaching its full form in North America, the incoming U.S. President John F.

Kennedy entreated citizens to 'ask not what your country can do for you, but what you can do for your country.' In the neoliberal context that has since taken hold, the entreaty might be reformulated: Ask not what your country can do for you, but what you can do for yourself.

Neoliberalism, the limits of knowledge, and the supposed limits of resources have brought a shift towards 'embracing risk,' according to Ericson and Doyle (2004: 30–1). The social and moral imperatives of socially produced forms of security and meeting of need have been superseded by a rhetoric and practice of reducing risk. Welfare states, as Culpitt says, are being reformulated into 'residual welfare societies' (1999: 35). Neoliberals have effectively created a negative association between welfare and 'dependency.' The word *welfare* no longer elicits ideas of the common good (Culpitt, 1999) so much as it conjures up concerns about an inefficient and unproductive workforce. The idea that *taking risks* can be seen as something positive and enterprising is restricted to the business world and those with money. For everyone else, risk has come to be associated with danger, and especially the danger of harming others or becoming a drag on the marketplace.

A substantial literature on liberalism and neoliberalism has emerged from scholars generally following Foucault. According to Foucault (1979), governing in contemporary liberal states means 'governing through our freedom' – that is, we are being governed by processes created through the assertion of our freedom and the autonomy to make decisions. This line of thought, often identified as *governmentality*, focuses less on ideology and policy content and much more on how governing is accomplished through techniques, technology, and practices of thought and action. A specific example, one taken up by a number of scholars of risk, is the contract as a form of relation between the individual and the state, a technique that, as Burchell (1996: 29) says, proposes (and sometimes insists) on active involvement by individuals and groups to resolve issues that formerly were the province of government. People are, in effect, invited to govern themselves, to supervise their relationship to themselves, and to act accordingly. The contract, as an element of the emerging discourse of a more 'active' state, provides a tacit criticism of the welfare state as a 'passive system of handouts' (Dean, 1995: 578). Dean argues that this shift to a so-called active state belies the idea of the minimal state often connected with neoliberalism. In fact, the state does not shrink but rather takes on new obligations of coordination, the provision of some services, and the categorization and monitoring of 'beneficiaries.' Thus, for some proponents of a governmentality approach, neoliberalism involves not so much a retreat from governmental intervention as a 're-inscription of the techniques and forms of expertise required for the exercise of government' (Barry et al., 1996: 14). The kinds of knowledge that government requires have been relocated to some extent outside the confines of the state and into the realm of the market, which may make government appear to be reducing itself. The individual has been repositioned from a 'social' being, governed through resort to social norms and forms, to a position of more autonomy, but one charged with responsibilities for planning his or her own life and being accountable for outcomes (Burchell, 1996). Some of these scholars urge us to see the positives of the neoliberal project, by which they mean the development of technologies of governing that allow more autonomy to individuals, an approach sometimes referred to as the 'responsibilization' of citizens. As we saw in the previous chapter, both Beck and Giddens see a potentially positive outcome of this direction in the form of 'reflexive citizenship.' Others express some concern about how particular members of the population will fare in this regime, especially those for whom autonomy is difficult or impossible to achieve and those who are unsuccessful or unlucky in their efforts (Taylor-Gooby et al., 1999; Barry et al., 1996)

Taking a somewhat different tack, Dean's work shows how recent practices of governing in welfare states are used for more than providing services and resources. In addition, Dean says, governing takes a form that seeks to 'shape the desires, needs, aspirations, capacities and attitudes' of the applicants (1995: 567). In so doing, an attempt is made to create governing practices that produce an 'active subject' capable of managing his or her own destiny, a subject that can hardly be distinguished from the neoliberal ideal of an 'enterprising self' (1995: 576). Dean concludes that analysis of social security from a governmentality perspective reveals that the character of social policy is very much dependent on technology, persistent routines of action, available expertise, and the nature of the bureaucracies that 'perform' governing. Further, he usefully shows how policy is enacted both within and outside of the usually recognized boundaries of government.

An alternate perspective on neoliberalism generally emerges from those placing themselves in the field of social policy and generally also on the 'left' side of the political spectrum. These critics demonstrate considerable concern about the 'death of the social.' They point out that social insurance mechanisms have worked to constrain tendencies of capitalist economies to create ever-widening income inequalities. Canadian social policy advocates such as the National Anti-Poverty Organization (NAPO) and the Canadian Centre for Policy Alternatives cite the 'shrinking social wage' (Mulvale, 2001: 84) and an increasingly regressive tax system as responsible for a widening gap between rich and poor. Problems like hunger, as indicated by the entrenchment and growth of food banks, and visible homelessness on Canadian streets are attributed by social policy critics to the dismantling of programs that helped to support people through previous economic downturns (Jackson and Robinson, 2000). These critics of neoliberal policies challenge the 'mythology' (Mulvale, 2001: 14) that social spending was the only or primary cause of the fiscal 'crisis' of the welfare state in the last few decades of the twentieth century. The increase in interest charges on the national debt in the 1980s and 1990s as well as decreasing revenue from corporate taxes are cited as major contributors to this problem (Ecumenical Coalition for Economic Justice, 1993: 33–40). Further, the high costs of social programs during some periods reflect high levels of unemployment, exactly the kind of social risk created by capitalism that the welfare state was designed to address in the first place. This critique suggests that efforts to dismantle welfare state programs and entitlements have been carried out under false pretenses. Claims that social programs are insupportable are to a great extent myths operating in the interests of corporate power and profit and at the expense of society's most vulnerable people.

Advocates from the left are also concerned about the future of equality rights in this neoliberal era. Women, racial and cultural minorities, people with disabilities, and other rights activists see neoliberalism to be erasing many advances produced through the welfare state (Teeple, 2004), even while acknowledging its deficits. The literature of governmentality that celebrates the benefits of autonomy generally tends to minimize or even ignore the social divisions of race, class, gender, and other 'isms' that are the focus of so much debate and discourse produced by social policy advocates and critics.

Rose (1996a, 1996b) takes a view of the present 'state of the state' that 'disturbs' the usual politics of left and right, modernism and postmodernism. He maintains that contemporary technologies and aims of governing are not simply a matter of the rhetoric and ideology of neoliberalism; nor should we imagine that certain political interests coherently planned the present circumstances. Rather, a confluence of critiques of the welfare state, the demands of many population groups for rights and a voice, the fracturing of expertise into domains now criticized as too authoritarian and exclusive, and other social trends have led to the individualizing and responsibilizing of citizens as well as to the auditing and accounting measures that now characterize governing. The political right, both Rose (1996a, 1996b) and Culpitt (1999) maintain, has simply been more effective than the left in finding a way to merge its interests with these developments; co-opting the meanings and technologies of 'risk' is a central feature of how this has been done.

Risk and Risk Management

Regardless of where critics position themselves on the political spectrum, there is general agreement that a fundamental shift has occurred, away from the welfare state as representing 'the social' and towards investing individuals with more responsibility for their own well-being. This shift is represented in virtually all aspects of life in Western societies and certainly in all of the helping professions. The individualization of 'helping' is clearly present in the intensifying professional focus on assessing and managing risk rather than on diagnosis and cure (Rose, 1998). In his influential article discussing the 'death of the social,' Rose (1996b) argues that the reconfigured terrain of governing detaches social welfare from the economy, creates new divides between people who are competent citizens and those who are judged not to be, and moves professional expertise into a position of being much more subject to governance than during the height of the welfare state. Giddens also argues that the crisis of the welfare state is not purely financial, as often theorized, but is also a crisis of risk management, a reality that requires a rethinking of the welfare state. Some risk theorists, in fact, argue that risk is replacing equity and need as the central concept of publicly delivered services (Fine, 2005; Kemshall, 2002).

Knowledge of risks takes on new political significance in this era; science and technology rise to ever-higher status because they have the capacity to both create and contain new risks. The space and power to identify and challenge or to conceal and deny risks similarly take on more importance, and the need to manage risk certainly foreshadows a reorganization of power and authority. Beck posits the existence of a 'techno-economic' sub-politics (1992: 186) in which government monitoring agencies and risk-sensitive media acquire new 'political and moral' strength and legitimacy in the risk society. In these conditions, the power to structure society 'migrates from the political system to technical, scientific and economic projects.' Thus, 'the political becomes non-political and the non-political becomes political' (1992:186). Political institutions then become administrators of something they do not control but must justify. This shift is altering the dynamics and politics of welfare states and is reflected in our case example presented in Part II.

Historically, risk management was seen not as an effort to eliminate risks but to acknowledge them (Clark, 2002). In the present era, risk, particularly in the human services, is viewed as something to identify, assess, manage, and eradicate, or at least reduce. The delivery of human services is now evaluated largely in terms of whether these goals have been accomplished.

To address these concerns, the sites of service delivery formerly focused on meeting needs are lately being devoted to the development and refinement of tools, techniques, and practices aimed at the management of risk. This is a focus that fits very well and is facilitated by the managerial approach characterizing neoliberalism and its concern with accountability. Managerial procedures of auditing, measuring efficiency, and instituting systems of accountability began to filter into socially financed policies and programs several decades ago. As neoliberalism has intensified and gained political power, these directions have also intensified and are now often referred to as the 'new managerialism.' The development of sophisticated computer software and large and easily accessible databases has no doubt improved the effectiveness of these directions.

Tsui and Cheung (2004) have summarized the basic tenets of the new managerialism. These include a strong focus on the market rather than on society or community, efficiency rather than effectiveness as the main criterion of success, money and contracts rather than care and concern as the foundation of relationships, and standardization as the measure of quality in the provision of services. In this scenario, professional knowledge is subordinate to managerial knowledge, and professionals themselves are less important than previously, since managers can carry out required tasks through delegation and the use of standardized controls. To a greater or lesser extent, these features of managing characterize and shape work and working conditions for employees of social programs. These not only attach themselves to risk, but they also shape and characterize the processes associated with the assessment and management of risk.

Conclusion

The U.N. Declaration of Human Rights says that every member of society has the right to social security and a minimum standard of living. It can be argued, however, that the loss of social benefits and social insurance, the loosening of loyalties to the social whole, and the 'responsibilization' of individuals work to change and diminish citizenship rights and entitlements, at least for some people. Those who are judged incompetent to manage their own risks and futures may lose personal freedoms and benefits accorded to others and which they themselves formerly enjoyed. Anyone falling below the established social floor could find herself or himself less able than before to make claims on the social whole. Even guarantees to a social minimum could erode and disappear (O'Malley, 2004). According to Beck, individualism has many meanings, not all of them associated with neoliberal thinking related to accountability and responsibility. Beck and others (e.g., Fine, 2005: 254) argue that individualization involves not withdrawal from society but increasing interaction with 'the social.' Individualization from this perspective includes individual rights, a demand that people be treated as unique individuals, and autonomy through social processes of recognition, as well as new forms of obligation and responsibility. A central basis for Beck's theory of risk involves the emergence of the 'reflexive citizen,' one who takes on the responsibility of knowledge and of reflexively acting on that knowledge. This new citizen would be informed, proactive, and 'less deferential.' However, not everyone has the capacity to do this (Hanlon et al., 2006). Beck's promotion of the reflexive citizen may even have inadvertently given credence to neoliberal rhetoric about individualism.

In the midst of disagreement about the nature of individualization, it is clear that Western liberal democracies are moving in the direction of reduced or at least changing forms of collectivity and towards the individualization of knowledge, responsibility for managing one's own fate, and perhaps new social groupings that reflect these changes: 'A new contractual relationship of the individual to the state is forged out of the increased perception of limits' to social insurance and services (Culpitt,1999: 50). At issue is the nature of 'the social' and the willingness of collectivities of people at national and local levels to spread responsibility for risk, to acknowledge social risks, and to share in the costs of managing and compensating risk: 'who better than the state,' Ewald asks, 'can guarantee the stability of insurance institutions?' (1991: 209).

There is dispute about whether the shift to individual forms of security really means that the social is dead. For instance, Fine (2005: 259), along with Douglas, believes that a risk society does not necessarily mean abandoning collective action, while both Simon (1987) and Beck argue that risk does not and cannot build social solidarity. And critics who complain that Beck's idea of risk-based government is a negative approach seem to prove Beck's point – a lot of contemporary government *is* negative, focused on bads and harm reduction. Our case study in Part II demonstrates this point.

Even some of the discourse of social policy is moving away from social equity and justice and in the direction of minimizing, measuring, and containing risk. Culpitt (1999: 8) argues that the success of neoliberalism has been in its containment of policy discussions and its success in refocusing them on what appears to be 'common sense' concerning fears about the future. Risk underlies and facilitates the maintenance of these boundaries. As taken up in neoliberal discourse, risk has acquired very particular and individualized meanings. Risk is associated largely with dangerousness, particularly dangers posed by designated risk classes to 'normal,' regular, tax-paying members of society. In this sense, the measurement of risk is meant to provide security of the person to law-abiding citizens, even if this involves curtailing the rights of people who are deemed 'risky.' Social issues leading to *economic insecurity* are elided from this discourse. Current definitions of safety and security do not include having a roof over one's head, enough to eat, or a regular and sufficient income. More and more, these definitions refer almost exclusively to protection from bad people and evildoers. Thus, risk provides a mechanism through which social provision can legitimately be replaced with 'physical repression' (Clarke, 2000, quoted in Mulvale, 2001: 86).

Accountability procedures, conducted through institutionalized risk management practices among others, increasingly lay blame for imprudence at the doorstep of the afflicted. Risk, in this context, is ideological. It deflects attention from social risks and problems; eclipses the idea of class; covers over gender, race, and other social divisions; and turns attention to the laying of blame for imprudence.

An important political feature of risk as it has been developed in neoliberalism is that it does not lend itself to social change. Risk focuses political attention and activity on fostering individual 'liberty' and security and away from pursuing social responsibility and justice, thus changing the traditional (if fragile) balance between society and the individual in liberal thought. The identification and management of risk as currently conceptualized and practised are deeply conservative processes. They imply the existence of normative behaviour that must be enforced through policing and consequences. As Culpitt puts it, 'risk and control are conjoined' (1999: 13). While the political left may also call up notions of risk, for example, in support of environmentally sound social policy, it is neoliberals who have most effectively deployed risk in the policy arena.

The shift to risk from need in social policy has led to the creation of new social categories. This occurs as a result of the discourse of risk, the eclipsing of the discourse of need, and also as a result of processes of measuring and accounting for people's behaviour and its outcomes – these are what Foucault referred to as 'political statistics' (1981: 245–6). People deemed to be less risky can be streamed into low-cost services or denied access to services, while those assigned to high-risk categories can 'legitimately' be policed by the state and its contracted partners.

It is in the uncertain context of this shifting terrain of power relations that helping professionals have found themselves asked to identify and contain risk, manage 'risky' populations, and take personal and political responsibility when things go badly wrong.

3 Risk and Social Welfare

Contemplating the radioactive cloud drifting across West Germany from Chernobyl nearly twenty years ago, the German sociologist Ulrich Beck famously observed that 'poverty is hierarchic, smog is democratic.'

Frickel (2006: 1)

When entering the Fraser Valley[1] in British Columbia, a vast expanse of rich farmland close by the city of Vancouver, it is impossible to ignore the soupy pale yellow haze that hangs over the valley on most days. At a glance, it's easy to agree with Beck that everyone in the valley is equally plagued by the quality of the air. However, this is deceptive. People with respiratory problems, pregnant women, and those who are either very young or very old are more likely to suffer as the smog alert rises.[2] Outdoor workers, especially those with jobs requiring strenuous physical efforts, will suffer more than those people who work inside. Ironically, people without cars of their own who walk and cycle and who least contribute to the smog are more exposed. Farm animals and crops are also affected, and those who depend on farming for their living feel the results.

The quality of the air declines the closer one lives to the Trans Canada Highway and other major arteries traversing the valley, where housing costs are lower and where more homeless people congregate.

---

1 The Fraser Valley corridor is the smog corridor with the second highest rating in Canada next to the Windsor to Montreal corridor in Ontario and Quebec.
2 See http://www.ecoinfo.org and http://www.ec.gc.ca/cleanair – for an examination of the effects of smog in the Fraser Valley.

While there are clear pockets of very expensive housing, real estate costs are lower overall in the Fraser Valley than in Vancouver, pushing people with modest resources to locate in the area in the first place. Many of the factors resulting in the Fraser Valley smog originate in Vancouver, an area with far better air quality.

At the same time, the capacity to respond to the effects of smog differs. Health Canada, providing advice to the quintessential middle-class Canadian, proposes that 'to minimize the risks' of adverse effects from smog we should:

- Check the Air Quality index in your community, especially during 'smog season' from April to September, and tailor your activities accordingly
- Avoid or reduce strenuous outdoor activities when smog levels are high, especially during the afternoon when ground-level ozone reaches its peak, and choose indoor activities instead
- Avoid or reduce exercising near areas of heavy traffic, especially during rush hour (http://www.hc-sc.gc.ca/iyh-vsv/environ/smog _e.html).

Obviously, people with greater resources are much better positioned to heed these risk-reduction strategies. Indeed, those who are wealthy can remove themselves from the brunt of the impact altogether. But, ironically, those who suffer most from smog and in fact least contribute to it are the least able to address it on their own. Moreover, by apparently failing to follow the advice to reduce their risks, they can be blamed for ensuing health problems. Their social context is rendered invisible in this process.

The perils of environmental calamities such as smog and other seemingly universal hazards are frequently undemocratic precisely because poverty is hierarchical, a point made by Beck and others but frequently overlooked. While it might be patently obvious that some people will be more susceptible to certain misfortunes and have far fewer resources for coping, it is remarkable how frequently this observation is ignored in popular and professional discourses. Early reports of the devastation of Hurricane Katrina made little mention of the people who suffered most acutely; the poor, black population of the inner city. Only later, as their plight became visually apparent, was it featured. A report on a longitudinal study of 11,000 British children and their use of alcohol was heralded in the press under the headline

'Child binge drinkers at greater risk of alcoholism, says study' (*Guardian*, 6 September 2007, 16). No questions were raised in the news report about whether and how socioeconomic factors may contribute to binge drinking behaviour among children, implying that all children are equally susceptible.

This chapter underscores the simple truth that discourses of risk frequently paper over the existence of significant inequalities. Risk thinking, with its emphasis on the scientific and rational, seems to be unhooked from considerations of power, politics, and injustice. We scrutinize how risk and the retreat from 'the social,' discussed in Chapter 2, have affected many social welfare programs that have shrunk and, in some cases, disappeared altogether. We focus on the Canadian scene over the past few decades, but similar changes are apparent in the United States, the United Kingdom, and other northern countries. Ironically, the reduction in social programs gives further traction to risk logic. Those who used to receive material and social supports are now more visible and seen to be 'at risk' or 'a risk.' Social programs are now sharply limited, so that triaging the people who need them through risk assessments appears logical. As we will demonstrate in the following chapters, these risk assessments focus largely on the characteristics of individuals and not on their social circumstances, thus feeding into the notion that risk and inequality are unrelated.

The analysis of risk and inequality is particularly important for human service workers who generally work with people who are considered vulnerable because of such factors as age, health, income, employment status, education, ability, or ethnicity. In fact, public health, education, and social services developed in recognition of collective responsibilities and to militate against the individual inequalities that exist within capitalist economies. As these public responsibilities are curtailed, clients and workers in human services are the first to bear the consequences. And, as we will examine in Chapter 4, professionals are those most likely to administer risk assessments designed to sort out those who 'deserve' to receive the limited available services.

The Hierarchy of Poverty

The conditions that neoliberalism demands in order to free human beings from the slavery of the state – minimal taxes, the dismantling of public services and social security, deregulation, the breaking of the unions –

just happen to be the conditions required to make the elite even richer, while leaving everyone else to sink or swim.

Monbiot (2007: 27)

Canada is considered to be one the wealthiest and most progressive countries in the world. It spans a vast geographical area of 10 million square kilometres – second only in size to Russia – and it is rich in natural resources, including fish, forests, and petroleum. Its population of almost 33.5 million people, mostly concentrated along the Canada-U.S. border, is composed of indigenous peoples, individuals of European backgound, and increasingly, people from less prosperous countries, all of whom live in reasonable accord – which is no small accomplishment. Canada's political and public institutions are stable.

Each year on 1 July, Canada Day, the media feature accounts from citizens about what they like most about their country. The most poignant stories come from recent immigrants and refugees, now mainly people from Asia, Africa, South America, and the Caribbean (about 13.4 per cent of Canada's population are visible minorities; Statistics Canada, 2003: 10).[3] They often tell harrowing stories of deprivation and instability in their countries of origin, and express gratitude towards Canada for offering a safe haven for them and their families. At the same time, Canada also compares very positively with its nearest neighbour, the United States, on many social indices including levels of tolerance and support for social programs. To complain about Canada in the face of these favourable comparisons can appear cranky, unappreciative, and even un-Canadian.

Yet Canada is also home to many citizens who live in deprivation. For instance, it is estimated that about 1.2 million children – one in six – live in families whose income is below the poverty line, a figure that has not declined since 1980 (Campaign 2000, 2006). The existence of abject poverty and marginalization in a country as wealthy and stable as our own is particularly intolerable. It is this comparison, between what we are and what we could be, that is important to make.

In Canada, and many other countries, the hierarchy of poverty has become steeper in the past several decades. The rich have become

---

3 Projections are that by 2017, about one in five Canadians could be visible minorities (Belanger and Malenfant, 2005).

richer and the poor, poorer, and the gap between them has widened: 'Broadly, if you compare *individuals* – average incomes per head of the world's richest and poorest people – the gap has narrowed, largely because China and India have made immense reductions in poverty. If you compare *countries* – the average income of one country and another – the gap has widened: more countries are lagging behind the rich nations than are catching up. If you compare incomes *within countries* – between the richest people and the poorest – then again the gap is widening' (World Bank, 2006: 9). This is true in Canada. Between 1970 and 1999 the wealthiest 10 per cent of Canadian families doubled their net worth while the 10 per cent at the bottom experienced a decrease in net worth of 28 per cent (Kerstetter, 2002). Data for this study were drawn from Statistics Canada surveys and excluded people living in specific communities such as reserves, military bases, jails, and chronic care facilities, suggesting that the gap between rich and poor would have been even wider had these groups been included. This trend has continued apace. A series of stories by the CBC over a few years sums up the trend:

- 'Canada's wealth disparity rivals Third World' (CBC, 13 December 2002)
- 'Canadian poverty rising despite economic boom' (CBC, 14 September 2005)
- 'Wage gap widening despite boom' (CBC, 1 March 2007)

An article on wealth inequality published by the TD Bank Financial Group notes that between 1999 and 2005, a period when total wealth in Canada increased considerably, the gains were not shared equally. 'The highest quintile received 71% of the total increase in wealth ... by contrast the lowest quintile saw its median real net wealth fall by 9.1%' (Drummond and Tulk, 2006: 2). A recent study demonstrates that this trend continues and that, in fact, the gap in earnings between the wealthy and the poor is wider than it has been for thirty years (Yalnizyan, 2005). What is more, the hours worked by Canadians increased by 200 hours per year, and this increase was borne by every group except the top 10 per cent of families, whose work hours remained constant. Further, the increase in income inequities occurred during a time of unprecedented economic growth and low rates of unemployment. The rising tide has not lifted all boats, rather only the yachts, leaving the row boats stuck on the bottom.

What might have been an uncommon sight twenty years ago – people panhandling and sleeping on the street, in bus shelters, storefronts, and city parks – is now an everyday occurrence in Canada's cities and towns. A poll and focus groups conducted by the Canadian Centre for Policy Alternatives (November 2006) confirmed that most of us are aware of these disparities and fear that they are increasing. The vast majority of respondents in this survey believed that the wealthy benefit most from economic growth and that our society is moving towards a U.S. model where disparities have been greater and more widely accepted.

The Wealth Gap

There are several reasons advanced to explain these growing disparities (Drummond and Tulk, 2006), mostly related to dramatic shifts in the organization of labour. During the past few decades, labour has moved away from waged work in union settings, such as manufacturing, to contract and part-time work primarily in the service and 'in sourcing' sector. Without doubt these changes are connected to the larger forces governing global economic development, as outlined in Chapter 2 of this book. *McJobs*, the term applied to many of these positions, has even been given an entry in the Merriam-Webster dictionary, an addition reportedly contested by Jim Cantalupo, the chairman and chief executive officer of the fast-food firm McDonald's, who complained about the accompanying definition 'low paying and dead-end work.' These jobs are most likely to be held by people with a fragile footing in the labour market: youth, women with children, and immigrants and refugees. For instance, in 2005 about one-third (34 per cent) of low-income children lived in families where at least one parent worked full-time for the entire year, an increase from 27 per cent from 1993 (Campaign 2000, 2006). The reluctance to improve minimum wages and index them so that anyone who works full year, full-time is assured a standard of living beyond poverty contributes markedly to this situation. For instance, in Ontario the minimum wage increased by 4.2 per cent in 2005 while 'the average CEO's salary in Canada increased by 39%' in the same year (Mackenzie, 2007: 2). Minimum wages that used to be tied closely to industrial wages have now fallen far behind while the numbers of workers relying on minimum wages have increased (Mackenzie, 2007).

Even those in reasonably comfortable positions have experienced wage stagnation. As funding for government services has been sharply curtailed, public service workers have been laid off and/or experienced wage reductions. Statistics Canada (2007) states that while the percentage of women with university degrees rose to 34 per cent compared with 21 per cent of men from 1991 to 2001, women still earn 18 per cent less than men do – down only from 20 per cent in the same decade – at least partly because salaries in female-dominated occupations such as health and education have not increased at the pace of male-dominated occupations such as engineering, mathematics, and computer science.

The demographics of Canada are also changing. The proportion of Canadians over 65 years of age – 1 in 20 in 1921 – had risen to 1 in 8 in 2001 and will likely reach 1 in 4 by 2041 (Health Canada, 2002: 3). Aging baby boomers have had more opportunity to accumulate wealth. The vast increases in the value of real estate have greatly enhanced the wealth accumulation of home owners, particularly those without mortgages, and have in turn benefited those older citizens who were well positioned in the first place (Drummond and Tulk, 2006).

On the other hand, newcomers to Canada have experienced a sharp decline in their economic well-being, partly as a result of job restructuring and housing costs. Overwhelmingly, immigrants and refugees settle in the three largest urban areas of Canada – Toronto, Vancouver, and Montreal – where housing costs are very high. While recent immigrants and refugees generally have increased levels of higher education over their predecessors, their settlement in Canada has been much more difficult than in previous decades. The findings of a number of studies have led to similar conclusions (Mwarigha, 2002; Ornstein, 2000; Pendakur, 2000; Reitz, 2001): 'During the last two decades there has been a dramatic downward shift in the economic status of newcomers to Canada. The groups of immigrants and refugees who have arrived in the last 20 years – overwhelmingly non-European visible minorities – are experiencing severe difficulties in the Canadian labour market and associated problems of individual and family poverty ... in spite of the fact that these recent immigrants are more highly-educated and skilled than previous cohorts' (Omidvar and Richmond, 2003: 1).

This economic struggle is made all the more difficult because immigrants and refugees from poorer countries are inclined to send a significant part of their wages to their families living abroad. Those new-comers experiencing some of the worst poverty and employment conditions are those who hold temporary work permits and who find domestic and agricultural employment, where labour standards are often unenforced. In the past, immigrants and refugees were likely to find entry-level work in jobs that required low skills but that were often well paying, such as those in natural resource industries and manufacturing.

Poverty has never been evenly spread across geographical regions in Canada. The incidence of poverty among children and their families illustrates regional differences. In 2004, those provinces with the highest child poverty rates – Newfoundland and British Columbia at 23.1 per cent and 23.5 per cent respectively – stand in contrast to Quebec, the only province in Canada where the poverty rate of children and families (15.6 per cent) has declined consistently since 1997 (Campaign 2000, 2006). This decrease is largely attributed to a range of family programs introduced in that province.

The gap between rural and urban incomes is frequently larger than provincial disparities (Beckstead and Brown, 2005). The long-standing poverty of indigenous peoples living in some of the most remote areas of Canada is stark evidence of this. However, increasingly Canadians are moving to urban areas. As of 2004, almost 80 per cent of the total population of Canada was living in urban centres (Canadian Council for Social Development, 2006), making pockets of abject poverty increasingly visible (Lee, 2000). The U.N. Populations Fund (2007) released a report singling out Vancouver, British Columbia, a 'breathtakingly gorgeous' city with a sizzling economy, as an example of one of the starkest images of urban poverty affecting a wide spectrum of poor people. Reported in the *Vancouver Sun*, the study states: 'but there is trouble in paradise. And nowhere is it more evident than in the Downtown Eastside – a two-kilometre-square stretch of decaying rooming houses, seedy strip bars and shady pawnshops ... Worst of all, it is home to a hepatitis C (HCV) rate of just below 70 per cent and an HIV prevalence rate of an estimated 30 per cent – the same as Botswana's ... A city with staggering wealth and soul-crushing poverty is far from unusual in the world's largest cities ... What makes the Downtown Eastside so different is that it is located in one of the most prosperous cities in one of the world's most prosperous countries' (quoted in O'Neil, 2007: n.p.).

Shaping the New Social Contract in Canada

While Canada has never undertaken a serious 'war on poverty,' it has a lengthy history of supporting programs that aim to address divisions among its citizens. In such a large and diverse country, regional disparities have long been recognized, and in fact, since the 1950s, equalization policies have been implemented based on the belief that all Canadians should receive equal access to public programs. Those provinces that have less ability to pay for public services receive equalization payments, while wealthier provinces do not. While not perfect, and indeed the source of considerable political tension, the principle of equalization payments has a lengthy tradition. Canada has also supported a basket of selective and universal programs in education and health care for those who, by virtue of age (Old Age Pension, Canada Pension, Guaranteed Income Supplement, and Family Allowance/Child Tax Credit) or seasonal employment (Employment Insurance), are unable to work. These programs have had considerable success in alleviating poverty for some vulnerable groups of people. Canadians are also aware that their country is a wealthy one compared with many others. Since the Second World War and the introduction of the Marshall Plan to assist in the redevelopment of Europe, Canada has, along with other rich, industrialized countries, extended its support to poorer countries primarily in Asia and Africa. While still falling short of international commitments and aspirations, Canada ranks tenth of twenty-one countries according to the 'commitment to development' index, which is prepared by the Centre for Global Development (2006) and includes such items as aid, trade, investment, and migration.

However, in recent decades the consensus that shaped these programs seems to have become fragile. Ehrenreich (1990) has an interesting proposition concerning the rise of fundamentalist conservative thinking in the United States during the 1980s and beyond. She suggests that it was buttressed by arguments against permissiveness, the hallmark of the liberal 1960s: 'Unwilling to blame permissiveness on capitalism, the New Right blamed the state. To the New Right, the most shocking and pernicious example of the permissiveness that gripped American society was located in the public sector, in the form of government programs to aid the poor. Welfare was a flagrant example ... The New Right's focus on social welfare programs guaranteed that the victims of right-wing policies would not, of course, be the business community, or even the hated New Class (professionals and managers) but the least indulged, least permissively treated segment of American society – the poor' (1990: 183).

Public policy debates in Canada similarly focused on defining the characteristics of individuals who are considered to be members of the underclasses. Because some people escape their impoverished surroundings seemingly unscathed, it is argued that those who do not are thus individually responsible. While arriving some time after the Reagan and Thatcher years in the United States and the United Kingdom, the governments of Mike Harris in Ontario (1995–2003), Ralph Klein in Alberta (1992–2006), and Gordon Campbell in British Columbia (2001 to present) introduced a similar basket of policies aimed more at demonstrating their retreat from permissiveness rather than their commitment to fiscal well-being. Reduced income taxes benefiting upper income groups and altered labour standards were the central ingredients in policies that scaled back public services, in particular income assistance. These government actions, largely consistent with policies at the federal level, softened the ground for some significant social policy choices that have affected those Canadians who are vulnerable to poverty and exclusion.

Cutbacks to Government Services

Building on the arguments of prevailing neoliberal thinking – in particular the predilection to 'blame the bureaucracy' (Savioe, 1993) – social programs in Canada and elsewhere have been seriously curtailed during the past two decades. As part of the 'debt reduction' strategies of the federal Liberal government, significant shifts in federal policies during the 1990s have had a far-reaching impact. The importance of the federal government in addressing poverty in Canada cannot be overstated; it has the capacity to make a significant difference throughout the country, even though basic social welfare programs are the responsibility of the provinces.

The bellwether policy heralding the shifting social policy regime in Canada was titled the Canada Health and Social Transfer (CHST),[4] a

---

4 The CHST originally included funding for health, education, and social welfare, but in 2004 the health funds were transferred separately (Canada Health Transfer) and the CHST was renamed the Canada Social Transfer. Health funds have increased rapidly while CST funds have not.

program introduced by Paul Martin as Minister of Finance under the federal Liberal government in 1995 (Battle and Torjman, 1995). The CHST was the outcome in part of a desire to curtail spending on social programs and in part to try to resolve many years of struggle between the provinces and the federal government, including the collapse of the Meech Lake Accord under a Conservative government and later the undermining of a potentially beneficial national social services review under a Liberal one. This struggle revolved around the reality that while provinces are responsible for administering health and welfare programs, the federal government uses its tax dollars to fund many of these programs directly, with or without provincial collaboration (English and Young, 2006). The CHST combined funding for health, education, and social welfare in one block transfer to each province and at the same time reduced national standards and the amount of funding that each province received. The cutback in funding to one envelope – social welfare – was considerable (Yalnizyan, 2005: 3), as the following facts attest:

- $8.2 billion cut in federal transfers to the provinces, 1995–98, representing a 30% decrease
- $4.2 billion cut in federal monies to social programs, 1995–98
- 1990–91 spending on social programs: 16% of GDP
- 2000–01 spending on social programs: 11.6% of GDP
- 1950: last time before this that spending on social programs was at such a low proportion of GDP

The social service envelope included in the Canada Health and Social Transfer was formerly entitled the Canada Assistance Plan (CAP), an imaginative policy introduced in 1966 that enshrined national standards for welfare policies and guaranteed matching federal funds for every dollar spent by provinces on social welfare programs. Under CAP, the requirements for federal funding were plainly stated:

- A province or territory had to provide financial aid or other assistance to any 'person in need' defined as 'a person who, by reason of inability to obtain employment, loss of the principal family provider, illness, disability, age or other cause of any kind acceptable to the provincial authority, is found to be unable, on the basis of a test established by the provincial authority that takes into account the budgetary requirements of that person and the income and resources available to that person to meet those requirements, to provide adequately for himself, or for himself and his dependants or any of them.'

• Initial eligibility had to be based solely on the needs test, and it could not include a mandatory undertaking on the part of applicants to work for their basic benefits.

Thus the core concept of CAP was 'need,' and while its definition was the subject of some debate, it nonetheless provided authority for the funding for a wide variety of income and social programs in Canada. These programs were cost-shared, with the federal government matching provincial expenditures on a 50–50 basis, with a national floor below which provincial expenditures could not fall. By contrast, the CHST left the provinces virtually on their own to fund programs as they saw fit.

Income Assistance

The immediate effects of the introduction of the Canada Health and Social Transfer were apparent in income assistance programs – fundamental programs for those using many human services throughout the country. Unmoored from the concept of need, some provinces took action to introduce stringent eligibility requirements and workfare programs, typical of the kind of welfare changes occurring in the United States and the United Kingdom (Lodomel and Trickey, 2001).

The effects have continued. Over the past decade the numbers of people in receipt of income assistance have been drastically reduced, and the benefits, always inadequate, have declined considerably. While the sharp reduction in the numbers of people in receipt of social assistance has occurred at a time when unemployment has been relatively low, it is also clearly the result of stringent restrictions enacted by most provinces. The overall numbers of people receiving social assistance have fallen from just over 3 million in 1993 to 1.75 million in 2003 (National Council of Welfare, 2006) in spite of increases to the population overall. Those in receipt of income assistance have always been among the poorest of the poor, but the depth of their poverty has increased substantially over the past few years. While the federal government has initiated child benefit programs, these have had little effect for lone parents on welfare. In many provinces, federal child benefits programs are deducted from provincial income assistance cheques. The National Council of Welfare concludes its report on income assistance on a sombre note: 'Welfare incomes have never been close to adequate anywhere in Canada. But the 1.7 million people – half a million of whom are children – who are forced to rely on welfare are being left farther and farther behind ... Ontario, Manitoba, Saskatchewan, Alberta and British Columbia hold the dubious distinction of recording the lowest welfare incomes between 2000 and 2005 for all four household types' (2006: 83). More than anything, these changes to income assistance policies illustrate the shift from what some governments like to call 'the nanny state' to the new realities of lean governments that espouse values of self-reliance and fiscal parsimony.

Employment Insurance

A second significant income program, originally titled Unemployment Insurance and developed after the economic hardship of the Great Depression, has been transformed from a modest but reliable source of income to the temporarily unemployed, to a targeted program aimed at returning specific persons to employment. This goal was the centrepiece of the amendments to the renamed Employment Insurance Act made in 1996, with a host of new policies aimed at limiting accessibility to income support provisions and placing emphasis on job readiness efforts. Eligibility was restricted through various measures including greatly extending the number of hours required prior to the payment of benefits. Levels of benefits and length of receipt of benefits were reduced. The outcomes were immediate and calamitous to many workers, particularly those with the most vulnerability to unemployment including part-time workers, youth, recent immigrants, refugees, and women. The Canadian Labour Council reported that 'the percentage of unemployed workers covered by the program in 1997 was less than half its level in 1989 – falling from 74 percent to 36 percent of the unemployed. Coverage for unemployed women was even lower with only 32 percent receiving EI in 1997' (as quoted by Torjman, 2000: n.p.). The gap between male and female beneficiaries has increased markedly since then, tripling between 1996 and 2004 (Battle et al., 2006). Ironically those excluded from Employment Insurance are similarly not eligible for the work readiness programs, the centrepiece of the changed Act.

It is not surprising that surpluses in the program were also immediately evident. Employment Insurance recorded a $26 billion surplus in
1999 (expenditures over revenues obtained through premiums from
employees and employers). By March 2001, the auditor general of
Canada, Sheila Fraser, reported that the surplus had grown to $36
billion, contravening the aims of the act itself in which premiums and
expenditures should match over time (Fraser, 2002: n.p.). Governments claimed these surpluses in their own budget reports, greatly
enhancing the appearance of their own financial performance. By
2008, in response to growing complaints, the government created a
new Crown corporation to manage the Employment Insurance
account and meet the requirements of the Act, including retaining surpluses within the program. While budgetary matters may be
addressed through these measures, the exclusion of many workers
remains.

Housing and Homelessness

Another key federal policy affecting workers and clients in human
services is social housing. Low-income Canadians are disproportionately affected by the lack of affordable housing, a problem that has
steadily worsened since 1993 when the federal government eliminated
funding for new social housing. Instead, provinces, territories, and
private markets were expected to meet the increasing need for low-
cost housing, particularly in urban areas (Shapcott, 2001; Hulchanski
and Shapcott, 2004). As a result, Canada 'now has the most private-
sector-dominated, market based housing system and the smallest
social housing sector of any Western nation, with the exception of the
United States' (Bryant, 2004: 218). Not surprisingly, those living in
'core housing need'[5] suffered most substantially. This population rose
by 33 per cent between 1991 and 1996 (Cooper, 2001), leaving one in
five Canadians in core housing need by 2001 (Drummond et al., 2004).

Evidence of how the housing crisis translates into harsh realities is
provided on most city streets, where an unprecedented number of
homeless people live hand to mouth. It is difficult to calculate the
numbers of homeless. In an article in the *Globe and Mail* this problem
was described as follows: 'Some jurisdictions use point in time counts,

---

5 Accommodations require major repairs, are crowded, and consume more than 30
   per cent of before-tax household income (Cooper, 2001).

which aim to determine the number of homeless people in a geographic area on a given day. Others use period counts, annualizing the numbers to determine the total number of individuals in a given year who are homeless. Some counts rely only on people staying in shelters; others exclude detox units, recovery houses or hospitals. Some don't include emergency shelters for abused women. Counting people who live hidden, under bridges or in alleyways, and those who are often on the move and don't follow a regular timetable is a difficult task' (Hume, 2006: n.p.).

In spite of these difficulties, the Calgary-based Sheldon Chumir Foundation for Ethics in Leadership released a report citing statistics from a wide range of organizations to estimate Canada's homeless population at somewhere between 200,000 and 300,000 people, with another 1.7 million struggling with 'housing affordability issues'(Laird, 2007). The report goes on to highlight dramatic increases in street counts of homeless people: Calgary's homeless population, for example, 'grew 740 percent between 1994 and 2006 ... an average 40 percent increase in homelessness every two years' (2007: 4). Laird cites poverty – not substance abuse or mental illness – as the leading cause of homelessness in Canada and identifies specific populations that continue to be overrepresented in homeless counts across Canada: children, Aboriginal people, the elderly, and new immigrants. Furthermore, for a variety of reasons, homeless counts may underestimate the numbers in these populations. For example, the most recent Homeless Needs Survey conducted in Victoria, British Columbia, points out that while 25 per cent of homeless people surveyed identified themselves as Aboriginal (a number almost ten times the percentage of Aboriginal people in the overall local population), it is likely that 'many homeless or unstably housed Aboriginal people did not participate in the survey for reasons associated with culture, discrimination and privacy. Some Aboriginal people do not use traditional service agencies, as they often are not culturally appropriate, so would not have been interviewed at many locations' (Victoria Cool Aid Society, 2007).

The vast increases in homelessness and unaffordable housing is in large part the result of government retreat from a national housing policy, reflecting not only an attempt by Canada's federal government to get out of the provision of services, but also its reliance on other levels of government and the private sector to step up to the plate in the absence of any particular incentives or resources to do so.

Child Care

Although a national child care program has regularly been promised throughout the past decade and more, it has never come to fruition. This is in spite of the growing numbers of mothers who are employed outside the home (approximately 76 per cent; see Kerr and Milshaski, 2005: 6) and the chronic inadequacy of approved and affordable child care spaces. Barriers to a national program include the fragmentation of responsibilities between the provinces and the federal government and the substantial involvement of the private sector in the delivery of early childhood programs (Friendly and Ferns, 2005) Quebec is the only province in Canada that has made universal child care a priority.

The story of a national child care program is one of missed opportunities and political timidity. The federal Liberal government proposed a national early learning and child care plan as part of their 2004 election platform, featuring a transfer to the provinces of $5 billion over five years for the establishment and operation of child care services. Negotiations with the provinces and territories began after the Liberals won a minority government, with most jurisdictions (except Quebec[6] and the territories) signing onto bilateral agreements-in-principle. Under these agreements, provinces were to build and operate their own early learning/child care (ELCC) system based on four principles: quality, universality, accessibility, and developmental programming. In analysing the agreements, the Childcare Resource and Research Unit of the University of Toronto noted that a variety of approaches to child care such as nursery schools, family day care and pre schools, available to parents in and out of the workforce and in all regions of the country were eligible for funding under proposed federal policy (Friendly and Ferns, 2005).

One of the first initiatives of the minority Conservative government following the 2006 election was the establishment of a 'Choice in Childcare Allowance' in place of the Liberals' national ELCC plan. The allowance – now known as the Universal Child Care Benefit (UCCB) – consists of a $100 monthly payment to all parents of children under 6 years of age, regardless of family income or the need for child care. In addition, the Conservatives proposed to spend $250

---

6 Friendly and Ferns (2006) have noted that a separate five-year agreement was reached between the federal government and Quebec in October 2005 to support investment in Quebec's existing system.

million a year to provide tax credits to employers for investment in child care spaces.

It was widely noted during the 2006 election campaign that the Conservatives' proposed allowance in fact amounted to a child benefit, rather than a child care program, since it would be provided to all families with young children regardless of need. In addition, critics pointed out that the Conservatives' program would do little to increase the supply of affordable, quality, child care spaces or to help families pay for child care (Battle, 2006). As one columnist's posting on Code Blue for Child Care put it: 'People who know anything at all about child care, like parents who need and use day-care services, know $1,200 a year, $100 a month, $5 a working day, doesn't come anywhere close to paying for it ... For-profit day care averages $722 a month in Toronto. Parents will search long and hard before they find anyone willing to look after their children for $5 a day.'[7]

In analysing the Universal Child Care Benefit and its impact on families, the Caledon Institute of Social Policy agreed that 'child care costs dwarf the proposed [Conservative child care allowance]. The most recent figures (for 2003–04 in most cases) indicate that parent fees for full-time centre-based care range, for infants, between around $6,000 and $12,000, and for toddlers and preschoolers from about $5,000 to $8,000 [per year]' (Battle, 2006: 2). Contrast these costs with the actual value of the UCCB, which for many families is considerably less than $1,200 per child under age 6 because the UCCB is taxable in the hands of the lower-income spouse in two-parent families (and the sole parent in the case of single-parent families).

The lack of approved child care spaces and the inadequacy of subsidies for those that do exist have a profound impact on many parents, particularly on mothers and children living in poverty. As one mother in our study stated:

> They [child welfare authorities] wanted me to find adequate child care that didn't involve someone coming to my house ... they wanted them in day care. I said that day care was really expensive ... I receive a subsidy but on top of that there'll be two or three hundred dollars a month depending on what day care we can get them into.

---

7 No reference provided – internet article posted by Code Blue for Child Care (www.buildchildcare.ca).

Low-income single mothers often face a Hobson's choice: get work (regardless of the hours and pay) to support your family (because income assistance may not be available and rates are inadequate) but do it in a way that does not compromise the care of your children (in spite of the challenges of finding and affording child care). Middle-income women, meanwhile, have in a sense been 'bought off' with an extra and not necessarily required $400 per month for any child under 6, rendering them less likely to protest the death of a national child care program.

While income assistance, employment insurance, housing, and child care are four policies under the government gun in the past decade, others have been similarly affected. For example, the newly elected Conservative government (2006) backed away from the Kelowna Accord, a multilateral agreement that held some promise to speed up land claims and repatriate services to indigenous communities. The overall impact of the loss of federal government leadership of social programs has had a significant impact on other programs, mostly delivered at the provincial level.

Reshaping the Non-profit Sector

With the demise of the Canada Assistance Plan and the pressures of mounting health care costs, provinces have little incentive to spend money on social welfare programs, including the many offered by the voluntary sector. Two particular funding policies have emerged, both of which have taken non-profit organizations away from their central purpose of serving particular populations and represent a shift from a pluralistic model to a neoliberal one (Scott, 1995).

The first is the use of non-profit (and in some sectors, a growing number of for-profit) organizations to deliver public programs through contracting processes (Ismael and Vaillancourt, 1988; Scott, 2003; Evans and Shields, 2000; Goldberg, 2004). As public programs have shrunk, the role of the non-profit sector has shifted from providing services supplementary to public programs, and often funded through core grants, to contracting with government to provide highly specific services. Frequently, these contracted services are time limited and focused on measurable behaviour changes. For instance, a very public dispute erupted in Victoria in 2007. Participants in a community mental health centre occupied it after the non-profit organization, the Canadian Mental Health Association, and the provincial government funding body agreed to close the centre. In place of its daily support program consisting of activities and meals, the association planned a targeted program designed to increase employment-readiness skills, something that many participants argued was totally unrealistic for many of those affected by chronic mental health problems (Harnett, 2007). Indeed, many voluntary organizations that were originally established to provide long-term supportive services and to advocate for social change, often at odds with government policy, have become instead the vehicles for the cheaper delivery of very limited public programs, frequently geared to short-term goals like employment readiness.

The second and related shift has been the overall cutback of public funds to the voluntary sector with the rationale that the strongest will survive on their own through the adoption of sound business practices: 'The voluntary sector in Canada is only now beginning to feel the full impact of neo-conservative policy, as governments are transferring significantly less money to the sector. The message has been received ... Voluntary organizations identify a need to become more competitive, to learn marketing and entrepreneurial skills, and to streamline management practices in order to increase organizational efficiency' (Salamon and Anheier, 1996: 4).

Particular organizations, those that are small, serving apparently less-deserving clients, and/or those whose activities are increasingly defined as advocacy, are clearly disadvantaged by these funding practices. With less capacity to submit complex bids in a competitive contracting environment, and without the resources or public approbation to mount fundraising campaigns, they are often passed over and many disappear altogether. The struggle of many women's organizations is evidence of this (Meinhard and Foster, 1996; Bradshaw et al., 1996). Grassroots and national women's organizations have experienced drastic cuts to the National Action Committee on the Status of Women and the Canadian Research Institute for the Advancement of Women, the closing of twelve of sixteen regional NACSW offices at the federal level, and the demise of many women's centres at the provincial level. While the protests were vigorous, in the end government cuts remained. The REAL Women of Canada, an anti-feminist group with extensive connections within the affluent conservative movement, provides the argument for a 'survival of the fittest' approach consistent with current federal government policy: 'REAL Women thrived without debts while feminist groups have collapsed. We have shown that a volunteer women's organization can remain vibrant and active without government funding. All it needs is the support of its members, which we are very fortunate to have' (*Reality*, 2006: n.p.).

The changes to the voluntary sector concurrent with cutbacks to government programs have particular significance for human service work (Baines, 2004). While the services offered by the voluntary sector have always varied from community to community, those services that now remain are less able to move flexibly to meet emerging needs, and they are particularly hamstrung in finding money for ongoing support services for people who are unable to enter the labour market and people who may require long-term support. Ironically, the reason for the emergence of many voluntary organizations, the need for community organizations to care for people often over a long period, has become the service that these organizations find most difficult to fund and deliver. This challenge has occurred precisely at the same time as there are fewer family and volunteer caregivers within the home and community.

It has also occurred as more people require the assistance of voluntary agencies, given cutbacks to government services. While these recent cutbacks have been enumerated in this chapter, one longer-term policy, de-institutionalization, has added to the numbers of people requiring assistance from voluntary organizations. De-institutionalization began as a mental health movement in the 1960s based on the belief that many people could lead productive and satisfying lives in the community rather than in institutions. Other groups of people, including those with physical disabilities and people involved in the criminal justice system, advocated for similar changes. The centrepiece of de-institutionalization required that funds saved on institutionalizing people were to be spent on community support services for them, and in some cases, control of them. The results of these efforts have been uneven. While many people who previously would have been institutionalized now live outside institutions, supports for them vary widely from community to community, and frequently such supports are so inadequate that people with serious mental and physical disabilities are left to fend for themselves.

Resistance to Change

This chapter has indicated that significant challenges have been facing Canadians over the past few decades, including the growing income inequalities associated with the shifting nature of the global economy;

rising employment rates among specific groups of people that have not reduced the problems of unemployment; low welfare rates, resulting in Canadians being 'paid to be poor'; and an increasing aging population that along with changing family structures make caregiving a more difficult family function (Jenson, 2004; Hay, 2005). Further, the inclusion of increasing numbers of immigrants into the labour market and the community and the redress of a century of dismal policies towards Aboriginal peoples are central. Policies that address social provision, social insurance, social inclusion, and social cohesion are crucial to guiding actions in the next decades (Boychuk, 2004).

This conclusion is hardly new. Study upon study has demonstrated that people who live in chronically poor conditions are far more likely than middle-class Canadians to experience reduced educational opportunities, specific physical and mental health problems, poorer employment opportunities, low birth weights and diminished life span, criminal justice involvement, and social exclusion, and that they therefore require additional resources from health and human services organizations to deal with these problems – nevertheless, there is a staunch reluctance to address poverty and inequality in a substantial way.

As outlined in the previous chapter, the reluctance to address social conditions and their impact is frequently presented in ideological terms. It is argued that people in poverty would lose their motivation to improve themselves and their willingness to accept any kind of work if they are provided with sufficient resources. Further, if some people escape these conditions seemingly unscathed, then why can't others? This latter question has led to research inquiries attempting to separate out survivors from others with the term *resilience* used to describe differences. Ironically, as we search for variables among individuals in the same socioeconomic boat, the boat itself remains unexamined. A related body of research examines variables that contribute to making people a danger to others. Socioeconomic conditions are often included as one variable in a host of others.

Frequently ignored in these arguments is that, while opposition exists to the use of government policies to substantially address significant problems facing the poor, this same opposition fades when government policy is used to buttress the resources of the middle and upper classes. Lower taxes and significant tax exemptions are often used as policy levers. A recent examination of the middle class across the world (Pressman, 2007) indicates that the middle class is declining across most Western nations and that those leaving the middle class are more likely to slide downwards than move upwards. Canada and Norway, where the middle class has grown substantially, are the exceptions. However, if the composition of the middle classes is determined on the basis of wage earnings alone, Canada's middle class shrinks considerably. Government transfers such as pensions maintain their growth. In fact, Canada directs only 22 per cent of its spending to the poorest 30 per cent of the population and 64 per cent to the middle 40 per cent, as determined by the Organization for Economic Co-operation and Development (Saunders, 2007). Another means for transferring government money to middle- and upper-class citizens and their companies is through the growing use of contracts. By cutting government services to the bone and contracting out a host of programs, the government can reward corporate benefactors. The reconstruction of Iraq is often cited as an egregious example of this practice. In another example, Monbiot (2007) has documented a case study of hospital repairs in Britain under the Private Finance Initiative, which allows corporations to build and run schools, hospitals, roads, and prisons. Because the private sector is interested in large projects and is not interested in difficult renovations, the study's author reports that a hospital was torn down rather than repaired, raising costs from an estimated £30 million to £410 million and resulting in the laying off of hospital staff to cover the expenses.

Another argument for resisting efforts to address social problems rests on the belief that issues such as poverty and disadvantage are simply too complicated to be tackled by any one government, particularly during the short span of an election cycle. However, our own history and the experience of other jurisdictions contradict this claim. Poverty for seniors was a significant issue for governments when the Old Age Security program for all citizens over 65 years of age was introduced in Canada in 1952. While many factors besides income security programs have changed since then, including the entry of women into the paid labour force in significant numbers, it is now true that a combination of universal and targeted programs for Canadians over 65 has contributed significantly to addressing poverty for this age group. Attempts to tamper with this success have been met with a firestorm of opposition from a group of citizens with considerable political clout. Canada also has a long history of delivering benefits efficiently and without stigma through the income tax system (Battle, 2001).

Other countries directing their wealth to income redistribution and to expenditures on education have fared well in addressing child poverty without sacrificing their ability to compete on world markets (Novak, 2007). After examining OECD countries by comparing levels of taxation and global ranking in economic competitiveness, Novak identifies three with the lowest rates of child poverty that nonetheless rank among the top five countries on global competitiveness (Finland, Sweden, and Denmark). He notes: 'Poverty is not reduced by having the largest amount of national wealth, but by how countries make use of the wealth they have' (2007: 27). Some optimists are now arguing that neoliberal notions of social policy are fading precisely because they fail to make the connection between the well-being of citizens and a thriving economy: 'Whether one talks about "social investment," "active social policy," or "productivist social policy," the idea is that to perform well an economy needs reliable and effective social policy. This idea goes against the neoliberal assumption of the inevitable trade-off between economic efficiency and social justice' (Saint-Martin, 2004: 3).

Conclusion

This chapter has demonstrated that economic and social supports for people living on the margins have diminished in Canada. There are more people living in precarious circumstances than before, and their situation is becoming more visible. The social hierarchy has become steeper, underscoring the considerable differences between the rich and the poor.

One might expect that the result of this retreat from social programs would be diminished overall government budgets and much leaner government operations. While this has occurred in some areas, for instance, expenditures on the Canada Health and Social Transfer and Employment Insurance, it is not true overall. Government expenditures continue to rise, year after year. Nor is it even true within those programs targeted for reductions. For instance, expenditures in the 2007 federal budget added $550 million to be distributed to the provinces to combat what is termed the 'welfare trap,' initiatives to encourage those on social assistance to move to employment. Other program costs rise. The number of police officers in Canada has risen each year since 1994. In 2005, spending on policing totaled about $9.3 billion, an increase of 4 per cent from the previous year and the ninth consecutive increase in policing costs in constant dollars. Spending is choosing.

We began this chapter with the proposition that risk thinking discourages an analysis of disparities. There are several ways that this occurs. As the opening example of smog illustrates, some risk talk assumes that 'we are all in this together, facing the same risks.' In addition, as we discussed in Chapter 1, risk takes our eye off present miseries, making these circumstances a less compelling reason for collective action. Instead, it focuses attention on making predictions about whether people are 'at risk' of some kind of future harm in some particular area. That they are living in immediate circumstances of deprivation and danger can be overlooked. In many situations, unless clients can be deemed to be 'at risk' or 'a risk,' human service workers are not able to provide the help that may so clearly be necessary. Helping others becomes dependent on calculations and not on responses to injustice.

Ironically, risk thinking can also allow us to mount programs and take action on those who are not in any particular 'need' at the moment but who share the characteristics of people who have been assessed as likely to do something bad in the future. In this process, social characteristics such as income, employment, housing, and ethnicity are not used to help people but to indict people.

Another way that risk becomes disassociated from social injustice is through ideological circles (Smith, 1990), and this chapter illustrates one such circle. Programs designed to assist people with the normal contingencies of living have been curtailed or eliminated so that people will 'help themselves.' As people apply for assistance from diminished programs, resources for these programs are diminished. Further conditions are imposed to curtail their use. Those requiring assistance yet not receiving it become more visible, and some appear to be threats or 'risks.' Other policies and programs to manage these threats are created, shifting work and expenditures to surveillance and policing activities. Cuts to social programs are further justified because these people come to be seen as undeserving of help (they are not helping themselves). The focus intensifies on 'these people' while their circumstances sink to the background of attention. Further, the argument goes, there is now even less money for social spending. The 'loss of social thinking' (Beck, 1992: 25) continues.

Of course, what is occurring besides this retreat from social thinking is a solidifying of power relationships. Those who have always enjoyed more than their fair share of social and economic power have even more power. Those at the bottom, less worthy of sympathy, have even less clout than they did before. Not only do they have less support from human service organizations, they also have less power to define their needs. Instead, they must accept the definition of their needs based on calculations of the risks that they may pose to themselves and others.

It is in the uncertain context of this shifting social world that helping professionals have found themselves asked to identify and contain risk, to manage 'risky' populations, and to take personal and political responsibility when things go badly wrong. The next chapter takes a closer look at how risk is translated into risk assessments that have been incorporated into a variety of professional fields and roles. In at least some professions, the job of risk assessment has become a major activity. The risks that professionals are asked to assess have been largely identified outside their professional purview, by academics, managers, and political exigencies. In the process of risk assessment, the primary focus remains on identifying specific characteristics of individuals while ignoring the characteristics of the larger social context in which they live. The disconnection between risk and inequality is further assured.

4 The Entrenchment of Risk Assessment in Human Services

Risk is a staple feature of human services. Professionals such as nurses, social workers, and psychologists often work with people whose lives are filled with challenges and problems and who have few resources to address them. The potential for 'bad things to happen' can be just around the corner. Not surprisingly, human service professionals express the desire to prevent problems rather than to apply bandaids after the fact. For them, calculating and addressing 'the risks' sound like promising activities designed to achieve this professional aim.

In recent decades risk has assumed a much more central role in professional thinking and practice, although often this is not explicitly acknowledged (Beaumont, 1999; Rycus and Hughes, 2003). Entering 'risk assessment' into a search engine with individual professions yields a staggering number of 'hits': for 'nursing' (about 1.2 million), 'psychology' (about one million), 'social work' (about 500,000), 'teachers' (about 100,000), or 'parole officers' (about 31,000). The prevalence of risk thinking and risk assessment in human services is no casual trend but represents a profound shift in views about human needs and professional practice.

In Chapters 1 and 2 we painted a broad picture of the discourses of risk. In particular we traced how risk thinking is reshaping our understanding of social welfare and collective actions, placing increasing responsibility on individuals for managing their fate. In Chapter 3 we examined substantial changes to social policies in Canada that are partly a result of this thinking and the impact that these changes have had on increasing inequality. More people are 'at risk' or 'a risk' in large part because of these developments. In this chapter, we focus on professionals in human services. We pay particular attention to how these various ideas about social welfare and risk have permeated human services and are restructuring organizations and the work of practitioners. These first four chapters set the broad context for our study of risk assessment in child welfare that follows.

Discourses of Risk and Risk Assessment in the Human Service Professions

There are at least two kinds of reports in the popular media that underscore the role of human service professionals in risk and risk assessment, loosely grouped as protection stories and self-help stories. On any given day we may hear stories about parole officers and psychiatrists who supposedly have recommended the release of violent offenders or mentally ill patients without attending properly to risk assessments, or about public health nurses who have failed to complete risk assessments on HIV-positive patients regarding their likelihood of practising safe sex. Recently, police in Victoria, British Columbia, were chided in the press for failing to 'carry out proper risk assessment' while chasing a car thief through busy residential streets. After the shooting at Virginia Tech, Stephen Porter, a forensic psychologist at Dalhousie University, said that the shootings 'should act as a catalyst for schools to adopt a "risk assessment tool" in which a counsellor would rate a troubled student for his likelihood to become violent.' What staff would be expected to do about students with high scores is not clear (Welsh, 2007). In fact, the media have been largely instrumental in focusing public and political attention on the risks of specific behaviours and crimes, attention that easily shifts as the next big scandal emerges in another area of risky behaviour and professional 'incompetence' (Parton, 2005; Tator and Henry, 2006).

While most of these stories accept unequivocally the presence of risk and the importance of risk assessments in predicting and managing risk, a few query whether these aims are always achievable. In a *Globe and Mail* article reporting on the fatal shooting of a police officer during a drug raid, the Laval chief of police acknowledged that death is 'an inherent risk in an officer's life. It's like flipping a coin. God willing, most of the time it falls on the right side. This morning it fell on the wrong side' (3 March 2007: A9).

Nonetheless, the general themes of these protection stories are consistent. Risk is a real thing with a potentially bad outcome. The meaning of risk in these stories often slips between the possibility of negative occurrences (the 'risk' of a given situation) and the potential of dangerous individuals ('risky' people) to cause harm, and the two ideas are often conflated. Another idea contained in many media stories is that 'at its core, as both a noun and a verb, "risk" denotes actions, agents or protagonists' (Hamilton et al., 2007). Something must be done about risk, and in these cases, at least, that 'something' falls to professionals. They must assess risk accurately and consistently, and they must manage its effects to protect the vulnerable and the general public as well. Indeed, many professionals feel the weight of these expectations and fear that their failure to guarantee this protection has undermined public confidence in their role.

There is another general set of stories, frequently told in the science and health portion of the news, in parents' and women's magazines, and in popular lifestyle literature focused on the latest 'risks' that have been uncovered and on advice from professionals about dealing with them. In these stories risks are also seen as real, but each is broken down into a particular set of factors that the general public is expected to protect itself against by taking prudent actions. From eating red meat (or not), drinking wine (or not), jogging (or not), we are pushed and pulled to pay attention to risk and to take action because professionals, armed with the latest scientific data, are advising us to do so. While many of these 'self-help' stories relate to health, we are also advised about other matters such as managing our personal safety (burglar proofing our homes and street proofing our children), and our economic security (managing our money and preventing internet fraud).

Failing to heed these warnings is tantamount to bringing on our own misfortune, yet our capacities and resources to do so are rarely mentioned. For instance, the Heart and Stroke Foundation of Canada recently invited television watchers to log onto its website and take their own risk assessment for heart and stroke disease, completing twenty-six questions about such things as family background, age, race, and lifestyle 'choices.' At the end participants are provided with a list of items scored as normal risks and elevated risks. This list is then further divided into those risks that participants can do something about and those that cannot be modified, for instance, age. Participants are then presented with an action plan that they are to undertake on their own or with the help of health care providers. This example is by no means unusual. We are frequently invited into this kind of risk assessment activity, presented as scientifically sound and as a positive addition to managing our lives. However, 'the concept of risk and assessments of the effectiveness of risk management in particular cases are used to distinguish between self and other: to project anxieties, to cast moral judgments, and to lay blame upon marginalised individuals and groups. In this sense, risk discourse is neither politically nor socially generous' (Douglas, 1992: 10).

Even so, professionals are largely sympathetic to risk thinking. This is perhaps not surprising, given their traditional focus on assessment as a central task, the complexity of the decisions that they make on a daily basis, and the media attention they receive when things go wrong. Kropp has noted that 'most professional bodies ... have ethical guidelines that mandate a duty to warn when there is risk of harm to an identifiable target' (2004: 687). This duty of care requires them to address clear dangers to vulnerable people. Further, the proliferation of literature on empowerment in the human service professions clearly supports the notion that the users of service, in partnership with professionals, should take charge of their own 'risks,' thus giving further currency to the concept.

A review of professional literature addressing risk reveals the overwhelming presence of risk thinking and the increasing role of professionals in responding to it. Most of the literature on risk in human services centres on a specific profession or field (see, e.g., Simon, 2005; Hoge, 2002; Shortt et al., 2006), although a few writers span risk practices across more than one discipline (Kemshall and Pritchard, 1996; Parsloe, 1999; Kemshall et al., 1997). For the most part, the complexities of the concept of risk itself, underscored in Chapter 1 of this book, are given short shrift in professional literature. It is assumed that professionals know what risk means and what their responsibilities are in dealing with risk. The opening lines of one book on the subject clearly illustrate this expectation: 'Risk assessment and risk management are now key issues for all practitioners and managers in the field of social care and criminal justice. Increasingly responding to the risks of others, preventing risks to vulnerable clients, or running risks to themselves is all in a day's work for the busy practitioner and manager' (Kemshall and Pritchard, 1996: 1). A typical professional article, in this case dealing with young mothers in foster care (Barn and Mantovani, 2007) presents several overlapping meanings for 'risk,' (mentioned 37 times in the text). The authors say risk can signify particular individual behaviours occurring in the present and labelled as 'risky' (sexual activity, use of drugs, ignorance of sex and contraception), and it can define a class of people engaging in these behaviours (young women at risk). Risk is also used to denote a set of current factors in an individual's life that, taken together, could indicate vulnerability. These include family background, age, level of education, and structural factors like inadequate funding for social services. Further, risk is used to indicate the possibility of misfortune in the future (risk of pregnancy, risk of social exclusion). While the authors do not formally define risk, they assume professional readers will share these various taken-for-granted definitions.

Although definitions of risk are not given much attention in professional discourses, there is considerable focus on scholarship and scientific research aimed at improving the efficacy of risk assessment instruments so that they enhance the capacity to predict certain behaviours or dangers. Much less attention is devoted to the task of addressing risks once they have been identified. And while the media have been quick to point out the errors of professional decision making, the notion that users of our services may be 'at risk' from our actual interventions has received little attention in professional discourses (Burke, 1999).

While an acceptance of risk and its implications permeate professional literature, it is also true that some scholars have underscored the complexity of risk thinking for human services (Beaumont, 1999; Krane and Davies, 2000). Much like the Laval chief of police, Parton (1998) suggests that rather than trudge down the path of continually trying to refine and improve risk assessment instruments and risk management strategies so that we have got it 'right,' we would be better to acknowledge publicly that it is not possible to eliminate risk. We should instead find spaces to rehabilitate the notions of *uncertainty* and *ambiguity*, concepts that used to be more or less accepted by many human service professionals. Parton's ideas have been expressed by others (Ferguson, 1997; Petersen, 1996), but they have not found significant purchase in professional discourses.

We also add that the notion of *taking risks* as a positive aspect of human growth may need revival. Indeed, professionals often suggest that their clients make considerable changes in their lives such as abstaining from the use of alcohol and drugs; moving away from undesirable partners, neighbourhoods, and friendship groups; and finding new employment – choices that may involve taking many risks. Many clients, particularly adolescents, are already engaged in risk-taking behaviour, which can be understood as part and parcel of their life stage. Yet positive connotations of risk are rarely featured in professional discourses, although they abound in our cultural values and lore captured in such sayings as 'Great deeds are usually wrought at great risks' (Herodotus, 484 BC – 430 BC) or 'Proverbial wisdom counsels against risk and change, but sitting ducks fare worst of all' (Mason Cooley, 1986).

In the following sections we will explore how these taken-for-granted notions of risk as something 'real and bad' that can be calculated through ever-improving scientific assessments play out in different kinds of risk assessment instruments used in human services and their applications in daily practice.

The 'Human Service Professions'

The term *human service professions* refers mostly to those professionals – such as nurses, teachers, social workers, probation and parole officers, psychologists, and others – who provide services within the mandates of public or quasi-public organizations of varying sizes and who are accountable both to their professions and to the organizations employing them. We recognize that many individuals in these professions work outside government or voluntary organizations in private practices or small co-operatives, but we are primarily interested in those whose work requires allegiance to state-funded organizations and who are most likely to be charged with undertaking risk assessments. We also know that many human service workers are not members of a specific profession, and in some cases do not have formal professional credentials, but are doing work guided at least in part by expectations of professional service. Clients are often unaware of the various titles and ranks of the people who are working with them, but they do expect some common organizational and professional orientation to the work.

The prospect of defining *profession* is almost as daunting as getting a clear understanding of the use of *risk*. Using as their benchmarks the traditional professions of law and medicine, scholars in earlier times focused on judging the state of an occupation according to the degree to which it demonstrated qualities such as a clear body of knowledge, requirements for long periods of training, autonomous decision making, relationships of trust with those served, promotion of acceptance and non-judgmental attitudes, and an ethos of collegiality and altruism guided by a code of ethics and self-governance (Wilensky,

1964). Many occupational groups such as nursing, social work, and teaching whose work took place within formal organizations were never able to attain this gold standard and were often referred to as semi-professions particularly because of their lack of autonomy and less 'scientific' knowledge base (Etzioni, 1969). The fact that they were largely female occupations was not lost on a number of scholars (Etzioni, 1969; Hearn, 1982).

More recently this trait approach has been found wanting, as it remains difficult to draw clear lines between occupations based on these characteristics. The commitment to a code of ethics is a feature of not only established professions, but a range of occupations from landscape artists, beauticians, information technologists, and others. The trait approach also obscures an analysis of how power works in defining professionalism (Evetts, 2006). Feminists have criticized this approach because it denies the importance of the artistic aspects of caring work, pays little attention to professional responsibilities of addressing social causes, and values empirical knowledge over other ways of knowing (Abbott and Meerabeau, 1998; Davies, 1995, 2000).

Another thread in this literature has focused on the functions of professions as a particular way of organizing work in contrast to the market and bureaucracy. One idea proffers that professions provide a civilizing force in market economies whereby highly regarded practitioners work for the individual and social good and at the same time engage us in paying deference to them. This is a model of professional and personal commitment that is at once both enlightening and colonizing (Davies, 1995). Talcott Parsons 'recognized and was one of the first theorists to show how the capitalist economy, the rational-legal social order (of Weber) and the modern professions were all interrelated and mutually balancing in the maintenance and stability of a fragile normative social order' (Evetts, 2006: 517). Not lost in the equation is the fact that professionals gained control of a market in exchange for their contributions to civil society.

Hanlon (1998) has suggested that the idea of professionalism is being used to flatter occupations into believing that they are gaining prestige and independence. Actually, argues Hanlon, professionalism is being redefined according to models of a management ethos and entrepreneurial spirit. Practitioners are encouraged to govern themselves according to the traditional and altruistic principles of professionalism, but without increases in pay or decreases in hours of work. This strategy seems to be paying off. The percentage of 'professionals' working over fifty hours per week almost doubled in the decade between 1991 and 2001 (Duxbury and Higgins, 2002: 46).

While these theories have merit in uncovering the layers of meaning and motives of professional work, they tend to obscure what may be the potential value of a professional approach to human services. Svensson (2006) conducted a survey of members of the Swedish Confederation of Professional Associations, asking them the question, 'What does the word professionalism mean to you?' Overwhelmingly, respondents emphasized the knowledge base inherent in the term, but the types of knowledge they reported included mostly 'practical know-how, experience and familiarity rather than theoretical and assertive knowledge' (2006: 588). They used such expressions as 'having the ability one claims to have' and 'to know what you are doing and why.' To a somewhat lesser extent, ethics and moral values and positive outcomes of the work were also contained in their definitions ('carry my work to a high quality for pupils'). This study fits with the findings of others and with the experience of the authors in the field of social work. Theories of 'how to help' can be generated mutually with clients, working within complex situations and particular contexts, and often bear little resemblance to textbook versions (Parton, 2003). Clients of the helping professions value acceptance, understanding, and talk (Howe, 1996; Callahan and Lumb, 1995) whereby they are able to review their experience and take charge of giving it different meanings than before. At the heart of helping is the process of engagement between workers and their clients, maintained through real conversations aimed at improving circumstances.

How risk assessment challenges these aspirations is not clear, and in fact contradictory evidence exists. On the one hand, there are suggestions that such assessments perpetuate a traditional approach to helping work based on positivist views of scientific knowledge. In particular, concerns are raised that the work of risk assessment is displacing the importance of relationship (Garland, 1997), the centrepiece of practice and professional codes of ethics. At the same time, there are numerous studies citing the potential of risk assessment to improve the decisions of human service professionals, a topic that we take up later in this chapter.

Human Service Organizations

Our experiences, from attending school, going to the public health clinic and hospital, calling the police or being 'called upon' by them, form our understanding of the purpose and functioning of human service organizations. As we know, these organizations vary greatly in size, aims, and operations, and there are a number of theoretical explanations designed to capture their purpose and functioning. One school of thought emphasizes their central purpose as the distribution of public programs with impartiality and skill. Hasenfeld, for instance, defines human service organizations as public or quasi-public institutions designed to 'protect, maintain or enhance the personal well-being of individuals by defining, shaping or altering their personal attributes' (1982: 1). Marxist and neo-Marxist views, on the contrary, contend that human service organizations exist primarily as vehicles for maintaining the power of the ruling classes, in effect, perpetuating class inequalities through a variety of measures, including the hierarchical organization of work, their stringent eligibility mechanisms, and their demands for compliance at all levels. Those espousing political economy perspectives build on the work of neo-Marxists but emphasize the importance of the myriad of interest groups that act on human service organizations, seeking to use them to advance particular agendas. This insight helps explain in part the highly contentious ground occupied by human service organizations such as public schools, hospitals, prisons, and welfare organizations, where various groups within and outside the organization battle for their views of what are permitted programs and desired outcomes.

While the purposes of human service organizations are contentious ground, so are explanations about their preferred structure and functioning. Certainly, theories of bureaucracy, with an emphasis on the formal aspects of human service organizations, their legal authority, and defined structures based on a 'chain of command,' have taken precedence. However, it is also recognized that human service organizations are, in practice although often not on paper, loosely organized structures in which centralized decisions and policies are adapted as they filter down the line to the street-level bureaucrats at the interface of policy and the needs of their clientele (Lipsky, 1980). In this view, human services involve rapidly changing, fast-paced situations where the discretion of those on the front line is often required. Further insights about the power and impact of human service organizations evolve from those applying postmodern concepts, particularly concerning how individuals internalize their norms and restraints, even in the absence of clear oversight. For instance, long after leaving school, many people still have dreams of being in a classroom, or trying to find a classroom (probably in pajamas) totally ill-prepared for the crucial examination about to be administered. Some suggest that we are moving from a period of faith in rational processes and commitment to linear progress, the modernist project, to a more chaotic and diffuse postmodern state where power is far less understood by examining formal systems only.

Insights from theorists are key to understanding what human service organizations are and why they perform as they do. There is also some agreement about their key characteristics. The central focus of human service organizations is people rather than products, and they have a public mandate, usually emanating from public laws and policies, to carry out their work. Human service organizations proliferated with the expansion of the welfare state from the turn of the twentieth century onwards, and they strike a bargain of sorts with those whom they serve: in return for receiving public services, participants 'expose significant aspects of their private lives to public scrutiny and control' (Hasenfeld, 1982: 4).

To meet their goals, human service organizations carry out two related functions. They categorize people, and on the basis of these categorizations they match programs such as care, education, counselling, and incarceration with the users of services in order to change them. The rationale is that these prescribed changes are good for service users and will promote the well-being of the community. Risk assessment offers promise in the task of categorizing individuals and may be one reason that it is so widely adopted. Risk assessment can be used as a sorting device to classify people, as well as a triaging method to separate those who need resources from those who do not, thus buttressing the classification system with a 'scientific' rationale. Risk assessment also has the potential to name specific behaviours and match these with specific action plans for change.

Individuals who come to human service organizations for some kind of assistance are frequently coerced into doing so, a fact that is particularly true for those considered dangerous to themselves or others. Even if they are not directly or indirectly coerced, individuals often have little choice about which organizations they will attend or who will provide them with service within these organizations. While there may be the appearance of choice, in actual fact choice has been reduced with the elimination of many services and the shoestring operations of those services that remain. In the past few decades the issue of choice has focused on whether to use public or private services. Presumably people who have the money to pay for services have more options than people who do not. Moreover, citizens are expected to use an increasing number of (often fee-based) services to assist them in becoming effective managers of their own risks.

At the same time, service users generally have little input into the policies or practices of human service organizations, a significant lack of power that is sometimes mitigated by advisory committees, client feedback mechanisms, and other initiatives. However, these organizations, with their authority to classify individuals, name behavior, and judge its meaning, can exercise considerable power over individuals and have a lasting influence on their self-concept. For instance, persons in mental hospitals are viewed and view themselves considerably differently from those attending university. Ambivalence about participation in public services has always been evident. In exchange for a certain loss of power and control, individuals may obtain services that sustain and/or greatly enhance their lives.

The Transformation of Human Service Organizations

As noted in Chapter 3, there have been vigorous attempts to transform human service organizations in the past two decades so that they more clearly reflect the aims of a neoliberal policy agenda. The goals of this transformation are to limit the numbers of people served through the use of rigorous classification procedures and the development of strategies to ensure that clients and potential clients become self-managers of their own risks – by quitting smoking, limiting alcohol use, maintaining their marketable skills, etc. At the same time, human service organizations are to provide surveillance of those considered dangerous to society and manage the behaviour of the most aberrant.

To accomplish these aims human service organizations are expected to change their approach to management, adopting what is loosely called the 'new managerialism,' described in Chapter 2. At the root of this approach are deeply held suspicions about the wastefulness of public service organizations. Accompanying discourses deride the sloppy management practices that are supposedly endemic to them. In this scenario, professional knowledge is subordinate to managerial knowledge, and professionals themselves are less important, since managers have the power to name the essential tasks and competencies of professionals and provide surveillance of their performance through audits and other controls. The introduction of risk assessment and risk management into some human services strengthens managerial practices, especially in fields where it is a central part of the work. In particular, risk assessment can shift the locus of power from professionals to managers through requirements for standardized practices and a focus on written and specific accountability measures.

The 'new penology' illustrates the application of this transformation in one field of human services. Changes involve the use of risk assessment, risk management plans, and technological surveillance prevalent in the corrections field at the present time (Kemshall and Maguire, 2001). The new approach is characterized by an emphasis on actuarial rather than professional decision making. In this scenario, processes of risk assessment and risk management, broken down into a series of steps requiring specific approval, are the central professional tasks. The new penology also involves an organizational culture that is focused on control and efficiency, with substantial paperwork required to document work practices. Probation officers often view this system as 'filling their in-tray with forms to be completed' (Beaumont, 1999: 137). Debates about whether corrections should focus on the rehabilitation or punishment of individuals have been largely displaced by this emphasis on the prediction and management of unlawful behaviour.

While this transformation might be viewed as a success by many in the corrections and other fields, the idea that business principles can simply be substituted for principles of human service delivery produces important contradictions in practice. A professional emphasis on care and concern for individuals suggests that the actions of human service organizations can and should be bounded by human rights considerations and moral values. While it may be sound business practice to dump excess inventory to make room for new products, human service organizations must think twice about discharging people who are in continuing need of care and protection in order to make space for new clientele. Certainly, such decisions can bring public disapproval when things go wrong, as in the case of a person who is inebriated, discharged from jail, and then dies on a public street, for instance. Technological advances in areas such as reproduction, stem cell research, and surveillance continue to exacerbate tensions between professional and business orientations. The sale of body organs or embryos for profit when there are willing customers are among many frightening possibilities.

While business models are also built to some extent on the importance of relationships with customers, the formation of relationships is frequently the *central* means by which human service organizations achieve their goals. Professionals skilled in using relationships to help people to make significant life changes require some autonomy in decision making. Attempts to limit this autonomy and to replace relationship building with more 'efficient' approaches continue to occur but are resisted by human service practitioners and their clients. Some practitioners are voting with their feet. In a spirited examination of the shortage of social workers in the United Kingdom, Harlow (2004) argues that the incursion of managerialism into social work practice is a significant force driving social workers, predominately women, out of the field and preventing others from entering. She argues that what attracts people to social work are relationships with others and the opportunities to make change, features of the work that are sharply curtailed under managerial systems.

Thus, while many workers in human service will attest to the changing nature of their workplaces and tasks, with an emphasis on the 'business of helping,' they also experience the chronic tensions created between this approach and their desires to work as professionals.

Yet risk assessment and some of its unintended consequences did not emerge only as a program of neoliberals with managerial ideas but has many roots. Within different professions, it is one expression of the long struggle in human services to perfect their central tasks: assessing individuals and treating or enhancing their behaviour. Although human service professional disciplines have developed largely in isolation from one another, the fact remains that they share similar purposes and histories. Most of those histories are told as a story of progress, moving from the isolation of individuals, usually in separate facilities or 'special classes' within ordinary institutions, to their integration into 'the community.' Theories of human behaviour have also shifted from those focused on the biological roots of behaviour to those incorporating social causes. Rose (1996c) traces this story of progress in one discipline, psychiatry, noting how the rise of the community care movement after the Second World War profoundly changed the practice of psychiatry. Over time, it moved from one in which psychiatrists were the experts in asylums, their domain, to one encompassing a much broader conception of mental health. Involved in this transformation were increasing numbers of individuals requiring service by many different professionals. Calls for interdisciplinary collaboration and interagency cooperation reflected this diversity of professional practices and sites. At the root of the community care movement is the desire to 'prevent' mental health breakdowns and to provide services and surveillance to those who would formerly have occupied institutional beds. It is not difficult to see how the conception of 'risk' and its assessment fits nicely with this long-standing professional agenda.

The Practice of Risk Assessment in Human Services

Given this context of 'progress,' it is not surprising that risk assessment has found fertile ground in the human services (see, e.g., Hannah-Moffat and Maurutto, 2003, for a sampling of their proliferation). The following review of risk assessment in several fields and disciplines indicates the wide range of instruments now in common practice:

- Psychologists and others working in the criminal justice system assess offenders at various stages of their incarceration (sentencing, classification, parole requests, release) to determine the ongoing disposition of the case (Monahan and Steadman, 1994; Hilton and Simmons, 2001). The use of risk assessment in corrections is widespread and long-standing, given the demands to predict which offenders can safely live in the community and/or minimum security facilities and which cannot.
- Police are called to a domestic violence dispute to determine the initial team of responders and to determine what should occur as the situation unfolds. An example is the B-SAFER risk assessment (Kropp and Hart, 2004).
- Nurses may use risk assessment routinely in their practice with patients to assess their likelihood of falling (Smith et al., 2006; Perell et al., 2001).
- Teachers are frequently required to complete risk assessments prior to field trips, often termed 'excursion management,' as well as assessments aimed at identifying children who are 'at risk' for mental health problems and poor school performance (Shortt et al., 2006).
- Social workers, psychologists, physicians, and nurses in mental health administer risk assessments on patients considered danger-

ous before admission and prior to discharge from hospital
(Langan, 1999).

Human service professionals not only carry out risk assessments
concerning their clients but they are also frequently the subject of some
kinds of risk assessment themselves as a part of hiring and ongoing
employment. For instance, criminal record checks are a kind of risk
assessment and have become mandatory for many human service professionals at the time of employment and afterwards. Drug testing,
another type of risk assessment, requires employees to submit to tests
as part of their employment contracts. These tests remain controversial
yet ubiquitous, particularly in the United States. Much of the controversy focuses on the uneven results of such tests. The rationale behind
these assessments is two-fold: those who have displayed certain
behaviours in the past or recent past are viewed as unfit for their particular positions because their performance will be directly affected,
and/or there is a perception that they are not capable or qualified.
Therefore, organizations could be held liable for employing them. At
the same time, employers must carefully balance the screening process
against human rights legislation, or they will find themselves facing
other kinds of pitfalls.

Further, workers in human services may require their employers
and/or unions to carry out and act on assessments of the risks posed by
the nature of their workplace and clientele. Occupational health and
safety standards in labour legislation often identify the importance of
risk assessment on a plethora of matters such as the prevention of violence in the workplace, the incorporation of individuals with disabilities, and specific activities outside the organization such as field trips.

Risk assessments, particularly those directed at clients, are generally
distinguished from general assessments by their stated goal of prediction and their tendency to focus on a range of factors that have been
selected to make this prediction possible. While they share many features in common, there are also wide variations among instruments.
Table 4.1 illustrates the various dimensions of risk assessments in
human services, presented as opposite ends of a continuum to sharpen
the differences among instruments. Clearly, these continua have many
gradations and it is unusual that any one instrument will reflect either
end of the poles. Further, risk assessment is constantly in flux with
instruments coming and going according to new 'risk' priorities, experience with implementation, and new research findings and political
considerations.

Table 4.1 Dimensions of Risk Assessments in Human Services, Showing Opposite
Ends of a Continuum

Developmental	Prescribed
Goals	
Aimed at identifying characteristics of large populations for attention	Aimed at identifying specific individuals within a population for attention
Mandate	
Discretionary administration within profession and/or organization	Required by law, regulations, and/or policy to be administered
Target population	
Aimed at populations who may have something happen to them – 'at risk'	Aimed at populations who may harm others – 'a risk'
Clients can request it	Clients have no choice about its administration
Clients contribute information to it and know it is being done	Information is largely gathered without client input and clients are generally unaware that it is being done
Science	
Reliability and validity of instrument open to consideration	Reliability and validity tend to be assumed
Practitioners	
Administered by highly skilled professionals	Administered by a wide range of occupations and professions
An occasional activity in practice	The main focus of practice
Structure	
A contingency model, incorporation of strengths	A standard checklist with scores focused on risks
Implementation	
The implementation of the instrument varies widely among practitioners	It is a goal to standardize the implementation of the risk assessment
There may be loose connections between findings of risk assessment and actions that are then taken	There are attempts to apply findings to subsequent actions, generally called 'risk management'

Goals

Most of the risk assessments in human services are aimed at identifying particular individuals within a limited population. For instance, who among an institutionalized population is most likely to reoffend or suffer a relapse? Which children reported to a public health agency are likely to abuse or neglect their elderly parents?

However, there are some exceptions where risk assessment is used to develop public policy, particularly in the field of health promotion. One example is the Pregnancy Risk Assessment Monitoring System (PRAMS) initiated in 1987 in the United States by the Centers for Disease Control to better understand why infant mortality rates were not declining as rapidly as they had been in the past. The risk assessment data are drawn from all women giving birth within a time period in a particular jurisdiction, with women deemed to be in 'high risk' situations sampled more intensively through written questionnaires or by telephone and using self-reported data. Data are aggregated and used for research and public policy making rather than intervention in particular cases.[1]

Mandate

Some risk assessments are clearly designed to assist practitioners in their clinical decision making. While practitioners may feel compelled to complete the risk assessment as a standard of effective practice in their organization or profession, they are not required to do so. For instance, risk assessments are widely applied within seniors' facilities to determine whether residents are likely to fall, an event that can be catastrophic for the frail elderly (Haines et al., 2006; Papaioannou et al., 2004). Data from the assessments may be used for redesigning the physical space and marshalling equipment and resources for particular individuals.

While organizations and practitioners may appear to have choice about the application of risk assessment, these choices are sometimes curtailed by the requirements of insurance companies, funding agencies, or auditors. For instance, under the recent policy in the United Kingdom, 'Every Child Matters,' local authorities appear to have some discretion about adopting the common assessment framework to be used by all professionals in different services dealing with children. However, funding to these local authorities from the central government could be curtailed based on their compliance with the policy (Parton, 2008). As seen in this example, the voluntary use of risk assessments in professional practice may be vulnerable to trends in liability management. As more and more organizations develop risk

---

1 See Centers for Disease Control (2006) for reports using these data.

management plans for themselves to curtail their own liability (Tremper and Kostin, 1997), they may be reluctant to allow the discretionary use of risk assessments in professional practice. They may be advised that if a risk assessment is not used with a client who suffers some calamity, the agency could be held responsible.

In an increasing number of fields, risk assessments are the responses to public scandals and demands for increasing surveillance and punishment of people at the heart of the scandal. In particular, recidivism on the part of sexual offenders, violent offenders, and abusing parents have fuelled a pattern of responses: tightening up the laws governing various human services or creating new laws, regulations, and policies to deal with particular offences or offenders; implementing protocols for professionals and community workers to communicate with one another and share information about clientele; and introducing or strengthening risk assessment and creating registers of clients. Child welfare provides an example. During the past decade or more, the definition of children requiring protection has been expanded to include the phrase 'who *are or who are likely to be*' (Government of British Columbia, 1996) maltreated or '*who are at risk of*' maltreatment (Government of Ontario, 1990; emphasis added in both cases here). These phrases clearly authorize the development and application of risk assessments so that practitioners can fulfill the predictive requirements of law. Similar developments have taken place in corrections and mental health (Hannah-Moffat and Maurutto, 2003; Kelly et al., 2002).

Target Population

The subjects of risk assessments are viewed according to the nature of their risk to others and their capacity and/or commitment to manage their own risks. Some people are viewed as highly dangerous to others: 'a risk.' In this case risk assessment is clearly intended to identify them and to control their behaviour. Others are considered to be 'at risk' from someone else and therefore deserving of protection and compassion. Yet these perceptions are not static. The template of the sympathetic and demonized client can shift as new risks are 'discovered,' often through public scandal, and previously identified risks fall from view. The development of the field of elder abuse provides a good example. The perception of the risk that adult children, usually women, will maltreat their aging parents has shifted from an unlikely occurrence to one deemed more likely, resulting in an increasing application of risk assessments designed to identify abusing caregivers. Changing perceptions of people who sexually assault children are also illustrative. The 'discovery' of child sexual abuse in the 1970s focused on perpetrators within the family, often people related to the victim. Ensuing scandals since then have shifted the focus first to the abuse of children within institutions by persons known to them and then to sexual abuse by strangers, the predatory pedophile, and the conflation of this image with homosexuality. Yet by all accounts a child, most frequently a girl, is still most likely to be sexually abused by a male person within her family (Trocmé et al., 2005); even though the attention of the public and professionals is fixed on 'the danger of strangers.' The community care movement has made significant changes to perceptions about who is a risk, sometimes in a positive direction. For instance, people with mental challenges who were formerly institutionalized and regarded as dangerous are now more likely to be considered acceptable community residents.

However viewed, clients of human service organizations are often unaware that they are the subjects of risk assessments. Owing to time or other pressures, workers in the human services may find it necessary to carry out assessments based on observation, files, and information from others, and without participation from those who are under scrutiny. The wide use of 'profiling,' which is really a risk assessment procedure, illustrates clearly that many people have no knowledge of the fact that they have been assessed for 'risks,' and because nothing may happen as a result of their profiling, they will not be alerted at a later date (Tator and Henry, 2006).

Less commonly, clients of human services may request risk assessments as part of their own risk management responsibilities. For instance, prospective parents, particularly those identified as 'high risk' because of age or genetic background, may ask for prenatal screening, bringing with it a host of contradictions. As 'good' parents who desire to manage their own risks and protect their future children from harm, prenatal screening may seem sensible to them. But the scores on most of the tests are by no means definitive, leaving parents to grapple with any number of probabilities about the health of their future children. Moreover, the focus of research in this area remains on the tests themselves and not on how they are used in practice by parents and professionals (Marteau and Dormandy, 2001).

Structure

The Brief Spousal Assault Form for the Evaluation of Risk (B-SAFER) is a good example of a typical risk assessment. Widely used in Canada in one version or another since the early 1990s, this assessment is designed for police and others with the aim of distinguishing serious situations from others (Kropp and Hart, 2004). The ten factors on the risk assessment include those focusing on the perpetrator's history of and attitudes towards spousal violence; violations of criminal or civil court orders; relationship, employment, and/or financial problems; substance abuse; and mental disorder. Accompanying the risk assessment are descriptors to explain what is meant by each factor and scales that practitioners use to classify the degree of risk, including descriptors for each level on the scale. Through this process people who are 'high risk' presumably will be identified and treated differently from people who are not.

While the B-SAFER type of risk assessment is most common, there have been some attempts to develop a contingency model of risk assessment (Gendreau et al., 1996; Monahan et al., 2000). In this approach, clinicians may pose a first question, the response to which leads to a decision tree with several options, further responses, and further options. The authors suggest that this approach produces a more reliable and valid prognostication and acknowledges the interaction among variables. While used in environmental risk assessments (see, e.g., Wong-Yim et al., 2006), this approach does not seem to have found purchase in the human services, perhaps because of its complexity.

Another innovation in risk assessment approaches is to include both 'risks' and 'protective factors' in the assessment, staunching in part the criticisms that risk assessment is all about the 'bads' and pays little attention to the strengths of a given situation (Shortt et al., 2006). To be even-handed, however, the assessment of 'strengths' would require the same process as 'risks,' involving the classification and measurement of strengths. The view of what constitutes strength can also be limited according to the definition of risks, so that the absence of risk appears logically and is supposed to be assumed as a strength.

Science

The scientific basis of risk assessment is highly contentious, and there are few fields where there is agreement about the reliability and validity of various instruments. Risk assessments are commonly divided into *consensus-based models*, composed of factors identified by practitioners, and *actuarial models*, which are developed from research on the characteristics of people who are most likely to fall into the risk category. Much of the literature on risk assessment in the human services suggests that actuarial models are superior to consensus models or to professional judgment alone in making accurate predictions (Barbaree et al., 2001; Serin et al., 2001; Austin and D'Andrade, 2005). However, this finding is nonetheless contentious, with a number of studies supporting one position or the other (Krysik and LeCroy, 2002; Hendryx and Rohland, 1997; Monahan et al., 2000; Hilton and Simmons, 2001; Haines et al., 2006). Further, the three types of assessment are frequently presented as discreet approaches ranging from the 'hard' science of actuarial assessments to the 'softer' approaches of consensus models and professional judgment. In fact, the construction and completion of actuarial instruments also requires individual judgment about behaviour and its meaning.

Developing an empirical science of risk assessment in human services is no easy task (Bourgon and Bonta, 2004). For example, Munro and Rumgay (2000) carried out a study examining the findings of forty public inquiries in Britain between 1988 and 1997 involving homicides committed by patients deemed mentally disordered. The authors suggest it is extremely difficult to distinguish between those persons potentially homicidal and others, citing the relatively rare incidence of homicide by persons with mental illness. The judgments of these inquiries noted the few instances where prediction was possible, that is, where individuals were showing clear signs of committing a violent act and the much more common occurrence where individuals were showing signs of becoming unwell again, and the situation could have been prevented by attending to their illness. The authors conclude 'that more homicides could be prevented by improving the response to patients who start to relapse, regardless of their assessed potential for violence, than by trying to identify high risk patients and target resources on them' (2000: 118).

This finding is echoed by others. Powell et al. (2000) examined the use of risk assessment to predict which patients would commit suicide in psychiatric hospitals, and Caldwell (2002) carried out a similar review on the current use of existing risk assessments to determine whether juvenile sex offenders should be registered as sexual predators under laws passed in several U.S. states. The studies reached similar conclusions: 'Selecting those most likely to engage in a specific behavior out of a population in which that behavior is rare is particularly difficult. If the behavior is sufficiently uncommon, the odds can become too long for any but the most robust methods to overcome' (Caldwell, 2002: 300).

Clearly, the less frequent the behaviour, the more difficult it is to predict because of the myriad of factors associated with any one action and the small numbers of cases available for examination. However, it is 'unusual' behaviour such as sexual assault and murder that causes the most consternation and results in pressure to develop and utilize risk assessments (Munro and Rumgay, 2000). Ironically, risk assessments designed to predict a fairly common occurrence – such as whether a mother living in poverty with several children and no employment will be reported again for child neglect – may achieve high degrees of reliability and validity but be of little practical use to practitioners who can predict this occurrence themselves.

Nonetheless, there is a strongly held belief that the science of risk assessment, while far from perfect, is improving and that it is only a matter of time before research will yield tools that will make possible the prediction of at least some dangerous or undesirable behaviours. Many people contend that to give up on this quest is to abandon long-held professional aspirations in human services: to ground work in scientific knowledge and to prevent behaviour that harms people. The other view is expressed far less clearly. It argues that science is simply not value free; even the items on the risk assessment and the evidence assembled to address these items is filled with decisions based on values. It further argues that professional practice is not only about science in the 'hard' sense but about the moral choices that must be made with and without scientific findings, particularly in a field that places value on human rights and social justice (Hannah-Moffat and Maurutto, 2003). The subject of terrorism provides a constant reminder of this tension. Should preventive detention occur for those whose profile indicates a high risk of their having terrorist connections even though the risk assessment itself is a blunt instrument and even though their loss of human rights and due process can be as damaging to social order as the potential harm they may potentially wield?

Practitioners

Risk assessments differ in the degree to which they are administered by individual highly skilled professionals or by a cadre of workers trained in a particular instrument. One of the most trenchant critiques of risk assessment is that it has the potential to be deskilling, in the sense that it introduces a checklist approach to practice. For instance, Kropp (2004) notes that while several kinds of professionals may conduct spousal violence risk assessments, including nurses, police, victim services workers, and psychologists, these practitioners have varying degrees of education, training, and experience with respect to spousal violence. Under these circumstances, it is unclear how well they will be able to 'assess risk markers involving mental health problems such as personality disorders and suicidal ideation' (2004: 687–8). The results of any one risk assessment may be used by several different professionals and decision-making bodies, all focused on similar items on similar scales (Parton, 2006). While this can increase interprofessional communication, as all are talking about the same issues, it can also reduce the opportunities for differing perspectives on the situation since the instrument encourages practitioners to discuss a limited number of factors and their scores.

The implementation of risk assessments can also be carried out as a sole professional activity requiring significant preparation and experience. It can be viewed as a logical extension of professional decision making, an 'aide memoire' for practitioners to complement their professional judgment.

For some practitioners, completing a risk assessment is an occasional activity and for others it is their main assignment, a factor that has significant implications for professional practice. However, even those practitioners who themselves use formal risk assessments only on occasion are frequently drawn into the risk assessments conducted by others. By its nature risk assessment requires professionals 'to collaborate with other professionals in a diversity of practices and apparatuses for the administration of risk across the territory of the community' (Rose,1999: 177). This organizing feature of risk assessment first became obvious to us when we interviewed social workers and parents in child welfare who consistently mentioned other professionals involved in some fashion in their child welfare risk assessments. Frequently teachers, police, and nurses were cited as providing information to complete the assessment. Lawyers often use risk assessments in the court process to provide evidence of child maltreatment or to defend parents against such accusations. Physicians, psychiatrists, and psychologists are often involved in risk reduction plans aimed at helping parents deal with mental health, addictions, and other issues. As well as members of established professions, we uncovered a cadre of other workers whose work is guided to some extent by risk assessment, including those who provide child care, family support, homemaking, counselling, advocacy, and other services. Whether they wished to or not,[2] all were drawn into the risk assessment process in child welfare, its values, logic, and work demands. As one mother investigated by child welfare workers said to us:

It's like they all are, they're all in it like together.

Implementation

Two particular issues related to implementation have relevance here: the acceptable completion of risk assessments themselves and the connection between the results of the assessment and what actually happens to reduce or 'manage' risk. The first issue relates to the question of whether practitioners carry out risk assessments as they are instructed to do so or use them as they see fit. Some may intentionally subvert their use. Studies exploring this question suggest that adopting risk assessment requires a shift in thinking for practitioners accustomed to dealing with people in the complexity of the moment. Even when practitioners see the information in the risk assessment as more or less accurate, they may question whether it is sufficiently trustworthy (timely and comprehensive) to guide their actions in the present and immediate future. Further, the process of completing risk assessments is largely an administrative one, driven by organizational requirements, thus taking professionals away from their work with individuals.

Risk management is not necessarily a logical step following from risk assessment. Kemshall and Maguire (2001) set out to examine how public protection panels charged with deciding the disposition of sex offender cases used risk assessments (completed by penal officers) in making their decisions. They found that the panel had the discretion to ignore the scores on the risk assessment, which they frequently did, instead using information gathered from others and their own impres-

---

2 Most child welfare laws in Canada and elsewhere require professionals and frequently members of the community to report incidence of child maltreatment and to provide information about the behaviour of parents and caregivers to child welfare workers.

sions. However, the researchers discovered that risk assessments played a significant part in determining which cases came before the panel in the first place – only those judged high risk. They note that the actual assessments themselves were often carried out by junior staff with little experience.

This study further discovered wide variations in the disposition of resources to those of highest risk; instead, most of the attention to all offenders occurred directly after their assignment to the unit. They note as well the 'inflation of the currency of risk classification': 'As more and more people are categorized as "high risk" (both because the overall number of registered sex offenders … is mounting and because of greater use of standard instruments rather than practitioner judgment), even the senior agency managers who sit on high-level public protection panels find it difficult to access all the resources they would wish for every such case. A consequence of this … was the creation in some areas of an informal category of "exceptionally high-risk" or "highly dangerous" offenders, to whom very close attention was paid, while the remainder of the officially "high risk" category were dealt with in more "routine" fashion' (Kemshall and Maguire 2001: 250). Actuarial scores mattered most in risk management for low-risk people who were frequently ignored or received only modest services.

Organizational traditions also play a large part in efforts to move police and correctional staff into the more impersonal approach of risk assessment and risk management of 'potential offenders' instead of dealing with offenders who have already committed crimes. Police were still attached to priorities of investigating crimes such as burglary that had already been perpetrated. However, researchers did note the movement of probation officer managers away from notions of rehabilitation and towards an affinity with surveillance and other control measures. The researchers also observed the tendency of organizations to put 'more time, effort and resources into processes of risk assessment than into actions to actually manage the risks' (Kemshall and Maguire, 2001: 253).

Areas typically ignored are the experiences of risk assessment for those being assessed and the eventual impacts on them and their lives. In an era where the study of diversity and the quest for social justice are hallmarks of many human services, the ways in which risk assessment may confound those aims is given remarkably short shrift (some exceptions are Hannah-Moffat and Shaw, 2001; Krane and Davies, 2000).

Conclusion

The concept of risk and the attempts to measure and manage it are deeply embedded in the human services. Our exploration of risk assessment instruments used in various fields yielded literally thousands of references and many parallel but largely unacknowledged developments across particular disciplines. In this literature the complexities of defining risk and the social construction of risk, featured in Chapter 1 of this book, are largely, although not completely, ignored. Usually, risk is presented as real and obvious: a sex offender harming a child while out on parole, a husband injuring his wife and children after the police leave the home, a person who is depressed committing suicide. Nor is there much effort to connect this emphasis on risk assessment in professional practice to ongoing efforts to reshape the responsibilities of the state for its individual citizens and their collective well-being, the subject of Chapters 2 and 3. We are daily dished up with announcements of cuts to one program or another and, at the same time, of increasing expenditures for surveillance activities supposed to protect us from an expanding menu of 'risks.' Given the pervasiveness of risk assessment and the rising expectations of professionals to do 'something' with less about people who are viewed as dangers to our society, this lack of inquiry is an important omission, one that operates to focus professional attention on individual rather than social responsibility for risks.

What is clear in this examination is the confluence of agendas that risk assessment appears to meet. For professionals, and particularly those whose professions come under public attack, it offers a promise to elevate their practice to one based on positivist scientific approaches. The long-standing mandate of professionals to provide assessments and relevant programs appears to be within easier reach when risk assessment is adopted. It also promises to enable professionals and their clients to predict what may happen, and it provides them with the authority to marshal some services in hopes of preventing tragedies.

Further, the struggles and tensions of interdisciplinary work may be eased if all are 'singing from the same hymn book.' For public service organizations and the politicians who answer for them, risk assessment suggests that explosive issues can be depoliticized. All that could be done was done and if procedures were not followed then those responsible can be identified. With risk assessment, decisions about resource deployment are clearly the province of managers rather than professionals, providing a tool to limit public expenditures – this is the 'sub-politics' of risk mentioned by Beck (1992). Risk assessment is also connected to risk management plans that many human service organizations are required by law to implement in order to meet insurance requirements for liability protection (Tremper and Kostin, 1997; Young and Tomski, 2002). Thus, the entrenchment of risk assessment in human services is hard to argue against, bridging as it does the often conflicting political, management, and professional agendas (Caldwell, 2002; Castel, 1991) in service of neoliberal goals.

Like 'risk' itself, risk assessments vary considerably across several key dimensions. Those aimed at the protection of individuals and the public share much in common and differ in significant ways from those that focus more on voluntary and self-help, not just in their content but in their administration as well. Not only has there been little clarity on this matter, it also appears that professionals and fields of practice have developed their approach to risk assessment largely in isolation from one another, rarely referring to similar instruments in other fields. Ironically, there is precious little interdisciplinary research and scholarship in the human services, when in fact, many fields share the same issues and questions. This professional isolation limits the exchange of critiques as well as the capacity to challenge the received wisdom.

Across all fields, and as seen in our own study, there is a great deal more attention devoted to the risk assessment instruments and their application than to the management of risk, once 'uncovered.' We were interested to discover the existence of very few studies examining how risk assessment plays out in practice and its success in meeting professional and management goals. While there is speculation that formal risk assessment changes professional practice, the directions and depth of these changes have received little empirical examination, a gap we address in our study.

What is the future of risk assessment in the human services? There is not much speculation in literature about the 'risk' of risk assessment in the human services. Do we envision a time when a generic 'human service' practitioner will administer tests across a range of fields that accurately predict who will do what, when, and where, and then prescribe what should be done about it? This seems hardly likely in the near future, but there are some trends that bear watching. The use of risk assessment to nail the responsibility for a wide range of dangers on individual human service practitioners is one trend (Rose, 1999). How risk assessment can blend the perspectives of various individuals and practitioners into homogeneous points of view, thus shutting down dissent and masking differences is another. How risk assessment can move thinking away from present experiences of social injustice and collective actions is yet another.

This examination of risk assessments across the human services helps to sharpen the focus for this book. For the most part, we will be examining the risk assessments that tend to fall towards the right side of Table 4.1; those that are largely mandatory, involve little choice by participants, and dominate the practice of those in the human services. Our choice to focus on these risk assessments and their application in practice is partly pragmatic; our expertise in practice and research rests in child welfare, a field where mandatory risk assessments have wide currency. But the choice also relates to the belief that it is here, where risk assessments are most deeply entrenched and prevalent, that an examination of their effects can be most revealing.

PART II

Part II develops a detailed analysis of risk and risk assessment based on our research project. Child welfare is a distinct field of social work practice mandated by law and carried out in some form or other in all welfare states. In these countries, society expects the vast majority of the care of children to be carried out by parents, with the state stepping in only when legal guardians appear incapable of doing so. Practice in the field of child protection is recognized as difficult and often subject to high-profile criticism by the media and the general public. Social workers have been cast as either wimps or bullies (Callahan and Callahan, 1997) when children within their responsibility have died. It is perhaps not surprising that risk assessment has taken hold in this domain. The ability to predict which children may be seriously harmed is certainly a vision shared by all who engage in child protection work, not only to save children but to save ourselves.

In Part II of this book, we look at the specific ways in which risk and risk assessment have entered into and helped to reshape the work of protecting children.

Chapter 5 examines the historical context of the development of risk assessment tools now in use. We also describe the usual clientele on whom risk assessments are performed, placing them in their social and economic contexts.

In Chapter 6, we provide a detailed examination of work practices involved in accomplishing risk assessments in child protection settings. The 'work' of both social workers and parents, mostly mothers, is described, showing how activities are justified, thought about, and coordinated. Chapter 7 moves to an exploration of what happens after a risk assessment is done. We especially examine disjunctures between the logic of assessment and the logic of managing risk.

5 The Institutional World

Risk assessment depends on the categorization of people on the basis of risk scores. It is hardly new to social work and allied professions to categorize people for purposes of deciding how to intervene with them; risk assessment seems to be the latest 'technology' supporting this approach. In this chapter we focus on child welfare work in British Columbia and Ontario, but we also provide a broader picture of the issues across Canada and other Western countries. As part of this scan, we introduce the people who are most frequently reported to child welfare agencies for abusing or neglecting their children. These are the people most likely to be the subjects of risk assessments and risk reduction, the topic of the following two chapters.

Categories of Social Services Clients

During the period between the First and Second World Wars social workers along with other helping professionals became interested in intelligence tests and taxonomies as a way of understanding their clientele. This interest reflected two related phenomena: the attractions of the growing fields of social and psychological science and the appeal of the eugenics movement which was sweeping across Europe and which, of course, later became discredited and feared as people learned of its consequences in Nazi Germany. Some of the 'scientific' categories established and embraced during this period appear to us now as politically incorrect at best and often dangerous and destructive. Tests for 'feeble-mindedness' were popularized in Canada during the 1920s, and the language of low intelligence categories began to appear regularly in social work files of the era. In child welfare files,

mothers were described as 'subnormal' and even as 'morons.' A
review of case files from the 1930s (Swift, 1995b) demonstrates that
social workers of that period were familiar with intelligence categories
and saw their work as involving the application of them to mothers
they visited. Their reasoning and evidence, however, can with hindsight be seen as shockingly judgmental. The labels attached to many
mothers by the child protection workers of the day cemented their
identities as inadequate and often resulted in the institutionalization of
children, mothers, or both.

Macnicol (1987) has examined the widespread efforts of various professionals in the mid-twentieth century to establish a 'hereditary social
problem group,' a project that he notes was crucial to the conservative
social agenda of the day. Macnicol traces British efforts to identify and
intervene with that 'submerged tenth,' described by Charles Booth
(cited in Macnicol, 1987: 297), who live outside the boundaries of citizenship and are alienated from conventional norms. In the early twentieth century studies of this hypothetical population, sometimes
referred to as 'social inefficients,' were sponsored by the eugenics
movement in hopes of finding a biological rationale for the steriliza-
tion of its members. Proposed indicators of membership included such
factors as receipt of public assistance, a criminal record, infant mortality, and a range of biological conditions such as 'mental deficiency' and
blindness. The good social standing of one's parents, payment of taxes,
school degrees, and even attendance at evening classes could facilitate
exclusion from this population. After examining a number of studies
from the interwar era, Macnicol concludes that this presumed underclass is a 'statistical artifact,' established through serious methodological contradictions (1987: 293). Among these contradictions are the conflation of biological and administrative variables and the inclusion of
very different kinds of people and problems into one supposedly
homogeneous grouping. Indeed, reading the history of 'scientific'
efforts to categorize people for the purposes of acting on and controlling their behaviour is embarrassing to read and should provide substantial cautions regarding present and future attempts at understanding people through categorizations and labels.

'Risk' as a Legislated Child Welfare Category

It is fair to say that projecting the risks of a child being harmed at some
point in the future has always been a feature of child protection work.

The very act of opening a case suggests that there is a child at risk of some kind of negative experience, in the judgment of the worker, the institution, or society. However, it is only recently that attempts to categorize parents or caregivers at various levels of risk for the purposes of determining intervention have been systematically and scientifically pursued.

Following an American trend, a debate arose in Canada in the mid-1980s about whether child protection authorities were involving themselves in private matters with far too little justification. Not unimportant at the time was the question of cost. The issue arose, after all, as the discourse of Western politics took a turn towards neoliberalism with its focus on making government and its costs smaller. In this context, government-sponsored child protection services might seem like the ultimate 'big brother,' carried out at substantial public cost. From this perspective, it seemed to make sense to raise the legislated threshold of child protection 'intrusion' into the private lives of families. In Canada, the idea of risk as a feature of law took on special significance during that period. In the mid-1980s, changes in Ontario's child welfare legislation were proposed, and a central issue was whether simple 'risk' or 'substantial risk' of harm to a child should be the standard of intervention in the interests of safeguarding children. At the time, the Ontario government favoured the higher threshold of substantial risk.

Child protection is well known to insiders as following a 'pendulum' pattern of policy, swinging from children's rights to parents' rights (Dumbrill, 2005). In periods favouring children, the levels of justifiable intrusion into parenting practices are set lower and encouraged. In periods favouring parents, the thresholds for intervention are set high, in the apparent interests of protecting the rights of parents to raise children as they see fit, unless they have inflicted actual harm. The policy of 'substantial risk' appeared to favour parents. After a period in the 1990s of intense media scrutiny in many English-speaking countries of the deaths of children associated with child protection authorities, jurisdictions swung back in favour of protecting children, hopefully before harm occurred. Thus, substantial risk became 'risk' in law, and an era of 'family building' ensued. Nevertheless, 'risk' had become entrenched in legislation, and most Canadian jurisdictions now use risk or similar wording as an important marker for intervention.

Ontario legislation uses the idea of risk in several sections. In Section 40(7)(b) and several similar clauses, risk justifies apprehension of a child without a warrant. The phrase 'there would be a substantial risk to the child's health or safety' provides direction to judges on the basis of risk. Following from Sections 72(1) and (2), even members of the public are required to make a report to protection authorities based on 'risk of harm to a child.' Legislation implies that parents too should know the salient risks to their children and protect against them.

Child Welfare Reform

It has become the norm for risk technologies to be introduced into child welfare practice as part of the aftermath of high-profile child death reviews. These reviews seemed to be strikingly common during the 1980s and 1990s, not only in Canada but in other Western countries as well (Smith and Donovan, 2003). This timing is significant because of the influence that media reporting can have on perceptions of risk. The extent of coverage, its volume, the kinds of information presented, the framing of the risks involved, and the symbols enlisted to represent risk all influence public perceptions of danger and can create pressure on authorities to dissolve or reduce the apparent threat. Salient risks are selected and deselected by institutions and individuals with authority, and they may be 'amplified' or 'attenuated' by those able to influence media coverage (Kasperson and Kasperson, 2005, 1996).

In Ontario, risk assessment as a technology began with a 'home-grown' tool, designed by an agency director, for the purpose of bringing consistency to the process of deciding which referrals to that agency would be investigated and which would not (Key Informant). This tool, never intended for broader use, was noticed by provincial authorities and revised for use across the province in the mid-1990s. At about the same time, a number of deaths of children in Ontario while under the care of local Children's Aid Societies were being reviewed and were receiving substantial press coverage. A relatively new and clearly neoliberal government was in power. In the wake of negative publicity about child deaths, this government determined to 'reform' child welfare in the province. Across the country, similar high-profile reviews of child deaths during the same period had created an atmosphere of change. Such reviews generally describe errors in judgment, unexplained oversights, and ill-informed practices by workers (Callahan and Callahan, 1997; Swift, 2001). They also typically point to vague or misguided legislation and systemic problems within protection organizations as the reasons for such deaths (Swift, 2001).

In British Columbia, 60 of 573 recommendations made by the Children's Commission in the mid-1990s dealt with risk assessment as an 'essential ingredient' for the protection of children (Government of British Columbia, 1998: 6). In Ontario, new recommendations, issuing from reviews in a number of other provinces, called for 'needed changes' and prominently featured risk assessment procedures to be required in provincial child protection organizations: 29 of the 428 recommendations issued by the Coroner's juries investigating Ontario's Children's Aid Society–related deaths of children called for the introduction of a 'comprehensive risk assessment' system.

The most prominent review of child deaths in this period was in British Columbia, resulting in the Gove Commission Report of 1995, which examined the provincial child welfare system in the wake of the death of a child well known to protection authorities. Calls for changes in the system were already under way at the time of this event, and the incoming New Democratic Party government was being encouraged to reform the system, including its guiding legislation, in line with its election campaign promises. The legislation was indeed altered, with the new version containing authority for the development of risk assessment by expanding the definition of a child in need of protection. The new law included the phrase 'has been or is likely to be' in its definition of child maltreatment (Callahan and Swift, 2007). Further, provincial child protection managers had already been introduced to a risk assessment model and tools at the time Judge Gove released his report, which not surprisingly emphasized the safety of children and the creation of the administrative apparatus said to be necessary to ensure it. Two recommendations in the report specifically called for a 'comprehensive risk assessment' approach to be instigated. Substantial changes in the training and practice of child protection soon followed (Callahan and Swift, 2007).

During this period, across Canada numerous inquests and reviews of child deaths occurred. Workers and supervisors involved in such cases were called to testify, and media coverage of this testimony frequently resulted in news items excoriating the workers in particular and protection services in general. Research on the effects of this public scrutiny points out the high levels of stress for protection staff. Research also connects negative media attention to high levels of staff turnover in protection services (Regehr et al., 2002). In addition, in the late 1990s, a worker in one Ontario agency was arrested in connection with the death of a child on her caseload. She was charged, along with the mother, with negligent homicide. Although these charges were eventually dropped, the effects on workers across Canada remain today. Workers still routinely mention this event and their reactions to it when speaking of their experiences in child welfare practice. An abiding fear of seeing themselves pictured and condemned in news media accounts of a child's death haunts everyone associated with protection work in Canada.

At the time the child death reviews were taking place, the Ontario and B.C. governments seemingly represented quite different political agendas. British Columbia was moving from a conservative governing party to a social democratic regime, while Ontario voters had just expressed their displeasure with five years of social democratic rule by voting overwhelmingly for a far right neoliberal government. Both new provincial governments, however, had solid support from child death reviews as well as public opinion as they began to introduce risk assessment as a required feature of child protection investigations. This change not only produced new work practices but, as Chen (2005: 245) argues, changed practice in such a way that 'the reality of children's existence [became] intelligible only in terms of their individual safety.'

Not surprisingly, then, risk assessment was not the only reform to be introduced. In keeping with the spirit of reviewers' recommendations, legislation in both provinces was changed to focus more clearly on the child rather than the family. Both provinces hurriedly developed training packages for new and existing workers. In keeping with neoliberal agendas of accountability, Ontario brought in a new funding formula, one articulated to the New York State risk assessment document that was eventually chosen by both Ontario and British Columbia as the required risk tool (Swift and Parada, 2004; Callahan and Swift, 2007), and one that tied risk assessment directly to accounting and auditing systems. In this way, an instrument designed to guide practice also, in effect, assigned budget responsibilities to workers because they were now required to calculate and translate their professional interventions into monetary terms (Swift and Parada, 2004).

The twin concepts of consistency and accountability became the watchwords of the new system. One of the most damning critiques of workers has been their supposed subjectivity and inconsistency in decision making. Workers have been criticized as thoughtless, sloppy, biased, and ill-prepared for their sometimes life-saving roles. The Ontario Coroner, following a series of death reviews in the 1990s, concluded that 'we have to educate all professionals involved with high risk children with a view to learning how to prevent deaths' (quoted in Chen, 2003: 211). From this perspective, it would seem reasonable that some form of standardized risk prediction tools be introduced, requiring everyone conducting investigations to cover the same factors and observations and to provide a consistent field of conclusions that workers must address. It would also seem reasonable that clear systems for tracking decisions should be developed for accountability purposes. These directions follow the same trajectory pursued in other jurisdictions and other service delivery settings. Smith and Donovan (2003), for instance, studied an American jurisdiction offering child protection services during this era. They document a route beginning with scathing media attention to child protection failures leading increasingly to an institutional culture of fear, mistrust, and blame. In this context, as Rose (1996c: 4) says, 'almost any unfortunate event becomes a "tragedy" which could have been avoided and for which some authority is going to be held culpable.' The prescription has been a heavy reliance on standardized assessments, which are supposed to predict and therefore reduce the chances of such occurrences.

Standard forms, especially those including numeric scoring, are presumed to increase consistency in decision making and ensure that the most salient risk factors are observed and rated. The introduction of various systems of accountability is supposed to further ensure consistent risk ratings. In our study sites, the new systems required workers to clear every single decision with their supervisors. The frequency of audits and the range of issues subject to audit were increased (Regehr et al., 2001). Computer systems were introduced for logging every action and requiring that every item be filled in. Standards of practice were revised to support the new regime. These measures created the potential for every action taken by workers to be documented and tracked and, in fact, for every decision taken at the supervisory level and above to be subject to review.

Child protection workers are generally rather suspicious of government-imposed reforms to their work, having experienced numerous plans to fix the system. As one B.C. worker said, following the Gove Report, 'We've had it square, we've had it diamond shaped, we're going back to round again' (Gove, 1995: vol. 1, 232). It is likely that seasoned workers were sceptical of the announced reforms in both British Columbia and Ontario, as well as elsewhere around the country. The public reaction from the child protection sector, however, was one of

unalloyed acceptance, one even of cheering the arrival of risk assessment. Most of the key informants participating in our study reported
feeling hopeful when risk assessment first came in. The previous
system was remembered by them as subjective and chaotic, and it was
hoped by those at management levels and many workers as well that
the new approach would improve services to clients by bringing order
to a disorderly system.

Consistency came to be seen as a high value throughout the system.
An important goal, according to the Ontario Risk Assessment Model
(ORAM), was to ensure that decisions would be made 'according to
clear, consistent criteria' (2000: 1), and the risk assessment tool, it was
claimed, would produce this consistency. Consistent risk assessment
decisions could be equated with good professional decisions, and at
the same time they could be equated with audits (Cradock, 2004), thus
fitting nicely with management goals. The case management auditors
looked for consistency, and the province wanted 'some form of consistency for accountability' (Key Informant). In addition, it was hoped
that consistency of definitions and decisions among different agencies
could be achieved. The idea of consistency came to be synonymous in
people's thinking with improved service. The possibility of consistently bad service was not mentioned.

In both provinces, official statements were made to the effect that
risk assessment was not to be considered a replacement for professional, clinical judgments, but rather a guide for workers aimed at consistency of service and investigatory activities (Gove, 1995; ORAM,
2000). However, this directive was perhaps more lip service than
reality in both provinces. One B.C. respondent said the new standards
quickly evolved as prescriptive rather than enabling; risk assessments
were redrafted into a set of

> must-do's … We moved directly into the lock-step approach that we were
> trying to get away from, which was 'you must do risk assessment.'

Risk Assessment Tools

Systematic use of risk assessment in child welfare practice began in the
early 1980s, and it gained traction by the 1990s in a number of English-
speaking countries. In the years since, formal risk assessment has
become 'tightly woven into the fabric of child welfare practice' (Rycus
and Hughes, 2003: 6). Of course, formal risk assessment tools do not

represent the first time that professionals in the field of child protection have attempted a systematized method of assessing potential harm to children. Brearley (1982) identifies the early 1960s as the time of the first systematic efforts to identify 'non-accidental injury' to children. Checklists designed to alert workers to 'risky' situations have been a fixture in child protection work ever since. In 1977, a group of medical researchers published an article claiming that new mothers at risk of 'abnormal parenting practices' could be identified with some confidence by following their recommended screening approach (Gray et al., 1977). One of the authors was the influential Henry Kempe, who is generally credited with the 'discovery' of child abuse. The authors acknowledge that specific factors required for accurate prediction had yet to be established. Their approach combined interview, observation, and a 74-item questionnaire administered to the mother in the pre- and post-natal periods. They found observations in the delivery room to be the most accurate predictors, and they offered a list of 'warning signs' indicating possible problems. These include what might seem rather obvious behaviours causing concern, such as 'negative, demanding or harsh' verbalizations by a mother to her newborn. Also included are much more ambiguous warning signs such as a lack of support for the mother by the father or family. These authors cite cautions in using such signs, indicating that the age and culture of the mother must be taken into account, and warning that 'varying combinations' of signs rather than any one indicator can signal 'possible problems.' It was not unusual in that era for such lists of signs to be culled from scholarly articles like this one and presented to workers in various agencies, with or without the attendant cautions.

Levanthal (1988) summarized the findings of eleven longitudinal studies that have attempted to predict the maltreatment of a child. Indicators include parents' personality characteristics such as high anxiety and the attitude of the mother towards her pregnancy. Also included are factors appearing on contemporary risk assessments such as abuse of the parent in childhood, cited in several of the studies, alcohol abuse, and known abuse by a parent of another child in the family. Some of the studies relied on the observation of parents, usually mothers, while others included checklists with weighted scores.

Recognizing the uneven distribution, implementation, and evaluation of such checklists, Magura and Moses developed a systematic approach, first published in 1986, called the Child Well-Being Scales. These were defined as a set of 'standardized client outcome measures' designed to assist managers in evaluating the effectiveness of protection interventions. Magura and Moses (2001) explain that the need for such measures resulted from an examination of the American child welfare system by the United States General Accounting Office. That body suggested in a 1976 review that the well-being of the program's target population should receive primacy in evaluation efforts, a recommendation that created pressure for the development of accountability measures by the system managers. Numerous efforts have been made to accomplish this goal in the United States over several decades. Even so, according to Magura and Moses (2001: 2), at the turn of the century, the field of child welfare still lacks agreed upon, valid, useful measures of the effectiveness of the services provided. Their own proposed scales represent a significant effort in the direction of trying to develop ways of measuring child welfare efforts and outcomes 'scientifically.'

These scales provide part of the logic and conceptual framework for comprehensive risk assessment tools developed later in the United States, including tools such as the New York model, which has been widely adopted in Canada. The Child Well-Being Scales involve the collection of information about the household, the caregivers, the child(ren), parental relationships, and behaviour and supports available to caregivers. These are, generally speaking, the categories of the New York tool as well. The Child Well-Being Scales also have a rating system, usually based on four or five points, as does the New York tool. There are about twice as many items of information on the Well-Being Scales as on the risk assessment, and the language is often framed differently. For instance, there is an item on both instruments intended to measure the caregiver's acceptance of the child. The Well-Being Scales 'anchor' description of a serious concern is 'parent is deprecating, resentful or angry' at the child. In the New York risk assessment tool, the anchor or marker for serious concern is that the caregiver views the child as 'evil or bad.' In the Well-Being Scales, a higher score indicates more positive parenting, while in the New York risk tool, high score equals high risk. Nevertheless, there are sufficient similarities between the two instruments to see child well-being as a major forerunner of some risk assessment tools, a fact acknowledged by key informants for this study. This development is not surprising, as the field has experimented for several decades with various kinds of tools that have built to some extent on one another. However, the conceptual shift from 'well-being' to 'risk' has proven to be significant.

Risk assessment tools remain essentially a list of variables (Gambrill and Shlonsky, 2000). Many models seem to represent a 'series of compromises' (Jagannathan and Camasso, 1996: 600), with most representing an unequal collection of 'individual, family, and broader sociological measures of risk.' As these authors note, models often end up representing organizational goals and oversimplification of criteria, which have impacts on the form and content of practices and discourses about risk.

We have a small window into the way risk assessment tools are developed in the Ontario Risk Assessment Model. The first step of the Ontario model determines 'eligibility' for services. This is the tool developed locally with research support and some community input for use in a single agency, but spotted and adapted for provincial use by the ministry responsible for child protection. A description of the history of what came to be called the Eligibility Spectrum says that 'some of Magura and Moses' (1986) Child Well-Being Scales categories and descriptors were incorporated into the tool' and that they have since been considerably modified (Ontario Association of Children's Aid Societies, 2000). A safety assessment and the risk assessment tool itself, both from New York, were then added to the process virtually unchanged, and a 'comprehensive assessment' was added later. 'It was never a system,' one key informant told us. We see in this description that although the model began with the idea of child well-being as central, the process continually veered towards the project of the assessment of risk. This process reflects Chen's observation (2005) that the logic of assessing risk requires a shift away from well-being and towards safety.

A report prepared by the Ontario Association of Children's Aid Societies (2000) suggests that many individuals and organizations have contributed to the refinement of the tool as time has gone on. However, examination of the tool shows that the two parts taken from New York remain unchanged. Rather it seems to be the addition of the comprehensive analysis and the implementation of the model that have been modified over time. Implementation of the model was influenced and modified by new legislation, standards of practice, and the provincial accreditation standards, as well as by field practice experience. The tool came to be overlaid with a work process based on many organizationally driven agendas. The process of creating a risk assessment model for Ontario illustrates how organizational influences enter into and shape the final product, so that it comes to represent an amalgam of organizational influences based on a tool developed well outside the local context (see Figure 5.1).

Theories Underlying Risk Assessment in Child Protection

As described in Chapter 4, there are two basic types of risk assessment, consensual and actuarial, and both are used in child protection work. The consensus approach, used in both British Columbia and Ontario during the period of our study, relies on ratings of factors identified through theory, research literature, and practice wisdom. According to a recent review of such instruments (D'Andrade et al., 2005), consensus tools often evolve into hybrids and tend to use the same instrument to assess all types of maltreatment of children, even though theories about the causes of abuse and neglect are usually different (Rycus and Hughes, 2003). The virtues of consensus tools are the collection and ordering of considerable information that can guide later work on a case. The other type of tool is actuarial. It is derived from statistical calculations that identify and weigh factors presumed to be predictive of future harm to children because they are based on large samples of past cases. In general, actuarial tools have tended to be used in the geographical area where they were developed (e.g., state or even county in the United States), and they use fewer factors than consensus models do (D'Andrade et al., 2005). Actuarial models are widely considered to be more accurate predictors of the abuse of children.

A variety of theories have been advanced over the years to explain the causal factors associated with child maltreatment, theories that find their way into risk assessment models, especially those of the consensus type. These run the gamut from sociological theories relating poor parenting to social and economic stress and psychodynamic theories focused, for instance, on the failure of parents to bond with their children. Given the presumed interplay among these possible explanatory factors, many researchers have suggested that a multi-causal approach to understanding child abuse should be taken (Brearley, 1982). Since very early on, a central explanation of child abuse has been the problematic childhoods of the parents themselves (Baher, 1976). Jones (1979) traces the 'cycle of violence' idea to Freudian theory. This line of thought posits that violence or abuse in childhood shapes the personalities of children, leading to traits that increase the chances that they will grow up to duplicate violent behaviour. This possibility supposedly increases if people have not dealt with their own anger

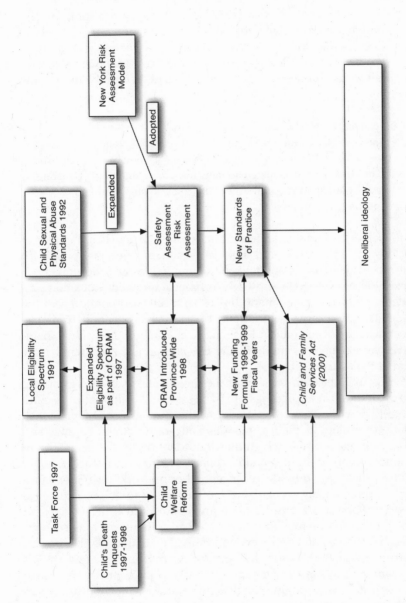

Figure 5.1: Mapping Child Welfare Reform

and have not developed appropriate strategies to handle these feelings. The cycle idea has been widely adopted by the helping professions and is used to explain not just violence but any repeated behaviour. Even clients internalize this thinking. One mother in our study reported that she avoided revealing her own personal history to protection workers because they always related her problems to 'the cycle':

> Interviewer: They've actually said that to you?
> Respondent: Oh, all the time. They want me to take groups for women like me. And I'm like, no. I'm not an idiot. I know it's a cycle. You know? I know I keep dating bad men. It's ... you know. But you telling me it's not [clap] ... You're right. I'm going to stop. You know? Like come on. Well anyways.

The cycle idea remains largely unquestioned in practice, in spite of various challenges to it, and in spite of the fact that many people do not repeat their own parents' behaviour (Breines and Gordon, 1983; Swift, 1995a). The cycle approach to practice in child protection preceded formal risk assessment, but it has been incorporated into the understandings and assumptions of risk assessment instruments. Most instruments include at least one item asking if the parents themselves were abused as children, and this is generally considered a key item of the assessment.

Cash (2001) has written one of the few available articles exploring the theoretical underpinnings of risk assessment as it applies to child protection work. According to Cash, the formal assessment of risk relies on ecological theory; theories concerning stress, coping, and crisis; and also on research studies that identify the characteristics of families involved in the child welfare system. Such theories and studies, she notes, provide a 'conceptual framework' for understanding and presumably recognizing families likely to abuse. Ecological theory in social work posits that family members create a 'system' and that they also are embedded within other systems, such as schools, neighbourhoods, and an extended family. Following this theory, risk instruments should account for both the internal and external systems relevant to the family. Stress, crisis, and coping theory points to moments of crisis bringing families into contact with child protection authorities. Individual and family coping skills and resources establish a foundation for understanding how individuals react to stress. Risk tools, according to this theory, should be able to identify both positive and negative coping mechanisms in a family.

Further, risk assessment instruments rely on previously gathered knowledge about the typical characteristics of 'abusive and neglectful' families. This approach relies on the idea that maltreatment of children is not the result of one influence acting alone but of several, often in interaction. Poverty, parental mental health, and the behaviour of a child are all elements identified in the literature as frequently present in child welfare populations, and which consequently should be represented in risk assessment tools (Cash, 2001). In reality, however, most tools in use do not represent a balance of these theories. Most of them focus intensively on the behaviour and cognitive characteristics of parents while de-emphasizing positive coping skills and broader social factors.

All models include categories of criteria, behavioural descriptors, procedures, and standardized forms to capture and record information. However, the risk assessment models used in child welfare practice differ considerably in their scope, purposes, and methods (Rycus and Hughes, 2003). At one end of the continuum, are tools and practices designed to classify families at the intake stage into high-risk and lesser-risk groups, in order to determine whether and what kinds of services will be required. At the other end of the continuum are models, like Ontario's, that become integrated with other information-gathering systems, analysis, decision making, intervention, and funding throughout the life of the case. Risk assessment was introduced by organizations in what many say was a well-intentioned effort to upgrade practice by standardizing the kind of information gathered. Many jurisdictions welcomed this innovation as a way of improving both the content and image of this work. Has it been effective?

Literature on Risk Assessment and Child Protection

The idea of risk in child protection, as in other domains, is commonly understood as likelihood, potential, or prediction. However, as noted in Chapter 1, risk is expressive of a number of shifting relations of power and brings many meanings into play. A number of different models for the assessment of risk have been introduced over the past fifteen years or so (Pecora, 1991; Michalski et al., 1996), and numerous benefits of risk assessment in child protection have been suggested. Among these are the possibility of broadening workers' perspectives

(Hornby, 1989); helping workers establish priorities (Cicchinelli, 1989); achieving more consistency among workers in identifying cases requiring protective services (Jones, 1996); and helping to manage complex cases handled by child protection authorities (Little and Rixon, 1998). Pecora's (1991) key study indicates that risk assessment procedures can help reduce 'bias' in decision-making processes.

At the same time, numerous problems and the limits of risk assessment tools themselves and their implementation have also been cited in the literature, almost from their introduction. A primary concern has been that risk tools quickly came into routine use in decision processes even though they had not been sufficiently empirically tested for validity and reliability. Their use as predictors of harm to children was brought into question in numerous publications (e.g., Pecora, 1991; Wald and Woolverton, 1990). Other studies show unclear conceptualization of tools (English and Pecora, 1994; DePanfilis, 1996) and uneven implementation (Ciccchinelli, 1989; Starr et al., 1994), problems that raise the question of what is being measured. Some authors claim that fundamental causal relationships were not well established in tools, bringing predictability into question, especially concerning the issue of child death (Trocmé and Lindsey, 1996).

Other literature moves beyond the benefits and problems of the tools to question the usefulness of the approach overall. Brissett-Chapman (1997) raises the question of how effectively culture and more specifically the effects of marginalization of specific populations have been incorporated into risk assessment tools and processes. Bell (1999) takes note of the 'inquisitorial stance' required by risk assessment, which stands in contradiction to the helping responsibilities of social workers. She also cites gender as an issue, pointing out the tendency to focus assessments on mothers. Krane and Davies (1999) examine risk assessment from a critical and gender perspective, finding the approach has the potential to 'entrench' oppressive relations. Goddard et al. (1999) ask if the tools associated with risk assessment are themselves 'instruments of abuse,' postulating that organizations may be better protected through this approach than are children. Following a review of problems with risk assessment in Great Britain, a 1995 report pointed out that the investigative approach represented by risk assessment not only wastes scarce resources on unsubstantiated cases but is not useful for client families (reported in Colclough et al., 1999). Others propose that since risk can never be fully controlled professionals should re-examine and re-emphasize their responsibilities to their clientele (Houston and Griffiths, 2000; Christie and Mittler, 1999).

Perhaps the most comprehensive recent review has been done by Rycus and Hughes (2003). Following an extensive literature review, examination of risk assessment tools, and a conference involving both researchers and users of tools, they reiterate the many concerns of previous critics. These authors state that the reliability and validity of risk assessment tools remains questionable and that there continue to be 'disturbing questions about all aspects of risk assessment technology and implementation' (2003: 6). Their report raises ethical and legal issues related to the use of risk assessment, including intrusion into family life unwarranted by actual harm to a child. Overall, this report casts serious doubt on most risk assessment models in use, including the New York model, which Ontario and British Columbia both used during the time of this study and which is still in use in a number of Canadian provinces: 'In practice, many child welfare professionals are making decisions about children and families with little more accuracy than flipping a coin, while believing they are using technologies that reduce subjectivity and bias, and that increase the quality of their decisions' (2003: 23).

The New York Model

The risk assessment model adopted by both British Columbia and Ontario originated in New York. It is a tool with twenty-three questions divided into segments relating to different aspects of child safety. In both provinces the assessment of risk is the third step in the process of investigation carried out by child protection workers. As we will see in detail in the next chapter, workers begin by screening referrals, usually on the telephone, through some type of eligibility criteria. If the case is eligible for service, a worker moves on to conduct an assessment of the immediate safety of the child(ren) involved. If there are immediate safety issues uncovered or if the worker has concerns related to a child's future safety, the case is kept open for further investigation. Only then does the actual risk assessment tool enter the picture. The task then becomes one of locating potential risks and their severity. Workers complete the risk assessment form, which is divided into five categories of 'influences.' These are the following:

- Caregiver influence, involving six questions concerning past abuse/neglect of the caregiver; drug and alcohol use by the caregiver; mental, emotional, and physical capacity of the caregiver to provide care; and the caregiver's expectations of the child.
- Child influence, including age under 2 years; child's response to the caregiver; behaviour problems; and the child's mental and physical development.
- Family influence, beginning with family violence; the family's ability to cope with stress; access to social supports; interactions among family members; and living conditions. This area comes the closest to flagging social conditions, but is framed in terms of the family's problems rather than deficits in the social context.
- Intervention influence, focused on the caregiver's motivation to be helped and cooperation with the interveners.
- Abuse/neglect influence, involving the access of a 'perpetrator' to a child; the caregiver's acknowledgment of responsibility; the severity of the abuse; and the known history of abuse of other children by the caregiver.

Within each of these categories specific risks are to be rated, for a total of twenty-three separate items. The final score is not the sum of these parts, however. Added later, and often given short shrift by busy workers, is a 'comprehensive analysis,' which is a written section designed to integrate the information found and rated in the previous stages of the process. The worker is supposed to base a final rating of 'high risk' (score of 3 or 4) or moderate to low risk (1 or 2) based on this analysis.

Risk Reduction Plans

Although the reduction of risk might be considered on the face of it to be the main point of implementing risk assessment procedures, the risk reduction elements of practice, described in detail in Chapter 7, have been underplayed in both British Columbia and Ontario. Certainly, one of the reasons for this was the unexplained but apparently politically driven rush with which risk assessment was brought in. Respondents in our study repeatedly described being under great pressure to produce the documents and software and to get training programs on the ground.

A second reason for inattention to risk reduction is the demanding nature of the 'paperwork' required to complete assessments. Actually, most of the required risk documentation is carried out on computers, and involves considerable time and attention to complete, since every screen must be filled out in order to close the file. Many workers complain that as much as 70 to 80 per cent of their workday is spent at their computers, at the expense of face-to-face time with clients. As one worker in Parada's study said, 'it gets to the point where we're so focused on documentation that our focus is diverted from the actual families … [this is] essentially an insurance policy to say, look, we did everything we could for this family and here are the papers to show that we did' (2004: 72–3). Time pressures and paperwork certainly are not new artefacts of service organizations. Lipsky (1980) pointed out several decades ago the disjuncture for front-line workers in all kinds of settings between recommended professional practices and administrative requirements. With complex risk assessments and increased pressures to demonstrate accountability, this disjuncture has simply intensified.

There is little if any evidence from our study that politicians and upper-level management in either province spend much time on the risk reduction component of the new system. Certainly this is not where budgets have concentrated resources (Gambrill and Shlonsky, 2001). There is a history in child protection, however, of employing standardized 'programs,' which clients are asked or required to attend (Smith and Donovan, 2003). These include parenting skills programs, anger management, budgeting, and alcohol and drug programs (Swift, 1995a, 2009). With the inception of risk assessment, this pattern of programming did not change to fit the identified risks of particular parents but rather intensified as a practice of making standardized recommendations. As American authors Smith and Donovan note, parents involved with child welfare 'commonly accumulate multiple certificates and complete multiple parenting classes' (2003: 556). And, as these authors also note, many services that might otherwise be needed by particular families are in short supply. In any case, there is very little evidence that these programs are effective in reducing risk to children (Gambrill and Shlonsky, 2001; Swift, 2007), an issue that will be further addressed in Chapter 7.

Recent Policy Shifts

In Ontario, the government has recently announced a move away from the consensus-based New York tool to an actuarial risk assessment model designed and tested in California. Actuarial models sample files of children and families involved in the child protection system, analyse paths of behaviour noted in files, and relate these paths to sets of characteristics and events to items identified as highly associated with a designated outcome, usually reabuse of a child (Gambrill and Shlonsky, 2000: 818). Actuarial models have been shown by many studies to be more accurate than consensus models like the New York tool, which is based on practice wisdom and 'expert' opinion rather than file review of actual cases. As Gambrill and Shlonsky (2000) report, this does not mean that actuarial models are without considerable difficulty. These authors examine a variety of problems with the approach, from definitional dilemmas to inconsistencies in implementation. Further, not all researchers agree that the actuarial route is necessarily the path to follow. Baumann et al. (2005) concluded that several actuarial models tested were not found to be superior to worker judgment in predicting abuse.

Nevertheless, Ontario moved to an actuarial model in 2007. The 'new' directions in Ontario and some other provinces such as Alberta, involve de-emphasizing risk assessment, focusing instead on a 'differential response' approach that directs workers to tailor investigations and interventions to the specific family and its problems. The 'new' approach involves a swing of the pendulum once more in the direction of supporting parents (Dumbrill, 2005). It also entails more emphasis on the care of children by relatives, a practice known as 'kin care,' in instances when the children cannot stay at home, and more 'community partnerships' with other agencies and services. These partnerships mean more referrals and contracting out of services by child welfare staff. Dumbrill's analysis of these directions in Ontario is that there are already some flaws in the plan. He points out that there is no instrument available to help workers decide which level of investigation is required, a problem that may very well lead us back to more pervasive risk assessment. The proposed collaboration between community agencies and child protection services is also potentially problematic, given the hesitancy of community groups to share information with protection services. Further, there is no existing model for collaboration, leading to the possibility of serious gaps in communication and services. Finally, Dumbrill says the new plan is focused mostly on strengthening agencies rather than on the families themselves. Organizations may well benefit, but it remains to be seen if resources will 'trickle down' to vulnerable parents and children.

Meanwhile, the actuarial model will still be a central component of the new plan. The model, taken from California this time, is shorter and includes separate scales for abuse and neglect. The items focus heavily on previous involvement with child welfare services, virtually guaranteeing much repeat business. Risk assessment remains entrenched in thinking and in practice, and the auditing and accountability systems positioned alongside risk assessment may even increase with the partnership component in place. In fact, the number and kinds of forms required to be filled out have proliferated in the new system (Ontario Ministry of Children and Youth Services, 2007). Now there are forms, some required, some optional, for family risk, reunification, child emotional well-being, adult alcohol and drug use, adult emotional well-being, family support, and mental health, among others.

The Children and Families in Child Welfare

While it is true that all families could be the subject of a complaint about the care of their children, the chances of having a social worker knock at the door are much greater for some families than for others. The system is reactive. Parents and children come in contact with the child welfare system because they and their situation have been reported by someone, a report that may be triggered in part by presumptions made about the family and its circumstances. Jones (1979) provides a graphic illustration of the probabilities that any one child aged 5 to 9 years in the United Kingdom will enter state care on the basis of key economic and social indicators (see Table 5.1).

Many other studies support the fact that parents reported to child welfare authorities have historically been drawn predominately from the ranks of the poor and disadvantaged[1] (Pelton, 1994; Lindsey, 2003; Fetherstone, 2006). In Canada, this issue was widely acknowledged by the National Council of Welfare in one of the first national studies of child welfare in this country: 'One fundamental characteristic of the child welfare system, however, has not changed appreciably over the years: its clients are still overwhelmingly drawn from the ranks of

---

1 It is clear that many people living in marginal circumstances are not reported for abusing or neglecting their children or that those with sufficient resources are not free from complaints about their parenting behaviour. But it is a fact that poverty and its attending problems present many challenges to children and their parents and that the child welfare system is more likely to hear about their struggles. It is also true that people living in poverty are more vulnerable to community scrutiny.

Table 5.1 Relative Probability of Entering State Care Based on Socioeconomic
Indicators: U.K. Children, Aged 5–9 Years

Child A	Child B
Aged 5–9 years	Aged 5–9 years
No dependence on social security benefits	Household head receives income support
Two-parent family	Single adult household
Three or fewer children	Four or more children
White	Mixed ethnic origin
Owner-occupied home	Privately rented home
More rooms than people	One or more persons per room
Odds are 1 in 7,000	Odds are 1 in 10

Source: Jones (1979).

Canada's poor' (1979: 2). A recent national study of child welfare families in Canada, limited because it inquired into source of income
rather than level, nonetheless concluded that in 2003 of the families
where complaints of maltreatment of children were substantiated 25
per cent were in receipt of social assistance or unemployment insurance or had no source of income (Trocmé et al., 2005) in contrast to
this proportion of the general population, about 5.2 per cent (National
Council of Welfare, 2006: 87). Another 12 per cent of parents involved
with child welfare held part-time jobs, multiple jobs, or seasonal
employment. While the rest apparently had full-time work, this does
not guarantee above-poverty wages for the family. As noted in
Chapter 3 an increasing number (about one-third) of low-income children live in families in which at least one parent works full-time for the
entire year (Campaign 2000, 2006). The lack of affordable child care for
many of these children would undoubtedly contribute to the numbers
of reports to child welfare for negligence. In fact, neglect is the most
common reason for substantiated child maltreatment (34% of all
cases), and failure to supervise is the most common reason for establishing neglect (Trocmé, 2005: 34).

   Child welfare, with its focus on the poor and their parenting, has
always paid particular attention to women and their behaviour,
without acknowledging the gender bias in its policies and practice
(Gordon, 1988; Risley-Curtiss and Heffernan, 2003; Fetherstone, 2006;
Callahan, 1993; Swift, 1995a). Many 'parents' reported to child welfare

are, in fact, single mothers (39 per cent in 2003 across Canada, reported in Trocmé et al., 2005: 74), and files are usually kept under the name of the mother, even when fathers are present. When fathers do reside with the family, they are frequently left out of the investigation and service plan (Strega et al., 2008).

Recent modifications to child welfare legislation have focused further attention on mothers and their responsibility for child protection. Reports of 'children witnessing violence,' a recent addition to child welfare legislation in many jurisdictions, have soared lately. In Canada, substantiated child maltreatment investigations involving such cases increased dramatically between 1998 and 2003, rising from an incidence rate per 1,000 children of 1.72 in 1998 to 6.17 and increasing in actual numbers from 8,284 to 29,370 cases in this period (Trocmé et al., 2005: 96). In the majority of these situations, women are being harmed by men but they are expected to protect their children from the sight and sounds of these incidents. The locus of responsibility shifts from fathers to mothers for taking action on inappropriate and often dangerous behaviour.

Children and families coming to the attention of child welfare are disproportionately drawn from the population of indigenous, colonized, and immigrant peoples. While poverty and its accompanying problems can be one factor, the history of racism towards Aboriginal and other minority groups in child welfare policy and practice is clearly another. Since provincial governments assumed responsibility for Aboriginal children and family welfare for those living off reserve in the late 1950s, Aboriginal peoples have been vastly overrepresented in the child welfare system (Johnston, 1983). Poor housing and homelessness have been especially significant for Canada's Aboriginal peoples. Colonial policies such as the creation of reserves, Band Council governing systems, residential schools, and child protection have featured moving peoples from their traditional lands into squalid conditions on reserves and into urban slums (Brown et al., 2002; Blackstock et al., 2003).

At present, available data suggest that from 30 to 40 per cent of Canadian children in care are Aboriginal with very few placed in Aboriginal homes in spite of legal or practice requirements (Blackstock et al., 2004; Farris-Manning and Zandstra, 2003). These figures differ substantially among the various provinces and indigenous groups. For instance, in Manitoba up to 68 per cent of children in care are Aboriginal and in British Columbia this figure has risen to over 40 per cent

(Foster, 2007). While the numbers of Aboriginal children are growing overall, these children still make up only 5.6 per cent of all children in Canada (Statistics Canada, 2001).

Tracking other cultural and racial groups in the child welfare system in Canada is not easy. The one recent national study on child welfare does not include an examination of race and cultural differences among the child welfare population. In the United Kingdom (Viner and Taylor, 2005) and the United States (Roberts, 2000; Hill, 2006), Black children enter the foster care system in grossly disproportionate numbers, a disparity that has increased over the past two decades. In 1998, Black children composed about 15 per cent of the population under the age of 18 years in the United States yet comprised 45 per cent of the foster care population (Roberts, 2000): 'the fact that nearly 60 percent of our nation's children who live in foster care are children of color goes largely unnoticed by most Americans. Yet these children, while under state-mandated care, suffer far worse outcomes – in terms of physical and mental health, educational performance, and access to basic services and resources – despite the hard evidence that parents of color are no more likely than white parents to abuse or neglect their children' (Hill, 2006: 1).

Family composition, race, poverty, and unstable housing are invariably connected. Families who experience frequent moves and other challenges of trying to raise children in inadequate or unaffordable housing are under particular stress and scrutiny (Cohen-Schlanger et al., 1995; Culhane, 2003). Further, the shortage of affordable housing affects the decisions of social workers about whether children are to be removed from or returned to their families. In a Toronto study conducted in 1992 and repeated in 2000, inadequate housing was identified as a factor in 18.6 per cent (1992) and 20.7 per cent (2000) of cases requiring social workers to decide whether to place or keep children in care (cited in Chau et al., 2001). Since the numbers of children in government care increased rapidly during this period, inadequate housing affected decisions for 61 per cent more children in 2000 than in 1992.

Overall, the numbers of parents and children involved with child welfare has increased markedly in Canada in the past decade. A national report comparing data collected in 1998 and 2003 concluded that the number of child welfare investigations increased 78 per cent in that five-year period from a rate of 21.52 per 1,000 children to 38.33 per 1,000 (Trocmé et al., 2005). Those investigations resulting in substantiated claims of maltreatment increased by 125 per cent, from 9.64 cases of substantiated maltreatment per 1,000 children in 1998 to 21.71 in 2003.[2] During a similar time frame, 1996 to 2001–02, the numbers of children in government care in Canada almost doubled, from approximately 40,000 to 76,000 (Farris-Manning and Zandstra, 2003). This remarkable increase in child welfare activities occurred during the time in which cutbacks to social services were in full flower, as outlined in Chapter 3. It also occurred when risk assessment was widely practised across Canada, one issue prompting the present study.

Although the number of children and families involved with child welfare has significantly increased, they are still most likely to be drawn from the populations facing significant disadvantages. It is also evident that a reduction in social provisions over the past two decades has increased the vulnerability of these individuals. Today's child protection workers are charged with carrying out risk assessments of these disadvantaged individuals and families with the aim of differentiating who among them can provide at least minimal care for their children and who might not. The social and economic circumstances in which these parents must operate are, as in the past, mostly excluded from consideration as risks to the safety of children.

Conclusion

There is a long history in the social sciences of attempts to understand and manage people through categories of science. In hindsight, such categories and the labels that ensue appear harsh and mean-spirited, and the supposedly scientific evidence supporting them has often long since been challenged and often disproven. When organizations and institutions adopt a 'scientific' approach for categorizing the clientele, the selected categories often result in the conflation of science with administrative requirements and information (Macnicol, 1987). In considering contemporary attempts to categorize and label populations served by institutions and organizations, it might be helpful to fast

---

2 The authors of the study note that 'the increase in cases of substantiated maltreatment appears to be partly attributable to a shift in the way that investigating workers classify cases, with a much smaller proportion of cases being classified as suspected (13 per cent in 2003 compared with 24 per cent in 1998, in Canada outside of Quebec)'(2005; 81). 'It is difficult to determine the extent to which these changes are the result of changes in child welfare policies and practices or changes in the types of cases being referred' (2005: 94).

forward ourselves fifty years ahead to try to imagine how these efforts might be viewed then. At one level, risk can and should be seen as another step in the long evolution of our society's attempt to 'know' its members, intertwined with our even longer-term attempts to control and manage certain groups of people. Referring to people as number ratings, as frequently occurs in the context of child welfare risk assessment, may not be kindly viewed by future professionals: 'She's a 1-1-A.'

Even if risk assessment is de-emphasized or abandoned, the era of risk will have left its mark on human services. Risk reconfigures issues. Organizations and institutions are internally restructured to bring themselves into line with risk thinking, concerns about liability, and the requirements of risk technologies (O'Malley, 1999). This process is in motion, and it will continue in child welfare and other human services.

Kemshall (2002) has convincingly argued that risk is replacing need and certainly equity as the defining concept in service delivery in the public services. Accountability procedures, rationing of services through 'sharpened' assessment, increased paperwork, and standardized pathways for service provision, she argues, all operate to link risk to new organizational forms that produce the way that front-line workers deliver services and provide 'McDonaldized care' (Fine, 2005: 262). Hoggett (1990) refers to this process as the 'remote control' of local sites through targets and procedures that are established outside the local site but applied to it. Professionals themselves are scrutinized through their compliance in filling out the organization's required standardized forms (Ericson and Doyle, 2004). The bureaucratically established categories on forms then become the basis for the development of future categories, including actuarial risk assessment tools, since this is the main information organizationally captured.

In Canadian child welfare, the ground was well prepared for the acceptance of this approach by the high-profile media reporting of tragic child deaths. It is not clear why media coverage of child welfare disaster stories spread across so many English-speaking countries in the past twenty years, and especially in the 1990s. However, coupled with pressure on governing bodies to be accountable for risk management, this trend caused a hasty resort to science, and often specious science at that, with a view to avoiding any appearance of inaction in the face of imminent danger (Ericson and Doyle, 2004). This history of the emergence of risk tools raises the question of how much government really responds to the science and how much to the single, but well-publicized, case. At any rate, it is now necessary to adjust policies because of 'unintended consequences' of some of the most thorough-going risk assessment practices. Although the appearance of change may be created by these new policies, risk remains well entrenched in Canadian child welfare policy.

Leiss (2000), echoing many risk theorists discussed in Chapters 1 and 2, notes that contemporary governments have more responsibility for containing and managing risk than they did in the past. He makes the point that in developing and deploying risk assessment science, governments have typically not opened their favoured models to public challenge. Risk models used in Canadian child protection, still well entrenched, rely on the more or less private use of tools and ideas that are presented to professionals as science and that have not been presented to wider audiences for public discussion or consultation. Leiss recommends that governments should be accountable for risk management, including the translation of science to make issues understandable to the public, examining possible outcomes of differ-ent approaches, and providing a decision method that cites both the challenges and the benefits of various options. This approach recog-nizes the limits of science and would require the employment of staff who not only have the requisite skills of science but the ability to manage the 'science-policy' interface (2000: 50).

Adams says risk management involves 'moral decisions made in the face of uncertainty' (2003: 87). Rose (1999) also discusses the moral aspects of risk management as they have been institutionalized in organizational life. However, the moral aspect of risk assessment has seldom been acknowledged in child welfare. This is perhaps not so dif-ficult to explain. Cradock (2004), for instance, points out that the sci-entific gloss superimposed on the assessment of risk conveys a sense of 'truth' that protects users from charges of moralizing and of too much governance of family life. These arguments raise the very serious question of whether we are actually imposing moral order on selected populations, disguised as scientifically based intervention.

6 In the Name of Risk

I have the privilege of presenting the B.C. Risk Assessment Model, a well researched instrument designed to predict future harm to children.
Director, Child Consultation Services, Risk Assessment Model (1996)

What have they thought of now?
Aboriginal worker

According to the review of risk assessment tools carried out by Rycus and Hughes (2003), the use of these instruments derives from concern about child protection tragedies and a wish to prevent other such tragedies. They were intended, these authors say, to assist and support workers in predicting future harm through the use of more rigorous and orderly procedures. Other authors describe an important purpose of the tools as the need to target scarce resources to those most in need, with a second purpose being the reduction of 'bias' in decision making (D'Andrade et al., 2005). Ontario's documents say that risk assessment 'makes it easier for the supervisor to ensure that the worker has taken appropriate steps' (ORAM, 2000: 1) and therefore assists the supervisor in the evaluation of staff. These and various other purposes claimed as the objectives of risk assessment flag an issue that plagues the field – what really is the point?

These suggested purposes signal but do not address and explore the historically specific circumstances, examined in earlier chapters, in which risk assessment arose. Risk assessments as they came to be formed, introduced, and practised in child welfare were not invented in a vacuum. The shrinking welfare state was producing diminishing resources available for human services practitioners to access. Discourses of risk as a common sense way of planning for the future had penetrated most professional sectors, and they had made their way into child protection legislation. Managerial practices had long since been intensified as part of the neoliberal project. These were some of the conditions and circumstances in which formal reviews of a number of child deaths related to protection services were held and publicized in most English-speaking Western countries. The outcomes of these reviews virtually all cited sloppy work practices as the main reason for child deaths. Both workers and the systems they worked in were cited as culpable and in need of repair. Reviews did not explore in any depth, if at all, the social relations of poverty, gender, race, and culture, described earlier in Chapters 3 and 5, that continuously play out in the practice of child welfare and related services. Nor did reviews place the presumed 'problems' in the context of shrinking resources available to both the clientele and the relevant state departments and ministries. Possible explanations for child deaths related to the social context were elided and lost from view, leaving workers and their work practices as the targets for change.

Manufacturing 'Bad Workers'

Of course, risk assessment has not completely altered the kinds of work done in the course of child protection work – far from it. In significant ways the organization of child welfare (Swift, 1995a) goes on as before. Situations involving potential harm to children are identified, and case files are worked up. Families are investigated, and plans for system-approved interventions are made and monitored.

A 'case,' of course, is always an expression of social and especially power relations of institutions and the society they serve. Institutional purposes determine the relevancy of the 'facts' to be assembled. Those facts are then organized in relation to the subject of the file, who comes to 'stand in relief' (Smith, 1990: 91) relative to others. The activities necessary to accomplish the construction of a case generally disappear in the process, and the case file, or text, comes to represent institutional reality. With the introduction of risk assessment, however, new elements were introduced into the thinking and work practices of staff, and new knowledge was required of front-line workers in order to fulfil their mandated responsibilities. Different discourses had to be accessed and incorporated into practices of thought, decision making, planning, and relating to clients. Workloads, especially as related to the new requirements for documentation, increased substantially. In addition, procedures revealing some of the actual activities involved in working up the files were introduced, specifically certain selected activities required of front-line workers.

For the period of our study, fear of error was a prominent feature of thought, speech, and decision making for workers. Meanwhile, important discourses, for instance, of racism and sexism, became even less relevant to the work process than they previously had been. Professional knowledge taught and used by social workers became secondary to management logic and the tools produced well outside the local sites of use. Power relations among the various actors shifted. Cases, as worked up in this context, reveal the new and shifting relations of power that they express and reproduce.

The very public excoriation of the system and its personnel carried out especially in the print media during the 1990s in Canada surely caused staff at all levels to cringe and seek cover. Even so, one might have imagined some pushing back from the child protection sector in response to the blame raining down on it, but this did not occur to any extent (Swift, 2001). Instead, the significant changes introduced in some provinces were met with acceptance, at least publicly. Managers and workers alike appeared to accept, at least at some level, that their work needed improvement. The reviews, the press, and certainly management agreed that consistency in data gathering and decision making was the top priority. Since organizational change generally proceeds from the perspective of system management (Rankin and Campbell, 2006), this choice was hardly surprising. Workers themselves came to feel that standardizing their work would improve outcomes and their own stress levels.

Many of the strategies adopted by provincial governments helped to ease workers' fears of the transition to a new system. Both British Columbia and Ontario engaged in vigorous hiring exercises; the prospect of new jobs for entry-level workers no doubt helped accelerate acceptance of the changes. In the period leading up to the introduction of formal risk assessment, selected staff members were consulted by the relevant ministries for input on the shaping of proposed tools. By way of justification of the proposed new regime, officials and managers frequently cited the numerous recommendations for 'comprehensive risk assessment' resulting from reviews of deaths. Workers were assured that their professional judgments would not be compromised by the use of the new tools. The guidance provided by the tools, they were promised, would enhance their practice and its outcomes. By the time the tools came into practice they were widely accepted not only as necessary but also as truly positive innovations in the practice of child welfare, supported by research and legitimized by their presumed objectivity. The already significant critiques of risk assessment published in both the United States and Great Britain played no evident role in this scenario. Risk assessment was here, and it was going to solve or at least mitigate the problems of disorder, subjectivity, and inconsistency, which reviews had 'uncovered.' Risk assessment would increase child safety. The structural and social underpinnings of many kinds of harm to children (Swift, 1995a) were not cited as part of the problem and were not about to be addressed.

The two previously described types of instruments that have been developed, consensual and actuarial, both rely on the study of actual protection cases and research literature in the field. It is common in documents to assure professionals that the tools they use are based on research and are not intended to replace but to supplement professional judgment (ORAM, 2000; Rycus and Hughes, 2003). As new instruments are brought in, the management of the organization or government department introduces practice standards, rules, and regulations to guide workers in their use and to connect them to other functions of the organization. In effect, then, risk assessment brings together three overlapping but often competing approaches to doing the work: science, managerial practices, and professional social work judgment, all aimed at improving workers and their work practices.

The Apparatus of Assessing Risk

The risk assessment apparatus introduced into Ontario, British Columbia, and several other Canadian provinces around the turn of this century demonstrates how textual mediation and coordination of everyday work practices operates. The many documents that comprise the system require constant attention to the texts by all of the relevant actors. Guiding documents like legislation and regulations cite the concept of risk and state the requirements for the use of risk documents. Tasks, speech, and reasoning practices of workers, managers, and collateral professionals must be geared to the completion of the several parts of the process, to the categories presented in computer-based files, and to the enumeration of 'amounts' of risk associated with these categories. Resources, including the worker's own time, are integrally linked to these documents. Training programs are developed to teach people how to think about the categories and the ratings on forms. Booklets outlining the 'competencies' required for the new work are written and distributed (Ontario Association of Children's Aid Societies, 2007). Information collected about families is extracted from the lived experience in which it was originally embedded and is reordered and articulated to organizational objectives. A 'virtual subject' is created in texts, one that the living person, whose life is supposedly represented, might not recognize should she be able to access the collected documents, which, of course, is highly unlikely. Meanwhile, information and aspects of experience not required by the relevant documents fade from attention. In child protection, this kind of file making has always existed. With risk assessment tools, we see a considerable intensification of these processes, including new and direct linkages between documented categories and management objectives. We also see the introduction of numeric scores that provide a gloss of 'truth' and objectivity to documents that previously represented merely the worker's subjective thoughts.

Our study traced some aspects of this shift and the experiences of workers and parents, mostly mothers, who experienced this form of work. Of interest to us are questions about the actual beneficiaries of the new regime. Whose power and interests are enhanced and reinforced through this reconfiguration of information, and whose voices and interests are suppressed?

Risk Documents and Practices

> Do we mean the probability of an occurrence, or the possibility of something happening, and are these the same? Or does chance refer to the uncertainty about whether a particular thing may happen? How are we to recognize chance – is a chance measured or is it an expression of belief?
>
> Brearley (1982)

In one of the only books on risk and social work, Brearley (1982) tries to unpack the meanings of risk for professional social workers. Risk in social work, he says, is clearly associated with predicting the chances that some loss will occur. But it is not so clear that events and outcomes *can* be predicted, or even that we know what we mean when we invoke risk as a way of doing professional work. Brearley asks us to consider what it is that we are afraid is going to happen, and with what degree of loss, and loss of what? Is it probable or merely possible that this loss will occur, and what would be the effects for various parties if it did?

The risk assessment documents with which child protection workers have been presented generally do not raise these epistemological questions. In the documents we studied, risk is put forward as a given. No debates about or definitions of risk are presented, and no discussions about the distinguishing features of probability versus possibility, or even of the feared potential outcomes of a situation, are held up for consideration. It is assumed that readers of the documents will all know, in general terms, what risk is and that they will have some common understandings of what is meant by risk for the children engaged in child protection investigations.

Investigations employing risk assessment tools can be relatively simple or extremely complex, as shown in Chapter 4. Our study sites represent the latter end of the spectrum. Several steps are involved, including the screening of referrals, carrying out a safety assessment, and doing a risk assessment. A worker is then charged with the task of developing a plan designed to reduce identified risks. Only one or as many as four different workers may have been involved in this sequence of tasks up to this point, with supervisors involved in advising and approving at points of decision. The entire risk assessment is repeated at regular intervals of a few months and also at any time that a subsequent concern about the family is raised. All these tasks are supposed to be done within specific time frames designated in standards and designed to ensure rapid attention to potentially dangerous situations.

In child welfare work, activity is focused on the case itself, meaning a family of caregiver(s) and a child or children, usually registered in the mother's name. Child welfare services, with few exceptions, do not focus investigative efforts on groups or communities or on social and economic policies that may create unsafe conditions for children. Risk assessment in child welfare means risks posed by and to specific individuals; therefore, risk assessments do not address social risks. The public apparently shares with professionals an understanding of risks to children to be those risks posed by parents and not those posed, for instance, by poverty. Were it otherwise, referrals to protection organizations would certainly skyrocket, given the 760,000 children in Canada who reportedly live in poverty (Campaign 2000, 2008).

Further, child welfare is a complaint-driven service. Investigations are confined to and focused on parents or other sanctioned caregivers, who are reported to authorities by a professional, neighbour, relative, or stranger. Children who are unsafe but who are not the subject of a complaint will not be assessed for risks by protection authorities. Recent legislation has included stronger sections dealing with professional and public responsibility to report concerns about a child's safety, but no doubt many children in unsafe circumstances go unreported.

Documents associated with risk assessment do promise that professional services will be offered to clients of the system in addition to the required investigations. British Columbia's case management model, for instance, is described as 'the much larger [than risk assessment] set of activities comprising the Ministry's overall practice model' (B.C. Risk Assessment Model: 14). Most tools include in their documentation the assurance that risk assessment does not replace professional judgment. However, workers' clinical judgments tend to merge with risk assessment in written descriptions of how the work is actually going to be done. British Columbia's risk assessment model, for instance, explains worker judgment as being 'the assessment of a child's immediate safety and estimation of the risk of future harm' (ibid.: 2), a merging of ideas that one worker described as social workers being 'co-opted' into doing risk work:

> I'll say it's a clinical judgment, but by picking a number, by rating the family by picking a number, that's in a sense your clinical judgment. (Worker)

The tendency to package professional practice with risk assessment is supported by the close ties that exist between risk assessment and 'standards of practice,' which are mandatory and establish basic performance levels of compliance (ORAM, 2000: 6). Standards generally read as prescriptive statements about how to do risk assessment. One standard, for instance, reads as follows: 'You must consult with your supervisor and have your supervisor approve your decision' at specified points in the process (B.C. Practice Standards for Child Protection: 11). Standards tell staff how to operationalize assessments of risk, and workers rely on them:

[Practice standards] are very explicit and they tell you basically how to conduct an investigation. So you cling to those practice standards unless you have a very good reason not to, and you clear that with your team leader, and sometimes your team leader clears that with the regional manager. (B.C. Worker)

Standardization, Science, and Culture

In popular parlance, the term *science* implies that standardized research methods and procedures have been scrupulously followed in order to produce reliable and valid findings that can be generalized beyond the subjects of the study. Use of the term *standardized* in relation to research procedures implies that findings can be trusted. While the official documents concerning the consensual risk assessment tools we studied do not specifically claim to be 'scientific,' statements do imply to readers that some form of science supports their use. Among the promises made, for instance, are that the tools will 'reduce the likelihood' of harm occurring to a child (The Risk Assessment Model for Child Protection in British Columbia, 1996: 10). B.C. documents state that British Columbia's risk assessment model is a 'standardized, well-researched and usable instrument' (The Risk Assessment Model for Child Protection in British Columbia, 1996: 10). Ontario's documents simply cite 'research findings' along with practice wisdom as the basis of the model (ORAM, 2000) Workers reading these statements in documents generally translate them to mean that the tools that they are required to use are 'scientific.' Virtually all of the workers we interviewed for this study harboured this basic understanding of risk assessment tools and therefore assumed the tools to be beyond formal question. However, they often privately wondered whether their investigations could actually predict future harm and whether the tool really 'works.' This gap represents for many workers a substantial but often barely conscious disjuncture between their own experience and organizational claims for the tools. Not mentioned in documents or by any workers interviewed are the significant critiques in the professional literature concerning the predictive capacity of these tools, critiques discussed in Chapter 5.

Potentially undermining any scientific features of risk assessment are the many managerial features imposed on the implementation of these tools. The managerial features of risk assessment allow for attempts at cost containment, accountability of workers and supervisors to upper-level management, and regular audits to ensure compliance with the system. Clearly, risk assessment has come to have multiple objectives; the prediction of unnamed future harms to children is just one of these.

A well-recognized issue in relation to the standardized approach called for by risk assessment procedures is that of accounting for the diversity of cultures among the people reported to child protection authorities. The problems of accounting for culture in such a uniform work process have been critiqued in the literature (Brissett-Chapman, 1997) and are noted often by workers. Guiding documents of risk assessment may address the importance of including culture in their instructions to workers concerning risk analysis: 'How risk factors are interpreted and analyzed should reflect an understanding of the complex interactions that occur between a cultural minority and a dominant culture. The B.C. Risk Assessment Model recognizes both cultural diversity and the diversity of abilities found among parents' (1996: 13).

For workers, this statement covers over a world of contradictions and 'hidden realities.' The instruments have not been built on the basis of cultural understandings but from assumptions of the dominant culture. Models in use in Canada can be described as 'whitey' tools (B.C. worker), 'very Westernized' (Ontario worker), based on urban experience, and more fitted to assess the safety of young children than adolescents, who, as one worker noted, love to take risks. On the ground, it is left to workers to discover and insert the complex interactions between Canada's many minorities and the assumptions and values of the dominant culture on which the instrument is most assuredly based.

Aboriginal peoples are known to be the most overrepresented in child protection populations, especially in relation to children in care (see Chapter 5). On some Canadian reserves, virtually the entire child population would have to be taken into care if the standardized risk assessment instrument were consistently followed (Ontario key informant). This is because of the excessively poor housing stock and living conditions on the reserves themselves, conditions that are the responsibility of the federal government. Further, Aboriginal peoples have their own experience and understandings of what constitutes risk to and well-being for a child and what can be done to reduce risks, understandings not accounted for in the standardized forms. The short time frames allowed for investigation create obvious problems of compliance in remote northern communities. Some Aboriginal groups decide to comply only superficially with the risk assessment process. It is a process heavily imbued with rigid rules and regulations developed well outside the local context. It is carried out almost entirely in written form and introduced into communities that have oral as opposed to written traditions. The focus of these tools is on the immediate caregiver, usually the mother, but they are used in communities that are built on extended family and band connections. Questions about history refer to a particular family's history; for Aboriginal peoples, history refers to problems that are the result of several hundred years of colonizing processes. Past hardships, viewed in assessment tools as 'risks,' are seen by many Aboriginal people as producing survival strengths. Risk assessment tools, like the organization of child welfare itself, represent urban lifestyles, but are used in communities that are isolated and rural. What does it mean, for instance, to rate a family living on a northern reserve as high risk on a scale for 'family isolation'? For them, risk assessment may seem to be just the most recent in a long list of strange and ill-fitting cultural devices used to disrupt and colonize Aboriginal cultures. As an Aboriginal key informant pointed out

Standardization is assimilation.

In urban areas, multicultural populations and sometimes highly charged racial divisions are the social context for conducting protection investigations. Workers conducting investigations may encounter any combination of languages, experiences of arrival in Canada, and cultural norms of child-rearing in the course of doing investigations. Finding competent translators, trying not to frighten people who have escaped from violent circumstances abroad, and behaving in culturally respectful ways while conducting the standardized investigation are part of the daily experience for workers, and will have effects on the outcome of the assessment:

They [family] may pass a sign that is of a very important resource that is two doors from them, but if they can't read it ... So then in our assessment a supervisor would say, 'Well there's a clinic next door to the family. Why didn't they avail themselves?' (Worker)

Instructions to have an 'understanding' of cultural complexities gloss over the amount of experience, knowledge, work, and skill required for accomplishing such tasks:

> So we talk about it when we're training, what it means to have a government official come to your door when you're a refugee from a country where that means your child will be disappeared and you will never see them again. So, we talk about that. But in terms of actually seeing it in black and white anywhere, it's not there. (Worker)

One common organizational strategy for reducing these difficulties is the practice of 'matching' the assigned worker to a family on the basis of culture or race. While this approach may seem practical from the organizational point of view, workers often view it as the dumping of cases onto workers identified as minorities:

> Most of my clients were other people of colour from similar racial, cultural background as myself. The assumption is that somehow I will work better with this population than anyone else ... And I can explain the North American cultural context in a way that will be palatable and they'll understand and they'll get it. (Worker)

For such workers, it may seem as though the organization values them as ethnically rather than professionally skilled practitioners. Of course, matching can itself be problematic for the worker in other ways:

> When I went to court with ... families from my culture, they would say, 'I thought you would understand. Of all people I thought you would understand.' (Worker)

> You know, that's one part of my identity. They miss the part where actually I'm a gay man, and my culture is very homophobic. (Worker)

While this worker may understand something of the family's culture, he must be careful not to reveal himself too much or he will be discredited, or worse.

Race, of course, is not mentioned at all in any of the risk assessment documents that we studied. However, racism at both the institutional and the personal levels is experienced by both workers of colour and parents of colour. Workers of colour assigned to white families may become targets of racism, while parents of colour paired with white workers may feel they are not understood. The documents assume a normative sociological subject for both client and worker: a white, cultural majority person who is heterosexual, speaks English or French, and subscribes, or ought to subscribe to the norms of the dominant society. It is assumed that workers and parents will adapt themselves to this reality, regardless of their own background and orientations.

> I remember there was a case of a Vietnamese family that I was working with, and that case presented numerous challenges. One, there was a language issue. You know? Where I had a hard time communicating with the client while building that kind of trust, but two, getting the information that was required. And I was under tremendous pressure from the supervisor because part of the challenge with risk management systems that was introduced is that it's streamed along timelines. (Worker)

The Work of Assessing Risk

In 1998 and again in 2003, the only nationwide surveys of 'cases' of child abuse and neglect in Canada were conducted. The purposes of these studies included determining the number of reports of investigation of child maltreatment conducted across the country and the number of 'substantiated' cases, that is, those in which it was determined that some kind of maltreatment had occurred. Findings from the 2003 survey (Canadian Incidence Study, 2005) showed that investigations were up 86 per cent (excluding Quebec), and the increase in the rate of substantiated cases stood at 125 per cent (excluding Quebec). These numbers are widely used by researchers, including ourselves, as an index of the state of child protection practice and its effects. Increasing numbers of cases could indicate that the new risk assessment tools were uncovering vast numbers of previously unnoticed children who were being harmed. Conversely, they could indicate something else – that standards for intervention were lower, as indeed they were, that risks were being overrated, that low-income people were struggling in the face of reduced resources, or perhaps other explanations. The numbers are at once both useful and problematic.

Smith (1990: 54–5) points out that the 'social facts' with which we work tell us very little about the actual activities of real, situated people that underlie those facts. The lives and activities of human beings from which the numbers are drawn disappear as 'facts' are gathered, categorized according to various schemes, worked up into formal reports, and presented. Events appear to have happened in the absence of actual people; they become 'cases' of abuse or neglect.

From our data, however, we can bring actual people back into the picture to help us explore how ongoing, coordinated work processes, accomplished by both social workers and parents, help to produce the facts of child protection via practices of assessing risk. Their actual activities provide a picture that is far less linear, straightforward, and objective than guiding documents would suggest.

Child protection is characterized by multiple problems, often messy life circumstances, and emergencies of all kinds. Both parents and workers face high levels of demand on their energies and both are underresourced for the work required of them. Many parents involved in the system have always been under surveillance in some way (Swift, 1995a). With the introduction of comprehensive risk assessment in Ontario and British Columbia, the levels and kinds of surveillance intensified for parents, and workers also found themselves scrutinized as never before.

One stated goal of standardized risk assessment is to create more order out of the chaos that is endemic to child protection. Documents repeatedly stress the importance of consistent content and procedure in determining whether and what kinds of intervention are required to ensure the safety of children. The unstated logic here is that more orderly work practices lead to better professional decisions, which in turn, produce interventions that will benefit clients by creating more order in their chaotic lives and parenting practices. Processes recommended in documents for accomplishing these goals create the impression that straightforward, clearly defined, and predictably sequenced steps are involved. The model used in Ontario during the study period, for instance, involved eleven 'risk decisions' in sequence from accepting the referral to closure. However, the work processes involved in carrying out even one risk assessment can be anything but straightforward, and they are typically behind schedule, sometimes by as much as months or even years:

The other reality is that the comprehensive form [risk assessment] is so tedious and onerous and if you did it properly it is virtually impossible to complete on all but a few files because it is so complicated. (Worker)

According to Welsh, 'in 73 per cent of [Ontario] cases, comprehensive risk assessments were not completed on time – every 180 days. At one [Children's Aid] Society the last full assessment was done almost two years prior to the auditor's visit' (2006: A1 and 7). The risk documents set out what appears to be an established, linear sequence: screening of incoming calls, determination of the 'eligibility' of the complaint to be investigated, determination of the present safety of the child(ren), assessment of future risk, analysis of risk factors, and the risk reduction plan. However, if a new issue arises, the sequence must start all over again at the beginning. In practice, workers often find that all of these steps are going on more or less simultaneously, in what one worker described to be a kind of 'secret process.'

For mothers, there is often no awareness that a complex set of procedures is in motion. The intervention of protection authorities likely seems to many parents to be 'one long case' (Mother), and they will usually be imagining that the worker wants and intends to stay involved with them indefinitely into the future:

They're out to get me. (Mother)

Parents' job is to give the appearance of good parenting, in hopes that the worker will not be able to find grounds to remain involved. For workers, on the other hand, there is a payoff in the form of a reduced workload if the case can be closed at the point of assessing safety. This spares them from the 'endless cycle of documentation' involved in the assessment of future risk. Workers struggle with the tension of missing something important, which encourages them to keep the case open, against the relief of 'moving the case along' towards the door.

The work required to accomplish the processes involved in assessment of risk in child protection during the time of our study is described in the following sections. Not every organization or worker follows the same procedures, of course. We focus on typical sequences described to us during the study period to reveal how workers and parents think about and manage processes of assessing risk.

Information Gathering

> Thorough information gathering at each stage of investigation and
> service provision is required to facilitate an accurate risk assessment.
>
> ORAM (2000)

As documents make clear, the risk assessment process rests on the
gathering of information concerning the circumstances of a family
about whom a complaint has been made. Documents are the authori-
tative voice about what must be done. They do not, however, address
the problematic nature of actually completing the tasks they order. It is
workers who must 'activate' these instructions, that is, gather and
verify information from a wide variety of sources as the first step in
producing an acceptable assessment.

Organizational documents usually call for very specific information.
To begin, a worker, often one specializing in intake and screening procedures, must determine if a 'complaint' meets organizational eligibility criteria. Some referrals are clearly ineligible. The target family, for
instance, may live outside the agency's catchment area. In those
instances, the call is recorded, any necessary referral steps are taken,
and the case is not opened. In more complex situations, screening is
accomplished by gathering information on a lengthy form. The worker
often begins by looking at any previous contacts of the family with
child protection authorities and/or police and by questioning 'collaterals' who know the family, people such as service providers, medical
personnel, and teachers. Often the family will be unaware at this point
that a complaint has been made. If the complaint is deemed 'eligible'
to be investigated, a worker, possibly a different worker, must next
determine the present safety of the child(ren) in the home. It may be
only at this point that parents learn of the investigation. As one mother
put it:

They come to the door with what 'we know.'

If safety concerns are established, a worker, possibly a different
worker yet again, will take steps to ensure the safety of involved children and will only then move on to conduct the formal risk assessment, which may also be done without the parent(s)' knowledge of the
processes and documentation involved:

They did a risk assessment on me using all the information they had.
They didn't actually ask me any questions. (Mother)

At each step, the process relies on gathering information. In our
study sites, and no doubt in many other locations, information gathered concerning future risks listed in the required documents is
entered and scored on a computer program designed for the purpose.
Risk assessment documents in use at the time of study score twenty-
three factors on a scale ranging from zero, signalling no concerns, to 4,
which indicates the highest level of concern. The number 9 is entered
for insufficient information. Workers are instructed that 9s 'should be
used rarely' (ORAM, 2000: 35). Each task also has time frames for completion attached, often quite short ones, which may mean that the
family can only be seen once for information purposes. Of course, a
worker must move quickly if immediate and serious safety concerns
are present. However, time frames in some jurisdictions are also
related to funding limits, as they were in Ontario.

Safety issues, time restrictions allowed for investigation, funding
limits, and constant pressure to produce information and scores
together create considerable pressure on the worker to come up with a
completed and scored document. Instructions on how to deal with the
actual problems of obtaining significant, relevant, and accurate information in these circumstances are not provided in the guiding documents. Informants may not be readily available; they may resist
answering questions, or they may not have relevant information. Past
files may take time to access, and they may contain inaccurate information. The family may be absent or in crisis, making it difficult for the
worker to acquire information relevant to the various steps of the
assessment. And, of course, family members may be not at all interested in providing information the worker wants to elicit, information
that can be used to 'judge' them, make them 'look bad,' and keep the
case open.

For workers, there is a kind of dual reality involved in collecting
information. Workers are concerned to gather the information needed
to complete the documents and close the case, if possible, and they are
also thinking about the information that will be needed to manage the
case should it remain open. They are generally concerned also to see
themselves as doing a 'professional' job, which means learning things
about the family that are not included in the risk documents. Given the

pressure to collect information in a hurry, the first concern of workers is to get in the door and get the family talking. In these circumstances, they generally do not have time to hear the parents' 'story.' The job is to be a very efficient detective, and to be seen by one's supervisor as such. Taking 'enough time' can result in a worker being labelled as 'slow.'

Not surprisingly, there is likely to be manipulation on both sides of this awkward interview. Parents being interviewed may or may not be told exactly what information the worker is after. Some workers show the whole risk document to parents; others, possibly the majority, try to construct a conversation in which the information they require will emerge. One worker took a laminated card of the risk items with her to interviews so that she could surreptitiously check that all factors were covered. In these instances, parents may never know there is a list of factors on which they are being scored. Some workers justify the awkward questions they are asking by saying 'there is a list,' but they do not share that list with the parents. Nevertheless, parents who have experience with child protection authorities usually have a good idea about what information they don't want the worker to have. They may learn this from past experience, through contact with other investigated parents, or by paying vigilant attention to the worker's interest in and reactions to particular issues. Experiences of their own past abuse or neglect are often concealed if not already included in what 'we know.' Since the witnessing of domestic violence by children has become widely perceived to be a circumstance that can result in the apprehension of children, women may wish to conceal this aspect of their relationships. Any physical discipline of children or instances of sketchy supervision will also likely not be readily offered. Mental health concerns and addictions may be downplayed, and even difficulties in coping will be shared only cautiously. This is a 'dance' between two parties with wildly different objectives in mind, although both may and probably do hope for the best outcome for the children. Many parents do not know that they are being rated on a list of factors, but they certainly know that the worker is looking for indicators that they are 'bad parents.'

Of course, the norms and standards of good parenting in Canada are not secret. They are widely displayed in the media and in everyday conversation with doctors, teachers, and neighbours. They are also embedded in risk assessment documents. Cleanliness, order, good health, knowledge of child development, absence of behavioural extremes, evidence of adequate resources, and a compliant and cooperative response to 'help' are demonstrated and rated in documents as zeroes or ones. The issue for parents being assessed is whether they are good enough to pass. Many see their job in the assessment process as 'proving' to authorities that their children are safe and happy and need to continue living with them.

One factor on most assessment tools that has intensified the problem of appearing to be good parents is an item that asks whether the parent(s) was abused or neglected as a child. This item references belief in the existence of a 'cycle' of violence in families, as discussed in Chapter 5. Parents have quickly learned that this item has special significance in the assessment process, and often cannot be effectively denied because the history of events is already in the file. It is part of what 'we know.' For workers, such a history tends to confirm the need to look for further problems because of their belief in such a cycle. Each new case opening recorded in the file adds weight to the idea that past history is a concern, even if the case was reopened as a result of a mother's request for services. As one mother was told:

> An opening is an opening.

For parents, there can be a sense that once this information is revealed there can be no escape from surveillance. The assessment of risk, after all, is premised on a belief that future child-rearing capacity can be predicted on the basis of past events, a belief that many parents seem to understand intuitively. They do not necessarily accept this idea, and in some cases are happy to point out their criticisms of it, as in the following example:

> But then, I find out there was reports about people phoning about my family, about things they did before I was even born ... I said what the hell is this crap? (Mother)

As many workers will acknowledge, if a child is not in immediate danger, and if the parent simply refuses to provide information, there is little choice but to close the case. Middle-class people who are reported are most likely to refuse cooperation. As one parent apparently said to a worker:

> No. I'm calling my lawyer. I will not let you into my home.

However, since most of the people who are investigated are poor, and without much recourse to legal or other advice, and in any case may be quite accustomed to having authority figures monitoring their lives, most investigations proceed as ordered. Further, many parents are aware that compliance and the appearance of an obliging demeanour can smooth the course of the intervention, and they try to appear cooperative, in hopes of a better outcome.

Data about the family obtained through these various manoeuvres have to be assumed by workers and the organization to be reliable. Workers know they are to limit their input of 9s, so it is often considered better to insert some information even if they are not sure of its accuracy:

> So we sometimes had to manufacture the information within that time-frame so that decisions can be made. You know? (Worker)

Workers also know that not everything they learn or would like to know about the family will fit into the documents they are trying to fill out:

> The risk assesssment … just sort of narrowed things down to an unreal set of facts. They might have all been true but it wasn't the whole story. (Worker)

Workers must develop methods of containing the stories they are told, in the interests of time, and they may find it necessary to cut off discussion when it does not fit their immediate informational needs, also in the interests of time. The job at this stage is to construct and reconstruct the parent to see if she or he fits into a designated risk group. Parents can have some input at this point, but they often feel the outcome has already been decided, and of course, they wonder how reliable the information is without their point of view included. Workers often share this concern, feeling, as one worker put it, that:

> a fundamental principle of assessment … is some level of trust and some opportunity for the client to [provide] input.

Even if the reported protection concerns remain unverified, the information provided during the investigation process will remain on file and can be accessed if another report is ever made concerning that same family. Information, whether accurate or inaccurate, can follow a family indefinitely. As one worker noted:

> We're asked to make life decisions [about] families with some flimsy kind of sketch of people's lives.

Rating Risk Factors

> You know, I can go in and do my investigation and score it this way. And someone else can go in and score it differently. It's a very subjective thing. (Worker)

The scoring of risk factors appears to provide substantial authority to the worker. At least in theory, risk assessment scores are the basis of prediction, and they establish the worker as an important professional, a producer of forensic evidence, someone with the socially legitimized power to act on this evidence. The assessment process is likely to be respected by other professionals, including lawyers, the courts, medical personnel, and the police. These professionals also use this type of evidence in their work; it is a familiar method of producing information and conclusions that can be assumed to be reliable:

> Lawyers love risk assessments. They [the tools] either say 'yea' or 'nay.' I mean it's for the lawyers. They have a different kind of thinking, in my view. (Worker)

Assessment procedures are also accepted and given credibility by auditing processes. The media reacted to Ontario's audit of Children's Aid Societies in 2006 by decrying the fact that many risk assessments were tardy (Welsh, 2006). The efficacy of the approach is not questioned; the standards that had been set and the procedures in place are assumed to be protecting children. What is recommended is more scrutiny of the Children's Aid Societies. The solution, according to one columnist, is 'minding the minders' (Di Manno, 2006).

Protection workers using sanctioned risk procedures have the authority to ask probing questions and obtain information from files and collaterals for use in court without the consent of the client. In their work with clients, workers often try to minimize the appearance of these powers in order to develop a working relationship, a skill they must learn on the ground since neither documents nor training focus on this tension in their work. Nevertheless, the questions workers ask of witnesses must be answered. Authority has been designated to workers to do the work in a certain consistent way, with instruments selected by legitimate authorities allowing them to intrude and order ongoing surveillance if the risk assessment scores are sufficiently high.

For workers, there is a kind of conflicted consciousness about the practices involved in rating parents on various risk items. The risk assessment tool is said to be scientific, suggesting that a rigorous and standardized process should be followed if reliable information is to be produced. Yet workers experience themselves and others as being subjective in the scoring of risk factors:

> Somebody might rate, you know, a spanking as, you know, 'Well that should be rated a three. Because I totally disagree with spanking.' And somebody might say, 'Well, it's a one.' You know, there is spanking. There is no law against it. You caution the parents, whatever. (Worker)

Guiding documents condone and, in fact, call for 'clinical judgment' to be used, something workers themselves generally speak of as 'subjectivity.' Accepting that risk assessment is scientific may lead workers to doubt whether they are doing the work 'right.' If it's scientific, where does subjectivity fit in? Do attitudes, norms, and opinions have a place in this work? Workers are asked by the process to conform, to stick closely to a 'consistent' process; at the same time, most workers want to use their professional skills and knowledge in the work, and they have been promised they can do so. The standardization of work practices discourages workers from questioning the process itself or the scientific basis of it. Privately, of course, many do:

> They are just saying this is what we should do. This is the trend in child welfare. But nobody is researching it … so it is just kind of there, and we are doing it, and I don't know if we are doing it the right way, and nobody is kind of looking at it. Is this effective? (Worker)

Awareness of their own subjectivity may produce moments of self-doubt, but since workers must clear decisions and risk ratings with their supervisors, this doubt can be somewhat assuaged:

> I check with my supervisor to make sure I'm bang-on with ratings. (Worker)

Of course, this process represents a kind of collusion that gives yet more weight to the scores:

Now that we agree, it's true. (Worker)

Certainly, there are significant spaces for workers to use their own judgment. In such instances workers are attuned to the fear of error instilled through experience and training:

It's kind of a rounding up. If you think it's a one, rate it 2. You err on the side of caution, if you know what I mean. (Worker)

You're supposed to have one of these bullets [descriptors] to decide the number. When in doubt, go up. (Worker)

I was trained to rate it higher in order to keep a case going. It's a safety thing to avoid missing a risk. (Worker)

Workers find other reasons to manipulate scores, including 'rounding up' ratings to ensure that clients will be eligible for needed resources:

So determining the numbers was also determining what the level of service that you wanted was so you knew how to fill out the numbers … in order to keep the referral up, people were actually embellishing information, or made to feel like they had to embellish information to put a person to that level of risk that they would fit into the eligibility spectrum for Child Protection Services. (Worker)

Important to notice is that *all* items on the risk assessment must be addressed and rated. What this means is that information is sought on questions that have nothing to do with the original complaint bringing the family to attention. As the assessment proceeds, the scope of investigation may very well be widened. Some questions mystify parents, and children are also asked to comment on issues that they may never have thought of before. An investigation concerning a father's visiting rights brought the following questions:

They asked [the children] if we laugh too much, if we ever topple over. (Mother)

The worker is required to score every item on the assessment form every time the risk assessment is administered, which may be many times on a single family. Experienced clients try to manipulate the worker's view of the situation to their own advantage, and workers meanwhile are attuned to producing enough knowledge of the situation to convince their supervisors that the scores they assign are justified.

Why are risk scores important? One reason is that child protection generally involves a series of workers carrying out different tasks at different points in time. Risk scores speak to subsequent workers, guiding their understanding of concerns on which attention must be focused. Once scores are entered into the database, they are there to stay. Even if they are based on inaccurate or incomplete information, they nevertheless live on in the file. Risk assessment scores produce a written history that will follow people in documents, even when the purported risks to children remain unconfirmed or are eventually 'reduced.' For instance, a mother who has at a previous time been reported for abuse, even if allegations remain unconfirmed, could be 'flagged' at the point of delivering a newborn child. This means that she will be subjected to risk assessment and likely ongoing surveillance, even if the assigned worker feels this constitutes inappropriate intervention.

Further, risk assessment produces a new way of categorizing clients, which they themselves may internalize:

I wasn't a very high risk. (Mother)

Those who have been assessed at a sufficiently high level of risk to warrant intervention will now be required to work at reducing this level in the eyes of the worker and his or her supervisor. Mothers repeatedly speak about trying to 'prove' to the child protection agency that they deserve to keep their children and that they are, in fact, good mothers. As we will see in Chapter 7, the effort to produce this proof may be onerous and ongoing. Those who do not manage to produce this proof may see their children moved to alternate care. Scores indeed do matter.

Analysing Risk

In documents, the responsibility for analysing the scores of risk factors to determine an overall risk rating belongs to the worker, with the supervisor's approval. In the New York model, there is no set method for arriving at this determination. The worker reviews the risk assessment scores to make this determination, looking at whether the majority of scores are high, moderate, or low, and also looking for specific ratings that may signal the need to increase the risk level. In practice, workers may be instructed to focus their final rating on 'key' factors. These are usually a parent's past history of being abused or of abusing a child themselves, the occurrence of domestic violence, mental health and/or addiction issues, and parents' willingness to cooperate.

Risk analysis, according to guidelines, is intended to be based on the risk factors and their interrelationships. Strengths identified in family functioning are to be included in this analytic process. However, strengths are not scored. Instead, a score of zero on each risk factor indicates the absence of identifiable problems, and by inference, becomes a strength. As one worker said:

Rave reviews are zero.

In a system focused on and requiring the production of numbers, narrative accounts will invariably carry less weight. Since families being assessed have already been found 'eligible' to be investigated, and since some immediate or future child safety concerns have been identified before risk assessments are done, any new evidence gathered increases the probability that risks to children will be found. A preponderance of zeroes is highly unlikely at this stage of an investigation. Hence, few 'strong' families are identified through this kind of risk assessment.

A significant issue for workers is producing a well thought-out risk analysis, given the already substantial amount of time required for the necessary paperwork, along with high caseloads. Workers are sometimes encouraged to take special time away from the office to do this work, and they are also encouraged to become as efficient as possible in the production of these reports. A task of supervisors is to teach and prod their staff of workers in this direction. One proud supervisor said of a worker on his staff:

He can get through three risk assessments in a day now.

Virtually all workers engaged in this work complain about the amount of paperwork involved. In Canada, strikes by child protection workers have been held, based largely on the impossibility of producing the voluminous recording required, and many front-line workers will admit that they are very far behind in completing required documents.

It is in the process of doing the analysis that workers are to 'individualize' members of the client family, to bring together the risks, life experience, and strengths of family members to develop a picture of their unique circumstances and the problems to be addressed. Because of the onerous assessment requirements, however, and because of the focus on consistency, this portion of risk analysis is frequently given short shrift, so that the itemized features of risk assessment receive considerably more attention than the unique attributes of the particular family. As one mother who had been assessed said:

[They] throw us all in one barrel.

Also, in a work process focused on risk, there is little emphasis on the identification of strengths:

There is so much emphasis on assessing risk that it's almost – people struggle to realize what is a strength in a family. But I think if you had a conversation you could draw it out of them ... I don't think there is a lot of acknowledgment. (Worker)

Workers are caught between contradictory directives. Standardization of the investigation process stands in constant opposition to professional analysis of the individual circumstances of particular families. Workers have incentives to resolve this contradiction on the side of using the prescribed items and procedures because they understand that the organization views consistency in this aspect of reporting as the most critical feature of risk assessment. Workers are constantly attuned to the need to gain approval of their assessment by the supervisor. Both they and their managers understand that evidence showing that procedures were followed is their own best protection in case at some later point harm comes to a child in the family being investigated. For this reason alone, it is likely that risk assessment in some form is here to stay. Individualizing and citing the strengths of the family have no organizational payoff for workers in this kind of system. In fact, a number of the public reviews of protection practice that led to the introduction of risk assessment castigated workers for being too focused on families, their problems, and their apparent strengths (Swift, 2001).

The conclusion of the risk analysis is the production of a final score. The situation is rated either 'low risk,' in which case the family is ineligible for further services (and resources), or it is rated moderate to high risk. This latter determination allows a fairly high level of intrusion to be instituted, including ongoing monitoring, court-ordered supervision, and the apprehension of children into alternate care. This rating is a double-edged sword, however, for it also allows resources and services to be provided. In fact, it is unlikely that the family will be served unless it is rated as 'risky.' Needs do not play a major role in this scenario.

Perceptions of 'Risk' on the Ground

In provincial child protection legislation, 'risk' essentially references a level of concern for child safety, justifying intervention by authorities. In the guiding documents that operationalize risk, no reference is made to the dense philosophical and sociological discussions outlined here in Chapters 1 and 2. Rather, risk is more or less assumed to be obvious. If a risk assessment has been introduced into practice, then risk is assumed to mean a finite number of factors included in the assessment tool, factors that can be identified, measured, and presumably reduced. Risk, then, is what we say today these factors are. If, as frequently happens, a jurisdiction adopts another assessment model, the implication is that the former factors are no longer risks. Thus, risk in child welfare is something of a moveable feast. Meanwhile, guiding documents are written in a declarative manner, are connected to the legislation in force, and therefore seem to make a definitive statement of what risk is.

One promise of risk assessment is that it produces consistency via a standardized way of conducting investigations. The listed risk factors provide a framework that workers must consult and that legitimizes and drives their ongoing practice. In turn, the framework narrows reflections about risk to the identified factors on the assessment tool as they relate to particular children and families they are investigating. Nevertheless, workers do not necessarily express consistent and standardized meanings of the idea of risk. Workers may see risk in some of the following ways:

- As safety for children
- As 'the negatives'

- As the problems they are going to have to address
- As variable from one community to another
- As the 'edgy' part of the work
- As 'the odds on danger of bad things happening' (B.C. and Ontario Workers)

Some workers have never thought about risk at all:

I just – I don't know. (Worker)

For workers, risk generally remains an uninterrogated concept. Consequently, the framework provided by the text becomes the reference point for coordinating their work.

Certainly, risk has a certain scary feel to it, both for workers and for clients. For workers, risk becomes something real that they must not miss in their investigations. If harm befalls a child later, workers were supposed to have seen it coming. For clients, as one worker said, risk pushes them up against a wall – it is something they likely fear to have mentioned and certainly must address if it is. For both workers and clients, risk is a 'thing' that must be identified and addressed. Parents know it is a 'thing' that may cost them their child.

Like workers, parents generally see risks as negatives. One mother said:

I always think that they mean high risk of, like, being a bad parent.

Parents often recognize that risk is cumulative:

The more things that happen, the higher a risk you are. (Mother)

Parents often speak of risk as something that is lodged in themselves and their family members:

I wasn't a very high risk. I was a low risk. (Mother)

I'm not a risk anymore. Now it's my children that are speech delayed that is the risk. (Mother)

Many parents associate risk with something they did or something that happened to them in the past and that therefore cannot be escaped or changed. These parents are frequently 'at risk' themselves. These parents often live in difficult, dangerous, and sometimes quite chaotic situations, many of which are not of their own making. The worker has to sort through the messiness of life to try and find the most dangerous, most harmful, most immediate potential harms to the *child* that can be fitted into the confines and categories of the assessment tools. Risks *to* parents are not supposed to be the focus of investigation; assessment tools do not capture such information except indirectly. Parents, after all, *are* the risk.

Workers often believe that they actually cannot do much to reduce the risks they identify, which by definition, represent something that has not yet happened. They are necessarily concerned with present problems and issues in the family that they know will have to be addressed; problems and risks are often used interchangeably to describe what they are thinking about:

> It's safety, it's problems. What are the problems here? And then [workers] switch around ... how much is the child at risk? (Supervisor)

Here, the supervisor is pointing out that workers frequently figure out what problems they are going to work on, and then they fill out the risk assessment to match this plan. As workers and parents grapple together with accomplishing 'the risk,' the idea of predicting the future frequently seems to get lost in translation. Understandings of risk on the ground are closer to danger than to chance, and to present problems than to predictions of the future.

We see in these descriptions that for the people involved in formal risk assessments, risk quickly becomes a concrete, objective reality; it is something that must be addressed. Although understood quite differently depending on an individual's location in the process, the notion of risk as a 'social construction' has little traction on the ground. This does not mean that there is no other understanding of risk, however. As we will see, doubts arise for both workers and parents as to what constitutes a 'real risk.'

Professional Work in the Risk Regime

The job of the worker is one of massaging disparate elements into an organizationally acceptable package that will pass supervisory scrutiny, a package that can stand as a legitimate record of what has been done and why. As numerous workers say, this task leaves little time for the responsibilities that professional social work takes to be important, notably building a relationship with the client and offering some actual help. One mother concluded:

> They don't help, they just write it down.

Of course, workers do attempt to help. But the imperative of producing 'the risk' clearly takes precedence for the organization.

For social workers, building relationships with families is seen to be a key professional responsibility and skill. With the introduction of risk assessment, many workers began to feel that relationships, through which they had previously tried to motivate and assist people in trouble, were removed to the back burner. Especially during the investigative stage, workers in a hurry to collect information often feel they are not doing social work any longer:

> So it's the whole relationship piece. To even try to build a relationship at the intake level, it's very difficult. Very difficult. (Worker)

Many workers feel they are going to be deskilled as professionals if they go into child protection work:

> My whole argument, or my hypothesis, about this whole thing, is that it has become such a tick-box profession. And child protection workers are really becoming administrative in terms of paperwork and they've lost their clinical skills. (Worker)

Mothers, too, feel the effects of a system that is focused on identifying risks rather than on providing caring and professional help:

> My boyfriend, my ex-boyfriend now, raped me ... What did they [child welfare] do for me? They took away my child and told me there's a cab waiting outside to take me to the hospital to give me a psychiatric assessment. Why don't you take me and my daughter at the same time? (Mother)

Certainly, the nature of the relationship between workers and their supervisors undergoes a significant shift in a risk regime that calls for all or most decisions to be approved by the level above:

He [the worker] kept running out to make phone calls. (Mother)

Supervisors assume less a teaching and supportive role, focusing instead on worker compliance with the rules and procedures. They have virtually no time to see families, so they become reliant on texts created by workers for the information on which they must base their own decisions. Supervisors themselves are, in turn, required to comply with organizational expectations:

I think often the supervisors are caught in the middle, right? So I don't think it's safe as a supervisor to say something that would be contrary to what the executive team expects. (Supervisor)

These organizational relationships 'set the stage,' as one key inform- ant said, for the worker-client relationship. In this scenario, people being investigated are at the bottom of an organizational hierarchy bent on compliance to rigid organizational requirements. Workers often feel that they are policing families rather than working with them, and they have formed what one worker referred to as 'unholy alliances' with other professionals, especially the police. Workers undoubtedly have increased power in this scenario over families being investigated. Workers raise questions not only about what profession- alism means in this context but also about their personal sense of ethics. Some are afraid they are 'losing themselves' in the quest to do the work required of them.

Conclusion

Currently, 'risk' greases the wheel of child protection practice in many jurisdictions, not only in Canada but in most English-speaking coun- tries around the world. Risk in this context is a powerful idea, one that justifies action and creates pathways to specific kinds of action to be taken. Risk also excuses inaction; if no organizationally sanctioned risks are identified, service provision is not funded, approved, or expected. Risk has become powerful because of its claim to predict future harm to an agreed-upon vulnerable population: children. Para- doxically, it is not at all clear that risk is commonly used as a predic- tive tool, and most of the literature that examines risk assessment tools critiques them for their weak predictive capacities (Rycus and Hughes, 2003). Even when doubting their predictive capacities, professionals may accept the technology of risk assessments without much questioning because of the promise of some protection for themselves. Risk flags the looming horror of 'missing something' in a case in which later harm comes to a child; accomplishment of risk assessment provides a shield against criticisms of stupidity, lax attention, and subjectivity, which have been the staples of high-profile critiques of child protection practice in the past.

Of course, the change of instruments and risk factors that organizations frequently make represent a deep contradiction for both workers and mothers. Risks and assessment scores from a previous era no longer have the same traction, but results remain in files. A child apprehended on the basis of those scores was still removed, and it can never be known if these families would have been treated in the same way had different risk factors been applied. This reality might lead to questions about whether it is the factors included in the risk assessment instrument or simply the appearance of socially sanctioned tools, presented as research based, consistent, and objective, that really matters. This, of course, is not the position taken by the vast army of researchers working to 'improve' risk assessment in child protection.

As Dean has pointed out, 'the significance of risk does not lie with risk itself, but with what risk gets attached to' (1999: 131). Risk does not seem to require exploration of its potential epistemological meanings in the professional context. The presence of a tool and its surrounding rules, regulations, standards, budgets, training programs, and audits supply its meanings. Even without definition, risk allows many kinds of actions to be taken. Information can be accessed by whatever means and can be assembled to justify specific actions that may in other circumstances be considered inappropriate. As organized in child welfare – and perhaps other human services – the apparatus of risk allows assessments to be made without input from all the relevant actors, most particularly from those being assessed. Family members may not even be aware of the factors on which they are being scored and the implications of these scores. The concept of risk allows and in certain situations directs professionals to control, scrutinize, and act on specific populations with public approval. In fact, if risk assessments are not done, and done on time, a public hue and cry can be raised. This is not necessarily the goal of professionals, but rather a form of power that has been accorded them from outside the immediate situation. It is a form of 'governing at a distance' (Rose, 1996c) that not only justifies surveillance and monitoring of troublesome populations but of professionals themselves.

Once it has been determined that risk is to be measured through scoring particular factors, opportunities for questioning and dissent are diminished, and alternative courses of information gathering and action that might be equally or more effective are obscured. Time and its declared shortage play a role in this respect. The rush to bring in risk assessment, often done under pressure of media attention and political will, creates an atmosphere in which questioning is poorly received. The fear of child deaths that pervades child protection adds to the sense that something must be done quickly, even though Canadian research shows that a very small proportion of child protection cases involve serious physical harm to children (Trocmé et al., 2005). The addition of strict time frames, legitimized by the importance of the activity but also fitting nicely with the managerial tendencies of contemporary organizations, creates a sense of hurry that staff find difficult or impossible to challenge. In any case, workers are often too busy carrying out the assigned tasks to spend much time in reflection. This does not mean workers never think about alternatives:

I wonder if there is not some other way to do this work. (Worker)

The centrality of risk assessment requires a kind of double consciousness for both workers and parents. For parents, the tasks are much the same as they were prior to the risk regime. Parents must appear to be as competent as possible, while not appearing so competent that needed resources will be withheld. They must manage and control the personal information they are asked to provide, while appearing to comply with the process. These contradictory tasks have been intensified with risk assessment because the factors and their scores are so important. If parents know they are being scored, they might seek to negotiate their scores with the worker. Even if parents are unaware of the scoring process, many have a solid sense of what is going to count against them, with non-compliance at the top of the list.

Workers are now involved in a process billed as scientifically based prediction, involving 'objective' empirical findings about the risks to a child's safety. At the same time, workers are dealing with the same problems they have always addressed with clients of the system: poverty, family violence and break up, and mental health and addiction issues. A significant task of workers in a rigid risk regime becomes one of squeezing familiar problems and needs into the prescribed categories of risk, sometimes manipulating scores in order to do what professional conscience tells them is needed. Without these steps, no action to assist people can be taken. Risk assessment presents life experience in simplified terms, as factors and scores. It is the task of workers, then, to sort through the complexities that they encounter, to match individual experience with the 'bullets' that presumably typify types of problems and to produce an individualized account that matches the template – all in a great hurry.

For workers, risk has intensified already existing contradictions in their work by narrowing the parameters of the field and the vision within which they can act. They tread a fine line between science, representing objectivity, and clinical judgment, representing subjectivity; between management rules and professional responsibilities; between paperwork and people work; between the consistency of work practices and the individualization of clients. The work of resolving these contradictions is largely invisible, even to workers themselves at times, and not likely provided for in training. In practice, as workers often notice, the objectivity of the exercise does not really exist – their ratings are by their own account subjective. All the same, workers' efforts are highly visible to management and must be accounted for and justified and must appear to be 'objective.' Files formed through the management of these contradictions then provide a permanent record of selected aspects of what has and has not been done.

Workers vary in their willingness and capacity to resolve contradictions in a way that is satisfactory to themselves and to their clients, and in their willingness to stay with the work (Harlow, 2004). Many choose to leave. Many are able to squeeze some kind of helping into their work with clients, but often with difficulty and invisibility. Sometimes they feel subversive in doing this and driven to hide these efforts altogether so as not to appear 'family friendly.' The ideal worker in this context, after all, is not the empathic, listening clinician. She or he is pragmatic, efficient, skilled at obtaining information quickly, always on the lookout for danger.

Risk does not enter the child protection terrain unaccompanied. Rather, risk brings with it a bundle of rules, regulations, standards, financial directives, and time frames, all articulated to complicated legislation. The ostensibly scientific basis of risk assessment provides legitimacy for the intensification of management control, and fear of deadly mistakes provides organizational personnel with a reason to follow the rules sufficiently to protect themselves.

Risk assessment processes and instruments promise improved safety for children. This apparently valuable goal provides a neat ideological cover for some important problems. In this presentation of risk assessment, the safety of children is assumed to rest entirely on their parents' behaviour, and safety is promised primarily on the basis of investigation and surveillance of those parents (Swift, 2001). Missing altogether are social threats known to endanger children, most notably poverty and poor housing. Workers are not directed to consider historical processes, such as racism and colonialism, that have produced harm to groups of children. The tools are demonstrably urban in their assumptions, and as will be demonstrated further in Chapter 7, they are largely based on white, middle-class ideas of child-rearing. They rest also on some unproven 'theories' of behaviour, most notably the notion of child abuse as a 'cycle' that must be broken.

Risk tools presumably at least provide guidance to organizations about what needs to be done to reduce those dangers that the organization has chosen to identify. In the following chapter, the relationships between risk factors and responses to risk are explored.

7 Reducing Whose Risk?

> Risk management is the human activity which integrates recognition of risk, risk assessment, developing strategies to manage it, and mitigation of risk using managerial resources. The strategies include transferring the risk to another party, avoiding the risk, reducing the negative effect of the risk, and accepting some or all of the consequences of a particular risk.
>
> Wikipedia (2007)

The logic of risk management holds that once risks are identified and assessed they must be dealt with in some fashion. The quote above suggests several strategies to address risk, but in child welfare at least, the stated strategies generally focus on reducing risk and its effects. For instance, a descriptor of a child welfare program states that, after families are classified into 'high risk, moderately high risk, intermediate risk, moderately low risk or low/no risk,' and those 'with a moderately high or higher risk rating are flagged for ongoing monitoring and service provision ... The social worker develops a service plan to address the areas of concern in cooperation with the family and other possible resources ... The Children's Aid Society social worker monitors the child, the family and the services provided to determine if the reasons for service continue to be present, and whether the services provided are addressing the risk issues. The case cannot be closed until the risk has been adequately reduced' (Family and Children's Services of Elgin County, 2006).

Precisely how risks are reduced or seen to be reduced through services provided to families is the subject of this chapter. One thing is clear from the outset. While a great deal of attention is paid to how to carry out risk assessment, a full sixty-nine pages in the Ontario Risk Assessment Model, the document in use at the time of our study, risk reduction receives much less attention, precisely eleven pages in the same document. But what instructions do exist for risk reduction convey an impression that there is a smooth, logical, and linear process between identifying risks, selecting those most important and amenable to change, matching these with appropriate risk reduction strategies, carrying out the strategies, and assessing the results. The complexities of this process, occurring within the often chaotic lives of social workers and parents[1] caught up in swiftly moving events, are largely unacknowledged.

In this chapter we explore how social workers and their clients translate the detailed assessment of risks into risk reduction activities within the context of real life challenges, organizational constraints, and professional principles. How do workers deal with what they know is needed and what it is possible to offer, and how do they fit their actions into the required template that governs the file? We trace what happens to the 'science' of risk assessment in the process of risk reduction work and how child safety, the expressed purpose of risk assessment, is affected. We also examine other purposes of risk reduction besides the stated ones.

Who's In and Who's Out?

At the outset, many people investigated by child welfare and even those who undergo risk assessment receive nothing else. A national study of child welfare in the United States that included the functioning of risk assessment concluded: 'Our NSCAW findings generally corroborate and extend those of other investigators in indicating that the vast majority of children who have a child welfare investigation will have the case closed at home with no ongoing services ... even though their families are often experiencing substantial difficulties in providing safe care for children who have a substantial level of developmental problems. The investigation is the primary

---

1 In this chapter, the words *parents* and *mothers* are used interchangeably to draw attention to the fact that it is usually mothers who are involved in the child welfare processes.

"service" that approximately 2.4 million children, and their families, will receive from their new involvement with child welfare services' (U.S. Department of Health and Human Services: Department of Children and Families, 2005: 11–12). These outcomes are true also in Canada. Even in cases where maltreatment has been substantiated, fully 56 per cent are closed following the investigation (Trocmé et al., 2005: 71). While this seems illogical, given the aims of risk assessment, it reflects the reality that services to address identified risks are limited or unsuitable or that some matters can be cleared up quickly. Further, a much larger number of parents whose risks are not substantiated (scored below the current threshold) will also receive no services beyond the investigation, except perhaps a referral. These families may duck the surveillance of the child welfare system, at least for the time being. What they will not be eligible for is assistance with the issues that may have led to the complaint against them. Thus, risk reduction activities occur with a minority of families who have been investigated. The families most likely to receive ongoing services are those that were reported to child welfare for reasons that fall into the 'neglect' category (not physical and sexual abuse, the most sensational child maltreatment cases reported in the media).[2]

What is also unacknowledged is that while complaints and investigations have risen markedly, in many instances it is the same people being investigated again, a point we take up later in this chapter. The parents who are required to undertake risk reduction activities after the investigation are likely to have engaged in those activities before or to have been connected to child welfare services themselves as children in government care. This is particularly true for Aboriginal people who make up the majority of those involved in child welfare in many Canadian provinces. The reasons for the involvement of Aboriginal people in child welfare are historical, well documented, and relate to the colonial policies of past and present governments. The *revolving door*, a term frequently applied to the field of corrections, is similarly applicable to child welfare. How risk assessment and risk

---

2 The national study of child welfare in Canada confirms that 'in cases where neglect was identified as the primary substantiated maltreatment, 57 per cent (an estimated 17,354 investigations) remained open for ongoing child welfare service – the highest percentage of the five primary categories of substantiated maltreatment' (Trocmé et al., 2005: 56).

reduction contribute to the construction of that door is part of our inquiry.

The Limits of 'Risk Reduction' Strategies

Child welfare work is filled with contradictions but one of the most compelling is the need to balance the child's right to live in a safe environment with the demands that social workers take 'those available measures that are least disruptive to the child, unless the child is in immediate danger' (*B.C. Handbook for Action on Child Abuse and Neglect*, 2003: 35).[3] While removal of children from their homes on a temporary or permanent basis is possible, according to legislation and policy it is to be considered only if other less-intrusive measures have been tried and failed or are deemed unworkable from the outset. These efforts may include providing supportive services to children and families, finding temporary placement with extended families, and removing 'offenders' from the child's home.[4]

However, taking the least-intrusive measures has never been straightforward. Legislation in most jurisdictions does not require that supportive services be provided in the same way as it authorizes resources to remove children from families (the words 'should' instead of 'must' are generally used in legislation describing support services). Because support services are not required by legislation, there will be varying and often limited resources for risk reduction activities.

Providing least-intrusive measures has also been limited by time constraints. Legislation restricts the length of time that children may be held in temporary care or that parents can receive supportive services before permanent decisions are made about the children's

---

3 B.C. Child, Family and Community Service Act Clause 2(b) states that a family is the preferred environment for the care and upbringing of children, and the responsibility for the protection of children rests primarily with the parents; (c) if, with available support services, a family can provide a safe and nurturing environment for a child, support services should be provided.

4 Support services for families are described in the B.C. Child, Family and Community Service Act, Clause 5(2) and (3). In accordance with Clause 5(2) the services may include, but are not limited to, the following: (a) services for children and youth, (b) counselling, (c) in-home support, (d) respite care, (e) parenting programs, and (f) services to support children who witness family violence. Clause 5(3) states that the initial term of the agreement must not exceed 6 months, but the agreement may be renewed for terms of up to 6 months each.

future. The rationale for such time restrictions is obvious. That there are children drifting between family and government care with no firm decision about their guardianship has been a criticism of child protection for many years. Legislative limits have been initiated to address this problem, at least in part. These limits also ensure that any risk reduction strategy must be time limited as well, often three to six months.

However, risk assessment has placed additional strain on finding the least-intrusive measures. In Canada during the period 1998–2003 when risk assessment was introduced in many Canadian provinces, the number of investigations rose from 58,201 to 114,607, and the incidence of substantiated cases doubled from 9.24 per 1,000 children to 18.67 per 1,000 children (Trocmé et al., 2005: 95). As the numbers of children identified as being at risk have increased, demands on the limited risk reduction dollars and on workers' time for engaging with families have been stretched accordingly.

The identification of risk is supposed to lead to some action to address the risk. In instructing workers about risk reduction, the Ontario Standards of Service (Standard 6) states that 'the worker prioizes the risk issues to be brought forward to and addressed in the Plan of Service' (ORAM, 2000: 34). As we learned in Chapter 6, there is a tendency for workers to score up if in doubt, and scores become higher as risk assessment becomes entrenched in practice (Leslie and O'Conner, 2002). Once identified, risks are permanently documented in the file. Thus, workers are faced with limited resources, limited time, and more families with high-risk scores that ought to be addressed in some fashion.

Given these realities, it is not surprising that the surest way to appear to reduce risk to children is to remove them from their parents, in spite of the admonitions for the least-intrusive approaches. In fact, this has happened. From 1979 to 1996 the numbers of children in care fell substantially, in part because of the declining numbers of children overall (Human Resources and Social Development Canada, 2006: Table 421). However, since then these numbers have reversed. In Ontario, the numbers of children in care increased from 11,260 in 1997 to 27,816 in 2007-08 (Human Resources and Skills Development Canada, 2005; Ontario Association of Children's Aid Societies, 2008). In British Columbia, the numbers of children in care rose sharply after the introduction of risk assessment in 1996–97, and by 2000 the largest ever total numbers were recorded (Foster,

2007).[5] The proportion of Aboriginal children in care, already very high at 31 to 33 per cent of all children in care, jumped to 37 per cent between 1998 and 2000 after the introduction of risk assessment (Foster and Wright, 2002: 124), and it stood at over 49 per cent in August 2005 (Foster and Wharf, 2007). While risk assessment cannot account for all of these changes, it undoubtedly has had an influence.[6] The cutbacks to social programs during this period have contributed to the desperation of many families, which in turn has led to more complaints and added to higher risk scores. As one worker observed about the rising number of children in care after the introduction of risk assessment:

> You know, I don't think it's easier to do this (risk assessment). I think it's easier up front. But in the long term it's not easier at all. When you come to children [who have been removed from their parents because of risk assessment] who are permanent wards, or who have no plan or any way to get out of the system, and have been abused in the system, is it really, was it the best plan for them?

While legislation and other documents profess the need for the least-intrusive measures, these measures have always been confined at the outset by dollars, time, and the volume of work, factors that have been intensified by risk assessment. During the period of our study, when risk assessment procedures were in full flower, a key approach to risk reduction was the removal of children from their homes on a full- or part-time basis. Ironically, in spite of many studies documenting the difficulties facing children raised in care, no risk assessment is completed as they enter care nor afterwards.

However, even with the removal of children from their homes, social workers are usually required to engage with families to reduce their 'risks' so that their children can return home, or, failing that, be placed permanently in a care resource, such as an adoptive or long-

---

5 Since 2000 the numbers of children in care have declined, in part related to the increased use of independent living agreements with youth and a backing away from application of the risk assessment model to all cases (Foster, 2007).
6 During this period, while the numbers of substantiated cases of child maltreatment rose sharply, the rate of children placed outside their home compared with substantiated maltreatment did not increase as markedly (Trocmé et al., 2005). Even so, the rise in numbers overwhelmed the system.

term foster home. This process is the subject of the next section of this chapter.

From Scores to Active Subjects

Risk reduction work presents several challenges. Social workers must pick up files containing risk assessments (frequently completed by other workers) and turn these 'high risk or moderately high risk' families into 'intermediate risk, moderately low risk, or low/no risk' families, as determined by the scoring system and within the limits of the time and resources available to them. And they can only do this if the file subject, the parents, and most frequently the mother, engages in this activity as well.

As we discussed in Chapter 6, assessing risk requires workers to isolate and evaluate a bundle of 'risk factors,' a process that shifts workers' gaze from the individual parent or child with particular problems onto the factors themselves, their interrelationship, and the scores. Instead of viewing people as individuals within a particular context, workers are encouraged to reduce them into specific factors to be scored. Workers even talk about parents in this fashion – 'she's a 1-1-A' – and parents sometimes have an inkling that they have been so labelled. In this process, the parent and sometimes the child are viewed primarily as objects of analysis; frequently family members have little input into how they have been defined.

However, addressing risk reduction requires a different approach. Viewing a mother as a passive and abstract collection of 'factors' and risk scores is not useful if she is to play the crucial role in the process of reducing her own risks, a central requirement of any risk 'reduction plan. Further, social work perspectives emphasize the importance of understanding individuals as unique persons located within a social context. Thus, an initial task in risk reduction is to reconstitute the primary caretaker as an active subject responsible not only for the present situation but for what the risk assessment instrument has predicted will happen in the future.

This transformational process appears in the family assessment, completed at the end of the risk assessment process itself and added to the risk assessment at the behest of social workers. It is the first time in the risk assessment instructions that workers are required to examine family functioning more broadly within their individual context: 'This assessment deals with broader child protection issues than does the risk assessment and identifies additional service planning issues to help address the comprehensive needs of children and families' (ORAM, 1998: 88).

In completing the family assessment task social workers speak most strongly about the application of their skills in developing 'the whole picture' and, where possible, beginning to engage with children and families. One social worker said:

> For me it's a chance to bridge it all together and ... the strengths and the not-so-good stuff, how did we get to the point, what's happened, and where to go from here.

The family assessment reflects social workers' ability to use their professional knowledge and skill in assessing family functioning and child development, and it stands as a written record of their abilities in this regard. In fact, completing a family assessment is a regular and valued part of professional social work, the place where an understanding of individuals within their particular context is the focus. And it is here that risk factors blend into real people (with real responsibilities to address). And because the family assessment often serves as a transferring summary between one worker (intake) and another (family service), the impressions of people are also transferred:

> I want to make sure my colleagues can pick it [the file] up and carry on. (Worker)

However comprehensive these assessments may appear, they have been circumscribed from the beginning by the overall focus on a specific list of risks and on the negative aspects of individual and family functioning. And because of the importance of making the connections between high risks and risk reduction strategies, workers are instructed to give attention in the family assessment to those risks that it is most important to change.[7] Parenting capacity and cooperation,

---

7 While detailed instructions are not provided about the development of the family assessment, standards state that among the many factors, an assessment of parenting capacity is 'critical, and it is cited as the most promising long-term strategy to protect children' (ORAM, 2000: 77). Parenting capacity is defined as 'the ability of a child's care-givers to make required changes within a time frame essential to the child's safety and well-being' (ORAM, 1998: 77).

drug and alcohol intake, mental health and domestic violence, and past maltreatment of and by parents are commonly identified as issues to be addressed. These factors relate to the behaviour of individual parents. Other factors cannot be changed (such as the ages of parents and children, the number of children) or appear to be beyond the scope of child welfare (housing).

Inscribed in these particular risks are ideas of child development, theories about cycles of violence, and bonding theories that already inform professional social work discourses and make workers appear to be sensible professionals, as well as informing their practical choices for selection. For instance, one factor, 'good knowledge of age-appropriate behaviour,' lends itself to teaching parents about developmental stages of children as part of their risk reduction plan, as though there were a universal standard; indeed, a focus on child development was a feature of many of the plans that we examined. However, this strategy raises many questions about the quality of the research that underpins theories of development, including its class, gender, and cultural relevance. Also, parents may experience difficulties producing the 'right' answers, depending on their language skills, education, and many other factors. A national study of parents with children under 6 years across Canada (Oldershaw, 2002) asked parents to comment on various topics, including their knowledge of the capabilities of infants and young children at various ages. Only 23 per cent of parents 'correctly' responded to particular questions about child development. Further, whether knowledge of child development as accepted by professionals relates to being a better parent has yet to be established.

Questions about the theoretical underpinnings of risk factors related to parental behaviour were raised occasionally by the parents we interviewed, but they remain largely unexamined. As one mother said:

> My dad never hit my mom. So it's not like I learned it. I'm not 'in the cycle.' You know? And my sister, her husband doesn't ... touch her ... So I don't know how it turns out. There's no guarantee.

However, the emphasis on the history of parental maltreatment, and on the resulting effects of the parents' maltreatment on their care of children underscored in 'cycle of abuse' theories, provides an essential unifying message to risk reduction activities:

> I am what I am because of what happened to me and it is up to me to break the circle, cycle, whatever. Your daughter will only date a man who

is going to abuse. And your kids will, you know, hate women, and beat them. (Mother)

The picture of the mother or parent emerging from the file is someone who is portrayed as an individual actor and someone whose own personal history and behaviour in specific areas presents risks to her children. Because many parents have had several risk assessments in the past that identified similar issues, the portrait can be one of a recalcitrant or uncaring parent who continues to bring this on herself. Social workers share this picture with parents as they sit down with them to talk about a 'risk reduction' plan. And as parents learn about the risks that have been identified, sometimes for the first time, they quickly figure out the central message: 'I am the risk,' a member of 'high risk' or 'moderately high risk family' who bears responsibility for what has or might ensue. Risk is personal.

Compliance

The input of the client is almost irrelevant in terms of ... the decision-making process, but the consequences are ominous for them. (Worker)

Parental compliance is an important part of the risk assessment process itself, and it is usually a critical item listed in the tool to be scored. Experienced parents know that it is in their interests to appear cooperative from the beginning even though their own version of events and their own efforts to meet their obligations as parents have been largely eclipsed by risk assessment procedures and policies. One mother experienced in child welfare investigations said:

It'll just make my risk go up higher by fighting with them.

However, the risk reduction process can really only proceed if parents are willing to undertake the assigned tasks, and for the first time, the importance of their involvement in the process is underscored in policy documents.[8] Gaining compliance or the appearance of compliance from parents to engage in risk reduction strategies is often not difficult. Parents are simply presented with the results of the risk assessment.

---

8 For instance, the Ontario Risk Assessment Model states clearly that the Plan of Service shall be developed with the participation of child(ren) and families (ORAM 2000, 79).

While parents may argue with some of the information, much of it has been collected from professionals whose word holds more influence than their own. Many of the items judging parents' behaviour are those that fit with popular views about what makes a good parent. These may coincide with parents' views as well. To argue with these items seems in itself to be an admission that they do not understand what makes for a good parent. Parents remember specific categories and their scores and talk about them going up and down during risk reduction:

I was a 4 and now it's gone down to 2. (Mother)

Parents are imbued with the language and logic of risk assessment and reduction as they become involved in the process.

When social workers sit down with parents to talk about risk reduction, they present them with the results of their risk assessment and also with a plan that:

Outlines the concerns and then outlines what we're going to do to help reduce the risk to the children in their home. (Worker)

And I really try to work with developing the plan in conjunction with the family ... Sometimes there are pieces in our work that we need to see that will reduce risk, and we need to be very formal with our clients and say these are the factors that I see are of concern to me and that would be of concern to anyone looking in on the situation and getting them to see that, see that these are factors that create a situation that makes it unhealthy for their children to be in the home. And if we can get families to buy into that then we're already reducing risk because they're already identifying 'Oh yeah.' I will then ... be the person that helps them reduce those risks. (Worker)

Whether the worker mentions it or not, parents understand that unless they comply with this plan, their children may well be removed from or not returned to their care. The situation leading to the investigation and the investigation itself are frequently highly traumatic. Under these circumstances, many understand that it is wise to cooperate or to appear to cooperate with the worker, sign off on the documents, and undertake the plans laid before them:

If the client says, 'Look I have difficulty with what you're proposing,' then that will be interpreted as a resistant client. (Worker)

The label 'resistant client' can follow a parent for a considerable time and result in added challenges. In fact, a recent study of child welfare workers in the United States indicates that 'level of cooperation' ranked highest in the risk factors influencing decisions made by child welfare workers about particular cases (United States Department of Health and Human Services, 2005).

One distinguishing feature of risk reduction plans, making them different from procedures in place before risk assessment was introduced, is their emphasis on increasingly precise behaviours to be changed, detailed tasks to be accomplished, and exact deadlines for achieving results. Because risk assessment instruments with their scoring system are used to measure change, they encourage this highly specific approach to working with parents. The reasoning goes that the more specific the behaviours to be changed, the more likely change can be demonstrated (and risks reduced). For parents and social workers dealing with sometimes overwhelming situations, these detailed plans provide a place to start, and they may provide some resources and a plan of action parents can undertake. Many parents are already familiar with the routines of having homemakers visit, entering treatment, and attending classes and programs. These programs may offer support and a valued structure to their days, particularly if they are struggling to manage their children or if they have had their children removed and are at loose ends.

However, there are some obstacles to gaining compliance with risk reduction plans. Parents usually have little input into the plans, and some of their major concerns such as money for food and transportation are not items in the risk assessment and thus are not usually available for inclusion in the risk reduction plan:

> You know, maybe if I was making $3,000 and was broke every month. But I'm getting $900. My rent is $700. So I'm not going to agree to budget counselling. (Mother)

By virtue of the standardized items on risk assessments and a modest array of available resources, many of these plans look remarkably alike and not necessarily appropriate to the situation facing individual parents. As one worker told us:

> When we're developing our plans, maybe we're not ... considering the unique situations of the various families. We say, 'Oh this is a case of poor

supervision. Well, this is what we did in that case, so we'll just include these in this plan.'

The result for many mothers is repetition:

> I took eight parenting courses, three anger management courses, and 18 months of family therapy. (Mother)

While agreeing with plans is in parents' interests, some protest. When presented with the plan, one father told the worker:

> OK fine, you want to play the hardball, I'll play the hardball with you.

One avenue of dissent is to retain legal assistance and move to court to fight for custody of the children. If it is even possible to retain one, a lawyer knows the value of risk assessment in court as well as the consequences if parents fail to cooperate. Consequently, a lawyer may well advise compliance with the plan.

Fathers are often positioned differently from mothers in relation to the risk reduction plan. Many fathers are simply ignored when the plan is made, especially if they do not live with the children. The child welfare file is opened under the name of the mother, and even fathers who want involvement may have little claim for inclusion in the risk reduction strategies. This is particularly true if they have been asked to leave the home as part of the risk reduction plan itself. Mothers know that fathers' defiance can jeopardize their case. They try to ensure compliance from fathers or to distance themselves from fathers' behaviour without further provoking their anger. As one mother stated:

> But I was just doing what they said to do. Darcy [her husband] was just the one who was enraged about it really ... He feels mad ... and he just felt really violated so ... I thought what if this makes more problems for us that we're upset about it? ... I was like, 'Shut up Darcy.'

Of course non-compliance can be a successful strategy for some parents, particularly those with resources. Social workers have few options except to go to court themselves if circumstances seem warranted. But this is time consuming with unpredictable outcomes, particularly if parents hire their own lawyer. As one worker said:

> I've closed cases because the parents just won't cooperate.

Social workers know that gaining agreement from parents to accept the risk reduction plan and engage in the activities required to complete it reflects on their performance as workers. Other workers such as homemakers, respite workers, and family support workers are frequently involved in risk reduction activities, and they, too, need to gain compliance from parents. These workers are generally employed in community or for-profit agencies contracted by child welfare organizations to carry out contracts for work with individual parents. In fact, a large portion of their agency budgets may be related to successful completion of these agreements. The specificity of these contracts, involving precise parental behaviours targeted for change, along with measurable outcomes, makes the tasks of these contractors more or less manageable and simultaneously legitimizes risk assessment and risk reduction processes. Mothers, too, will be judged by their willingness to accept the risk reduction plan and to engage others, mostly fathers, in its demands. One worker advised parents:

Make sure you are in compliance throughout.

Compliance for social workers also involves filling out numerous forms and keeping files up to date. Risk reduction plans clearly spell out what is to happen to reduce risk, name responsible parties, and specify criteria and deadlines for completion. They form a record of action for which supervisors, workers, and mothers can be held responsible:

No one wants to be responsible for something really bad happening ... that's what all this paperwork is about. (Worker)

This record of accountability can and has been used to monitor worker and mother performance, and to justify subsequent decisions about children in court.

The imposition of standardized plans or at least plans with limited applicability to individual circumstances does not fit with social work values, which encourage the involvement of people in the definition of their problems and the selection of actions to remedy them. Yet, ironically, risk reduction work is seen by many social workers as the place where 'real' social work is possible, in contrast to the investigation stage where social workers are viewed and view themselves as policing. Social workers often see themselves as 'different' from and more caring than their colleagues. They try to squeeze out extra resources for their clients and connect in a genuine way with families they work with:

> I can't even explain to you my approach. It's just very different than other people. Like I said ... I'm not abrupt. I try to join with families as much as I can. (Worker)

Yet it is a struggle to feel professional, and social workers observe that while some of their colleagues 'treat families with respect and anything else we would expect social workers to do,' some of their colleagues do not appear to be struggling in the same way but simply 'going with the flow.' Seeing themselves as different from others helps them to comply with the demands, if not the spirit, of the process. Perhaps also this is a strategy to hide from themselves their own complicity with a system of which they disapprove.

Managing the Risk; Managing the Contradictions

The actual work of risk reduction looks remarkably similar to what has always happened in child welfare: mobilizing services for parents within their own homes, involving parents and sometimes children in programs in a variety of different local or regional organizations, and removing children from their homes on a short-term basis during the day or week or on a full-time basis for temporary or permanent care. All of these approaches may be required within any one risk reduction plan. For instance, children may attend a day care program during the week and respite care on occasional weekends while the mother takes medication and attends a psychiatric day program, works with a homemaker within the home to develop 'home management skills,' and attends a parenting program to learn about disciplinary approaches considered appropriate by the child welfare organization. The social worker assigns the work to a variety of different service providers, mainly through contracts, tracks progress, and decides when further action must be taken or the case closed. *Plus ça change, plus c'est la même chose.*

That risk assessment has not led to any significant changes in the kinds of services offered to children and families is at once surprising but, on reflection, an outcome that could have been anticipated. As we noted earlier, the core risks identified for work in the risk reduction plan relate mainly to changing the behaviour of parents and children, something that has always been the focus of child welfare work. Agencies in long-standing relationships with child welfare are 'experts' in this work. Risk assessment did not bring with it any new technologies to diminish risk, and in many cases it has reduced attention to family work because funds have been diverted to the intensive risk assessment stage. In the end, the elaborate process of assessing risk, based ostensibly on scientific principles, has not brought with it significant changes to family service work.

However, the governing logic of risk assessment persists through the risk reduction process. It holds that once risk reduction activities have taken place, then a repeated risk assessment will determine whether, in fact, the risks are now low enough for children to be in the care of their parents. Thus, social workers are instructed to replicate risk assessments to measure progress, based on the assumption that the original assessment contained accurate information and accurately identified and measured risk and that the subsequent activities addressed those risks. This in itself represents increased attention to paperwork and inserts, again, the risk assessment process into the activities of risk reduction:

> They didn't actually ask me any questions. They just did the risk assessment on the information they had and my progress that I had been going through. [This risk assessment] was better than my other one. It was a lot better, but I still rated high on my ... my history stuff. (Mother)

If risk assessment scores were inflated to begin with, as is often the case, then it is not surprising that the scores will appear lower at a later time (Lyle and Graham, 2000). Further, as Barber et al (2007) point out: '...it could also be that the link between risk assessment and case closure actually works in reverse; that is, workers do not conduct an impartial risk assessment leading to their case decision, but rather they make their decision to close the case and then record ratings aligned with that decision. Such a phenomenon ... would be expected under conditions where workers are placed under external organizational and/or legal pressure to close cases prematurely or according to some externally imposed timeline' (21).

As one social worker told us

> I'm thinking of closing my case. And they [supervisors] would say, 'Well just do the risk assessments.' And if it rates low enough then I can close it. And if it rates too high then I can't. (Worker)

Certainly, strategies designed to give the appearance of success in meeting the goals of the plan are not lost on clients. One mother whose husband worked during the night and who slept surreptitiously at her home during the day made her point clearly:

> As long we weren't living together, and I didn't, you know, sleep with him and stuff, they closed the files.

However much it appears as business as usual, risk assessment has intensified many of the long-standing tensions in family service work. Because risk assessments identify more issues than previous assessments, the plans themselves contain more activities. Carrying out the plan is largely the responsibility of parents, usually mothers, accompanied by a growing cadre of specialized workers with expertise in family support programs such as homemaking, parenting classes, and anger management, as well as other professionals such as nurses, physicians, psychiatrists, and alcohol and drug counsellors. Specific goals in the plan are matched with specific activities led by particular workers. The sheer time and effort required for the accomplishment of risk reduction plans has increased accordingly (Brown, 2004). Given that there may be several items to address in the plan, and limited time to accomplish goals, parents are often working full-time at their plan. Employment is frequently out of the question during this period.

Unemployment insurance or income assistance programs offer very limited income, well below poverty levels for most families. The latter program often requires a reduction in monthly allowances when children are removed from home, forcing parents to move to smaller quarters, a factor that may be held against them when they try to have their children returned. Not uncommonly, a parent's week may look like this one:

> He's coming here twice a week to do his parenting stuff. He is a recovering drug addict and alcoholic. So he has ongoing supports through the week so he does probably three support groups a week ... and on top of that he does his visits with his girls. So he has two overnights a week and all day on the weekends and that kind of stuff. Add [construction] work on top of that, it's just not possible. (Family Support Worker)

Ironically, the increased work of risk assessment may stand in the way of parents maintaining or resuming the care of their children. Meanwhile, social workers are increasingly occupied coordinating this cadre of workers and completing documents to demonstrate that risks are being addressed.

The site of much of risk reduction work is often the mother's own home. Family support and child care workers may arrive to assist her with parenting activities, homemakers may assist with household tasks, and social workers may drop in to check on her and the children. While these activities are coordinated through the risk reduction plan, at least on paper, it is left to the mother to work out the logistics of the comings and goings of various workers who may change frequently during the life of the contract. The pressures to be an efficient case manager as well as a 'model' parent in the presence of these workers are considerable. The risks identified in the plan may fade compared with what the mother thinks workers are looking for. Mothers mention the importance of 'impression management': keeping a clean house, having polite children, making sure workers are greeted graciously and that they are home when workers drop by, behaviours that they perceive to be important to family support workers and social workers, even though these behaviours are not part of their risk reduction plan.

They [family support workers] told me like, 'You're different from many of the women that, you know, get their kids taken away,' stuff, and I'm like well for sure. They notice little things, like I wash my children's hands, you know, even though he's one and she's two, I still wash the hands before we eat. You know, I ask to go to the kitchen and grab a ... a, you know, a little bit of Sunlight and a rag, just to wipe off the area where we're eating. You know, I go the extra mile to vacuum up after us, and stuff like that. (Mother)

Mothers must assess the preferences and peculiarities of workers moving in and out of their homes and change their tack accordingly. While the list of formal behaviours to be changed has expanded since risk assessment was introduced, there also remains the informal list, the guesses that mothers make, to ensure that they pass the risk reduction exercises.

Risk reduction work also occurs in specialized agencies, sometimes located in the local community but often requiring travel time and expense. In urban centres, agencies may be contracted for very specific programs necessitating many different trips for different programs.

Attending programs can mean many hours spent on public transportation, often with children in tow. The relationships that parents
build particularly with staff during these programs may be highly
valued. However, because of the specialized natures of the programs
and their sometimes distant locations, these relationships generally do
not continue past the contract. Parents are frequently torn between
responding to these workers and confiding in them while understanding that these same workers are required to report on their behaviour
to social workers in charge of their case. Further, parents may assess
that it is not advantageous to form relationships with other participants whom they may perceive to be poor parents (by virtue of their
being members of the program). They fear that they will be 'tarred
with the same brush.' Demonstrating their difference from other investigated parents to staff was a frequent strategy used to achieve a
passing grade in the contract. Ironically, while building social support
is an item on the risk assessment instrument, it is difficult to achieve
within the realities of the risk reduction strategies.

The work of risk reduction is demanding and time consuming. At
one level, parents are attempting to meet the written obligations of the
contract without appearing to resist its logic or the way it comman-
deers their scarce resources. The programs are clearly focused on
changing their behaviour, thus reinforcing their understanding that it
is they, not a set of factors, that are the risk to their children. Their
living conditions and financial circumstances are seen to be largely
extraneous. At the same time, parents experienced in the ways of child
welfare work know that there are informal and subtle ways to work at
risk reduction that may count as much as the contract. Appearing to be
in charge of a well-kept home, presenting well-behaved children and
partners who do not cause trouble, while distancing themselves from
others in the same boat and remaining cordial and cooperative with a
cadre of workers who enter their homes frequently and sometimes
unannounced are key tasks in this 'impression management.'

Clearly, some parents are advantaged over others in managing these
challenges and contradictions. After an exhaustive study of the work
of mothers in risk reduction, Brown concludes: 'They must become
familiar with the working milieu of government and overcome the
barriers of an overloaded, understaffed bureaucracy, in order to carry
out what is expected of them in a "cooperative" and "consistent"
manner. To be successful this requires core competencies including
effective organization and communication skills, persistent research

and problem solving ability, production of appropriate emotional responses, as well as significant amounts of patience and personal resilience. These skills are employed in a highly scrutinized, time-sensitive working environment in which authorities focus on finding gaps or inconsistencies in their performance' (2004: 125–6). Mothers are like unpaid workers in the risk reduction industry, carrying out jobs that are crucial if the whole enterprise is to continue:

> So it's a juggle but it's possible, it's possible. It may not be as possible for somebody who hasn't gone out of their way to take a look at everything as closely as I have. (Mother)

The 'good' client, not necessarily the one at highest 'risk,' may attract additional resources, a not uncommon phenomenon but one that is particularly evident in systems that reward compliance. Those who lack knowledge of or sympathy for middle-class orientations, those from other cultures, and many who are experiencing a major life crisis may not fare as well. This latter fact is crucially important given that most of the clients involved in risk reduction work are there because of their 'neglect' of children, a cause clearly related to resources. That most of these parents are not from the middle class, are not white, and have not experienced positive relations with government agencies puts them at additional 'risk' in this system.

Even when parents achieve acceptable levels of performance in the specific skills and knowledge identified in the risk reduction plan, they may be required to undertake further work in order to keep their children or to have them returned. A family support worker said:

> 'I need you to do a, b, c, d,' and then the client does a, b, c, d and says, 'Well, how come I can't have my child back?' and the worker says, "Well, now you need to do e, f, g, h.'

This phenomenon has been noted previous to the introduction of risk assessment (Weller and Wharf, 1997; Callahan et al., 2005; Rutman et al. 2002) but risk assessment exacerbates it. Even though parents may have mastered some particular tasks in a specific period of time and can demonstrate performance in these tasks, workers may feel that such specific behaviour is insufficient to permit continued care of their children. Yet specific behavioural change is what is demanded by the risk reduction approach. Workers are aware of the larger challenges facing parents that require long-term attention, some of which cannot be addressed within the risk reduction contract either in the short term or at all: issues such as insufficient income, poor transportation, unstable housing, tenuous connections in the community, mental health breakdowns, and alcohol and drug misuse. In addition, there are frequently long waiting lines for specialized services.

Extending the time of the contract is a mixed blessing for mothers and workers. Workers (sometimes with parents' approval) will add items to the risk reduction contract so that they can continue to provide resources to parents who are struggling. Workers often choose to add more specific items to the risk reduction plan to buy some time for more change to occur. Or they can add items to challenge parents who may well fail and thus buttress the worker's case in court for removing or keeping children in care.

Parents, meanwhile, may be wishing to have child welfare workers out of their lives:

> I wouldn't say anything if I was getting depressed, having any rash thoughts. I wouldn't say if I was overwhelmed … anything that would give them reasons to stay open. (Mother)

Or a parent may want to keep contact and her case open, thus remaining eligible for resources, however small:

> The social worker has been giving us bus passes and stuff … if she was to sign off I might lose some of my benefits. (Mother)

In this case, the mother must accept surveillance and the chance that her continued contract with child welfare can be used against her.

At the same time, social workers are often reluctant to extend contracts. The satisfactory completion of the contract reflects on the abilities of family support and social workers and the integrity of the risk reduction process itself. Moreover, workers may need to deploy the scarce dollars for risk reduction to others, particularly since the numbers of cases have risen markedly since the introduction of risk assessment. Workers may even be ordered to close a certain number of cases for budgetary reasons (Key Informant). Always, the worker must take care in making any decision to extend or terminate a contract, as risk assessment and reduction documentation shines increased light on workers' and supervisors' actions and affirms their accountability for decisions.

Social workers are busy creating and monitoring contracts with a variety of workers, who are engaging with parents who are, in turn, busy fulfilling their part of the contract. At the same time there are some significant contradictions that must be managed as well. These include the 'science' of risk assessment versus the reality of risk reduction; the professional mandate to individualize versus the organizational imperatives to standardize and control; the need for parents to be in paid work versus the demands of the unpaid work of risk reduction; the need to be part of the team versus the need to distinguish oneself from others; the 'identified risk reduction activities' versus the unspoken tasks of impression management; and the need to move the case along versus the possible consequences of closing it.

Not surprisingly, an undercurrent of disquiet permeates risk reduction activities, a sense that if all of this is done and documented children will be safe, together with a sneaking suspicion that this work may be largely unrelated to children's safety. Certainly, this unease on the part of social workers and mothers stands in stark contrast to the certainty and confidence of the risk documents and the risk reduction plans themselves.

Surveillance

The risk assessment and the risk reduction plan serve as documents that coordinate the activities of parents and workers in a variety of different sites and provide measures to indicate change in individual family circumstances. They indicate when cases should be opened and closed. They also provide a means to monitor what supervisors, social workers, and contract workers are accomplishing, and they are used by management, including audit teams, to measure the work. In some cases these documents determine what contracts will be renewed with what agencies, what disciplinary action may be warranted, and what resources are required for any one child welfare office or agency. They are the paper trails, and as such, they provide a system of monitoring the actions of many people.

Parents do not see this picture. They see fragments of risk assessments and risk reduction plans. Workers may explain the process to them but parents are unsure when the risk assessment/reduction process started and ended. For many it seems to simply go on, even after the worker has stopped visiting. Most parents we interviewed could not answer whether their case was closed or not, as there seemed to be no consistent process for notifying parents about case closure. Even when parents knew that their case was closed, they remained apprehensive:

> They said they were definitely coming back whenever they felt like it, and 'don't smoke marijuana around your children, and we'll be coming back to see if you do' ... I was like, whatever, and that was it. I've never seen them. (Mother)

For these mothers, risk procedures are a 'panopticon,' like Bentham's prison design, a tower from which each individual cell can be viewed (Foucault, 1995). As in the prison design, those in the cells cannot tell when and if they are being watched, and so they learn to monitor themselves as if they are always being observed. Clearly, risk assessment and reduction have sharpened the bureaucratic sense of what is going on, but they leave the process highly ambiguous for parents. Parents' sense of being under surveillance never seems to disappear, and apparently for good reasons.

A recent study of child welfare trends in Canada (Trocmé et al., 2005: 54) indicates that in the majority of children's and family situations where maltreatment has been substantiated, previous reports had been made about the family (overall, 63 per cent). This figure is even higher in cases where neglect is the primary category of maltreatment (73 per cent) (2005: 54). Moreover, 38 per cent of these cases had been closed for a year or less, a figure that rises to 48 per cent for neglect cases (2005: 55). A comparison of these data with similar data collected five years earlier indicates the increase of repeated investigations. The authors state: 'From 1998 to 2003 the incidence of substantiated maltreatment involving previously investigated children increased by 134% from 4.86 per 1,000 to 11.35 per 1,000 children' (2005: 99). These data show that there is a high rate of repeated reports, with a large number of these cases opening and closing within the year, a trend that has increased markedly and that is even more evident for those cases identified as neglect. It was during these five years that risk assessment was introduced in many Canadian jurisdictions. Indeed, parents are wise to think that they will have many repeated involvements with child welfare. As one mother acknowledged:

> Since the first, I guess I've had 14 openings.

These findings are supported by studies in other jurisdictions. A national study in the United States,where risk assessment is standard practice, notes: 'the families of children who come to the attention of child welfare agencies on any given day have very often been there before. The family issues that led them to be investigated at this point appear to be persistent. More than half of all children/families have had prior reports of maltreatment to the agency, and 30% have prior CWS history (not including investigations)' (United States Department of Health and Human Services: Department of Children and Families, 2005, n.p.).

Clearly, risk assessment is only one variable that contributed to this change. As Chapter 3 indicates, risk assessment in Canada coincides with resource reductions for welfare state programs, making the target group of child welfare clients more vulnerable. Moving cases quickly through the system within specified timelines and insisting on highly specific behaviour changes of the parents has become a large part of the work. The social and economic problems of many families, including resource deprivation, are unlikely to be solved with this approach.

There is another feature of risk assessment that contributes to this 'revolving door' and the ongoing surveillance of parents. As we noted in Chapter 1, risk as an actuarial concept depends on past history to predict the future. In child welfare the assessment of risk relies heavily on parents' past histories as children themselves and as adults. As such it is a highly conservative process, reducing attention to the parents' capacity for change and focusing instead on their probability of repeating past behaviour. Parents are aware of how the past will be held against them:

> Well I'd been told while I was still pregnant by the community service workers that since I had been raised in foster care that they would put a higher standard on me. (Mother)

This fatalistic and pessimistic approach stands in stark contrast to the signature beliefs of many professions: that people can grow and change.

Workers themselves have a sense of being watched, given that they must complete forms, repeat risk assessments, and face audits, censure, and even dismissal. Not surprisingly, those working away from urban centres, or with ethnic communities, who are experienced or 'hard to replace' appear to pay less attention to the surveillance system. For them and others, it is a parallel universe that they acknowledge but do not respect.

Concluding Remarks

This examination of the work of risk reduction demonstrates that the goal of preventing *future* harm to children, the stated objective of the risk assessment policy, has been largely displaced. What remains bears some similarity to what has always happened in child protection: individual parents are engaged in supportive programs with the hope that these programs will help them to be sufficiently capable parents at present and for the immediate future. However, risk assessment has sharpened some features of this reality and has intensified the contradictions endemic in the work.

The goals of bringing science to bear on child protection problems, a central pillar of risk assessment, seem lost by the time risk reduction measures are implemented. Indeed, most research efforts in risk assessment have been placed on identifying key risks and improving the predictability of risk assessment instruments. What to do with those 'risks' once identified is not the focus of research or even of significant organizational efforts. This very point is a subject of debate regarding screening young children for possible autism. While several groups including the American Academy of Pediatrics argue for improving diagnostic tests and mandatory screening, others, including Canadian pediatricians, oppose mandatory screening. The problem, they say, lies in the potential costs of mandatory screening, including the numbers of false positives that will likely result and the reality that, once diagnosed, services are simply not available. Moreover, fewer resources would be available for providing services, given the cost of screening (Gandhi, 2007). Unfortunately, this debate has not yet occurred in child welfare. Our search for studies examining the connection between risk assessment and risk reduction and studies assessing the outcomes of risk reduction in human services yielded very little (Kemshall and Maguire, 2001; Brown, 2004).

Further, there seems to be scant organizational curiosity about the usefulness of risk reduction, even though participants in our study raised questions about its outcomes. Certainly, data on repeat investigations in the Canadian Incidence Study (Trocmé et al., 2005) suggests that the effectiveness of risk reduction strategies used to date is questionable. Evidently, the science of risk reduction interests very few. One existing study, by Flynn and Bouchard (2005), examines several intervention programs routinely engaged in by child welfare agencies. These authors conclude that only one study team published a paper producing a reliable evaluation of their program design (MacMillan et al., 2005). However, even the MacMillan study did not report levels of significance indicating that their intervention was successful with this client population. Flynn and Bouchard conclude that there is no convincing evidence available that these programs provide effective interventions to parents who are assessed as high risks to their children.

The theories underpinning risk reduction are largely deterministic and behavioural in nature, leaving out the rich contributions of psychosocial and critical theories that underpin much of social work. Ironically, the idea of breaking cycles of violence/abuse that helps to justify the risk assessment approach to child protection is not applied to the risk assessment/reduction process itself, which snags the same 'offenders' again and again. Once in the system, it is difficult for a core group of parents to leave it. A child welfare cycle is created and perpetuated. This is not surprising since the system translates social circumstances into individual troubles, fails to address these troubles with significant resources, and uses the history of that failure to indict parents again. Instead, it is the parents who are seen to be repeating 'the cycle' of maltreatment, while the system and social relations that catch them in their net remains unexamined.

Risk reduction aims at producing 'risk managers' for contemporary society. According to this 'risk society' thinking, parents need help in learning risk management skills if they are to be better parents. They must accept that professionals know best about risks: professionals confirm the existence of risks and their harmful qualities, they identify and measure their strength through tests and scores, and they prescribe what should be done to address them. The risks and remedies are standardized and apply to everyone. The risks that professionals identify in child protection, and in other fields, increase as a result of the behaviour of particular individuals, not because of the context in which they live. The remedies to address risk then lie in changing those behaviours. Clients are instructed in new forms of conduct, supported with the help of various experts. Asking for a significant amount of help puts parents at risk of appearing incompetent, while asking for too little appears as non-compliance. The sense of being watched and of watching oneself, in turn, is ever present.

While the documents require workers to focus on specific risk factors, the people before them and the situation that they are in may bear scant resemblance to these factors. Workers talk to families and children in their world and hear their stories about what is happening and why. The more they listen and respond to people, the harder it becomes to manage the discrepancy between the file and the reality:

> It's not just paperwork. It's real life. It's people. It's feelings. They're children. (Worker).

However dubious the outcomes for social workers and parents, risk reduction makes clear who is responsible for dealing with risk – the front line. This process of downloading responsibility has sharply curtailed the liability of the senior levels of government for child protection and has clearly identified who is to be blamed when things go wrong. Front-line practice has become risky business.

The idea that risk work with its attention on behavioural change has other purposes besides producing 'better parents' or even better 'risk managers' is not lost on some workers and mothers. They wonder if it covers up a moral agenda unfolding beneath the surface of their activities: a process of rewards and punishments based on beliefs about what makes good parents and good citizens. Mothers suggest that the list of tasks and their frequent repetition may have more to do with gaining compliance and meting out some kind of punishment than with attention to the safety and well-being of children:

> I kind of got the impression that I wasn't allowed to hire a cleaner. I got the impression that I wasn't allowed to have someone help me. That was not allowed. That would be too easy. I would be getting away with it ... I would be not learning what my duties are. (Mother)

We began this chapter by naming different strategies to address risk. We have documented several in play in this chapter, most particularly reducing risk to some by assigning it to others. One of the identified strategies is not evident: accepting some or all of the consequences of a particular risk. In other words, acknowledging that with the state of science and the vagaries of the human condition, it is not possible to prevent all risks to children. It appears politically impossible for governments to admit that they cannot protect all children all of the time or even to engage in discussions about the challenges of doing so. In the midst of writing this chapter, other child welfare scandals have occupied the media. Blame is tossed around. New procedures will follow, and more resources to investigate child deaths will be commandeered. Nowhere is there discussion about the 'real risks' facing many children, not just death at the hands of their parents or caregivers, but hunger and shelter and want. To raise such issues is to acknowledge our failure in these areas. Nowhere is there talk about the limits of science and the fact we are all vulnerable to risks that cannot be predicted or prevented. Better to focus on the introduction of improved tools and tighter procedures, along with the shortcomings of particular parents and individual social workers. Who benefits?

PART III

In the final chapter of the book, we explore the relevance of the study for human service professionals. Risk is placed in the context of relations of ruling and the relations of power expressed by this concept. The meanings of risk and the effects of its apparatus are revisited, with a view to understanding the many effects, especially ideological effects, of this innovation. Alternative ways of thinking about risk and risk assessment are proposed, with a focus on social justice.

8 'What Have They Thought of Now?'

The most effective way to restrict democracy is to transfer decision-making from the public arena to unaccountable institutions.

Noam Chomsky

Our study involved risk assessment procedures taken to extremes in a specific context of fear, reinforced by neoliberal politics. Our purpose in this concluding chapter is to demonstrate how local practices such as these are 'hooked up' to larger social forces and how they help to reproduce ruling relations, that is, those relations that 'connect us across space and time and organize our everyday lives' (Smith, 1990). We also consider how these practices help to realign power relations not only at the level of policy decision makers but right down to the smallest corner of everyday professional work. We trace these connections in this chapter and examine their consequences, focusing especially on the power relations of risk, since it is in these relations that professionals reproduce discourses and practices of domination, however inadvertently. In the conclusion we examine some alternate ways of thinking and practising, framed by the concept of social justice. We begin the chapter with an examination of the relationship of risk and global capital, arguing that capitalism in its current form is the engine of ruling and power relations.

Risk and the Dynamics of Global Relations of Capital

A revised world order is under construction, albeit haphazardly and with no identifiable grand design. This redesign involves an intense focus on security. For many human service professionals, security issues related to flows of refugees, immigrants, and trafficking of human beings are especially relevant. As corporations, motivated entirely by the lure of increased profits, encourage national governments to relax controls over business practices and reduce social benefits, substantial low-wage labour markets develop, often crossing national borders. The national state finds itself facing a contradiction between encouraging globalization of wealth and creating the circumstances for social reproduction of labour and consumption. In this situation, the state produces new 'risks' through its near total support of market forces and through necessary attempts to codify and manage risks (Robertson, 1999) to further corporate interests. At the same time, the political imperative to reduce taxes and cut welfare programs means fewer resources available to deal with 'risks' (Kemshall et al., 1997).

The populations in contact with child welfare, juvenile justice, criminal justice, and the mental health system are often society's most vulnerable people, those most marginalized by the individualizing society now under construction. They arrive at this point through an array of social and personal processes. Social processes such as immigration, complicated by the globalizing economy, punishing social policies, and periodic economic downturns provide the social context for personal troubles. These troubles then become complicated by innate capabilities, life events, life decisions, and the health of individuals. Many people, perhaps a growing number, are not particularly useful in the new global economy. Where once they might have taken low-paid labour – Piven and Cloward's 'reserve army of labour' (1993) – many of those jobs are now exported to other countries where even cheaper labour can be found. Programs, including risk assessment, offer 'creaming' processes that select the most promising clients for some kind of retraining and impose behaviour management and surveillance on the rest. Obsessions with security provide the justification for these intensifying functions of the state.

As a society, we have never resolved the problem of 'these people.' Attempts to institutionalize, sterilize, incarcerate, and control them have gone through various phases. We are in the latest phase, one of identifying the less fortunate and more vulnerable people among us as 'risky' individuals and legitimizing various forms of 'education' and control in our treatment of them. Some, the most competent, healthy, determined, and frightened, will succeed and perhaps improve their own lives and the lives of their children. They are driven to 'prove' they can do it. Others – many in fact – will not succeed. These people are pretty much throwaways, not useful in the economy and inconvenient to society. The social task has become to reduce the burden that such individuals impose on the rest of us. They do continue to perform a social use: they provide an example to the rest of us of who we don't want to be.

The national state, meanwhile, seems content to move from its former role in promoting social welfare to one of supporting capital and the free market. Risk is central to some of these changing forms of governing, including the direct enlistment of the professions to do the on-site identification and management of difficult populations, to engage in ongoing surveillance of certain groups of people, and to instil within 'risky' individuals the mantra of self-management thinking. In the process, professionals have not only been co-opted to do the dirty work but human service workers may very well find themselves under substantial surveillance and control. Seen in this light, discourses of risk are capable of performing very extensive forms of controlling the 'conduct of conduct.'

As we see in this study, risk and its technologies, applied to individuals, have the capacity to create categories of people who can 'legitimately' be treated as different, as risky, and who can therefore be subjected to surveillance and controls that others escape. Risk categories can allow the law to intervene in people's lives and deprive them of social and civil rights, even where no evidence of harm to anyone is actually demonstrated. The people most affected may not even know that a risk assessment has been done 'on them,' the categories they have been assigned to, or the basis of the scores justifying controls on them.

Our example has been child welfare. For parents and children caught in this web, the result can mean surveillance and separation for very long periods of time. The official knowledge created through institutionally sanctioned documents such as risk assessment instruments is the salient knowledge that governs social relations and forms of discipline and control, while knowledge developed locally and through lived experience is devalued and made to disappear. A new risk assessment tool may cancel out risk items and scores that formed the basis of clients' involvement with child welfare services, but it will not cancel out the effects of surveillance, controls, and separations. Risk can and has become part of a punitive apparatus that not only lays blame and establishes responsibilities but punishes. Risk has the potential to be part of the 'law and order' agenda, with concrete practices and an ever-expanding net. Examples from other arenas of professional practice are easy to find. Probation and parole services offer a long-standing illustration. For prisoners, risk assessment practices, as Loury (2007) points out, can mean support disappears as prisoners come to be seen not as persons but as risks. And according to Loury, we know what to do with risks – 'we keep them locked up.'

Risk, Modernity, and Postmodernism

Our study has demonstrated that modernity is alive and well and living in human services practice, sustained in part by risk and its technologies. We have presented a substantial amount of evidence demonstrating the standardizing and homogenizing processes that characterize modernity, supported by unquestioned positivist science and attention to the 'rational individual' who learns and abides by universal truth. The 'new managerialism' aids in this project through its standardized practices of efficiency and accountability. As Amin (1989) has noted, capitalism, and especially global capital, requires and is facilitated by a universal science that discovers and distributes truths about human nature and about the organization of the social world. In this context, individuals are to be treated equally through standardized practices based on objective science. Social class, race, gender, and other divisions are glossed over in this 'equality' project.

The postmodern challenge to universal truth and authority remains largely unrealized in these circumstances. Widespread acknowledgment of the existence of many kinds of realities, the fracturing of the social contract that supports the welfare state, and social legitimization of 'identity' as a genuine issue and concern have been to some extent conscripted by the neoliberal project. In this scenario, identity is bonded with risk – the risk of being an immigrant, of being young, of being a person of colour, of not speaking English, of being mentally ill. This fracturing of the social whole, also illustrated by the move from social to individual risk, has resulted in substantially weakened social movements, now recast as 'special interests.' Social equality is redefined in terms of standardized templates, with members of identity groups reduced to seeking exemptions from these standardizing procedures. Their experiences and knowledges are almost completely subsumed by standardizing processes such as those of risk assessment.

The traditional welfare state, of course, was often accused of universalizing tendencies, and the neoliberal approach to the welfare state has not reduced this propensity. Technologies of governing, including those of risk, instead, continue and even intensify this direction. In addition, risk technologies help to move attention from well-being to safety and security. In so doing, blame and liability can be downloaded from elected officials and upper management to front-line workers and service users, who are increasingly expected to become risk managers.

Both Beck and Giddens suggest that in this era individuals will necessarily become 'reflexive' citizens. One of the more serious questions raised by risk and its assessment is the question of whether we actually will become more reflexive and active in our engagement with society or whether we will become automatons (Robertson, 1999), following the managerial rules and procedures required in organizations in order to manage the fears amplified by 'risk' and its technologies. Another concern raised by Lash is that there will be 'reflexivity losers' who do not have the time and resources to do this reflecting and acting. 'Just how "reflexive" is it possible for a single mother in an urban ghetto to be?' he asks (1994: 120).

In summary, the universalizing directions of modernity continue and are intensified in many respects in the neoliberal era of the welfare state. This tendency, according to some theorists, will be countered by the newly reflexive engagement of individuals, a premise questioned by others and challenged by our own study. First, most people, including professionals and certainly service users, are not positioned in relation to relevant settings in ways that allow an overall view of their own circumstances. They are, in Gramsci's terms, subaltern social groups. These are groups working on the basis of a '"common sense" that is a fragmentary result of the sedimentation and ideas' of other groups, generally elites, with different experiences and social positioning in society (Ives, 2004: 78). Second, as Lash (1994) points out, available resources will surely play a central role in anyone's ability to engage in reflexive activity. Power relations play out in this field of homogenizing pressures, limited perspectives, and uneven resources for reflexivity. In the next section we explore these power relations through the prism of risk.

Power Relations of Risk

Ruling relations, mentioned at earlier points in this book, connect and coordinate people's activities across space and time (Smith, 1990). Power relations are viewed as actual activities of people coordinated to 'give the multiplied effects of cooperation' (Smith, 1990: 70). Ruling relations are not necessarily oppressive in Smith's terms, although they may be. The complementary notion of power relations clearly does express positions of dominance and subordination. By viewing activities carried out in specific sites as mirroring these generalized and generalizing relations of ruling and power, it is possible to develop a deeper understanding of how our society is organized and, particularly, how ruling is accomplished and reproduced. Following Smith's methodology, texts that coordinate everyday work and activity are especially important in developing such an analysis. Texts define, order work processes, propose values, instruct our thinking, and frame our activities, and texts are therefore key to appreciating how we ourselves come to be implicated in reproducing these relations.

In our study, it is clearly shown that texts are significant as organizers of professional work. We acknowledge that these guiding texts of risk have created a terrain that is increasingly difficult for both professionals and service users to challenge effectively, and we further acknowledge that risk texts and discourses are only one of a number of mechanisms that create this effect in the contemporary world of work. We argue, therefore, for the importance of careful analysis of social and power relations by human service workers as a step that can produce more effective identification of and challenges to oppressive relations of ruling. We focus next on specific work practices, made visible through our research, as a means of illustrating how the power relations of risk link everyday activities to the complex social relations of the society we live in. Left unexamined, we argue, these practices create and recreate positions of dominance and subordination through 'multiplied effects of cooperation,' and constitute barriers to effective social action.

Objectifying Risk

There are competing discourses at work in defining the meaning and relations of risk. Risk is an abstract concept widely debated by academics. Risk is an actuarial concept, with mathematical rules guiding its determination. And risk is a professional concept used to organize work and legitimize interventions into people's lives. However, there are significant disjunctures between the academic literature about risk and actuarial techniques for calculating risk and between theory and the professional discourses of risk assessment. Ultimately, it is the technological, objective strand in discourse that dominates the literature of human service professionals who administer risk. Professional literature reflects an understanding of risk as a real, objective 'thing,' an object that can be identified, measured, and managed. In taking up and acting on this aspect of discourse, professionals help to entrench the idea of risk as an objective reality, at the expense of other kinds of meanings.

Participants in our study virtually all treated risk as unquestioned, objective reality. Clients in our study came to see themselves as the embodiment of risk. They regarded the results of their assessments as potentially true, even as they marshalled evidence to demonstrate that the assessor was mistaken. Because the consequences of the assessments were so serious for them, they generally began to cooperate even when they considered the assessment to be flawed. They accepted, often with bitterness, their assignment into a risk class and began to march to the music played for them.

When translated into risk assessment, the risks contained in documents and the risk scores become fixed, thus reinforcing the 'reality' of risk, establishing a truth that becomes difficult to dispute. The reality established in documents of risk stands in contradiction to the fluid nature of life experience. Risk as it appears in organizational documents can only be 'updated' periodically, while the life conditions of the service user continually shift and change. Although at one level professionals may try to address changing realities, they must simultaneously attune their own activities to the documentary reality appearing in forms in order to satisfy organizational objectives. Professionals have completed these documents by squeezing fragments of life experience into pre-established and standardized categories. In the process, most life history, everyday experience, and the service user's own version of events are excluded (Krane and Davies, 1999). The information captured by risk assessment categories and scores becomes the reality of the service user's life for as long as she remains involved with representatives of the organization.

Practices involved in treating risk as an actuality that can be seen and measured cover over the intensifying power imbalances that give professionals, as speakers for the institution, substantial voice while service users are silenced. Thus, a new category of society is created, one that is threatened, demoralized, fearful, and ultimately, compliant. There is no actual evidence in our empirical study that any of these procedures actually increased the promised safety of the children involved, raising again the question of the actual purpose of the exercise.

Accepting Official Knowledge

Closely related to practices that objectify risk are practices of thought and speech that reflect practitioners' acceptance of official versions of science and knowledge as the legitimate versions to incorporate into their work, often against their own better judgment.

The marketing of risk tools as scientific has important effects. Workers in our study generally believed that the tools they were using were scientific, even though they often did not see the results of their assessments as particularly accurate. Nevertheless, the risk assessment scores that they produced were taken as the information needed for future work – belief in science generally trumped workers' own experience. Consequently, information known but excluded from the categories called for by assessment tools became less legitimate information on which to base workers' professional activities. The selection of risks to be addressed is, as Douglas (1992) says, a matter of social organization. However, Douglas's trenchant commentary on the social selection of risks is not accounted for in practice since risk assessment tools are generally portrayed as representing the universe of knowledge about risks in a particular arena. In reality, of course, only a narrow band of information, issues, and activities become officially recognized risk assessment items, but questions about the socially organized processes of selecting these items have not been taken up to any great extent in the literature of risk in the human services. Thus, the official risk factors appear to be synonymous with 'risk' – they can be taken as the truth of risk and as all we need to worry about.

Notwithstanding faith in science, there can be considerable slippage in practice in the use of ideas that claim calculations as the basis of their credibility. On the ground, it was apparent in our study that risk was generally equated more with danger than with any mathematical calculation of probabilities. Danger, as Kemshall et al. (1997) point out, does not have the 'aura' of science that risk has; we have not heard anyone speak of 'danger assessments' in the course of our work. This displacement of words is significant. Workers doing risk assessments are not so much considering the 'chances' that something might happen, in spite of the scientific wrapping of the tools, but rather searching for dangers lurking in the corners of the case. People with high risk assessment scores, therefore, may easily come to be seen as dangerous people, bringing their social standing into serious disrepute.

Seldom officially noticed in the work of assessing risk is the disappearance of the knowledge of services users, a stance that can easily be justified if the clients are treated as dangerous. Posed against tools produced by the scientific community, clients' ways of knowing and talking about their own lives and experiences appear to be mere subjectivity, presented in defence of their risky lifestyles. Risk assessment technology certainly can provide considerable power to the professional, particularly in work with reluctant clients, since the tools in use appear to reveal 'truths' that the client is hard put to dispute. We do not mean to suggest that the 'science' of the risk assessment process automatically blinkers front-line workers and professionals. They are not automatons, as some have suggested, but active, reflective professionals who are attempting to piece together a plan of work, based on organizationally required documents and procedures. Professionals no doubt take many opportunities to understand the people they are trying to help, but the official knowledge desired by the mandating organization for its purposes almost invariably takes precedence.

Professionals have a history of seeking scientific tools in order to improve practice. In fact, most professions are defined to some extent by the unique scientific knowledge on which they base their practice. In this regard, technologies of risk, especially if cast as scientifically based, can elevate a profession and imbue the individual professional with considerable credibility. At one level, 'scientific risk assessment' lends new authority to the expertise of professionals. This, as our case example shows, works well for lower-ranking professionals, often women, who must deal with physicians and judges who are at the top of the professional hierarchy. In this process, the positivist science spawned by modernity is reinforced and given new life, while critical science with its focus on exploring how surface appearances are produced loses credibility or disappears altogether. At the same time, though, this kind of science constrains these same professionals, because of the knowledge base from which they must work.

Positivist science is grounded in the beliefs of modernity, promising continuing progress and ever-improving prospects for human life. It is a testament to the continuing strength of modernity that we may not think to question this premise. Positivist science asks us to be the subjects and perpetrators of experimentation on the route to that better life. It often does not question the damage done along the way, and very often the poorest and most marginalized people, as we have seen, are the test subjects for new science. Increasingly strict ethics reviews of research studies appear to promise protection for research subjects from unknown harms resulting from experimentation. If we were proposing a research project testing out the risk assessment instruments used in British Columbia and Ontario child welfare, our proposal would, in fact, have been governed by stringent scrutiny and guidelines in the best interests of our participants; our actual study was indeed so governed. However, once the experiment is freed from the bonds of the scientific community, no such guidelines or scrutiny apply. When risk assessment instruments such as those used in British Columbia and Ontario were officially adopted by provincial governments and their agents as the tools to use, through processes known only to those most closely involved, no protections for potential subjects were included or even discussed, as far as we know.

We noted during the course of our study that the risk factors identified in organizational documents have changed. Some have been deemphasized, some have disappeared altogether, and some new factors have appeared. Each new version of the relevant risk factors is couched in scientific language and sold as a better version than the last. The effects for those people previously scoring high on now defunct risk documents and factors, however, remain unchanged. Children were placed in alternate care, parents were closely watched, mothers were required to engage in various kinds of 'helping' exercises. While improved 'science' may appear to justify a new risk assessment tool, we might consider asking these families how they felt about being the guinea pigs for experimentation of poorly designed tools and the practices that accompanied those tools. Should we perhaps apologize to them for the intrusions into their lives that were based on ideas that we have now decided were faulty? Clearly, the power exerted by the use of these risk assessments continues on long after the tools are gone.

Coordinating Work Practices

The very existence of clients, in this case 'risky' or dangerous people, provides the rationale for the employment of a great many people. Figure 8.1 shows how one risky mother and her child act as the focal point for and legitimation of the activities of many professionals in different fields of practice.

The idea of risk, as we have shown, has the capacity to coordinate a variety of professionals operating in different arenas. Risk texts and

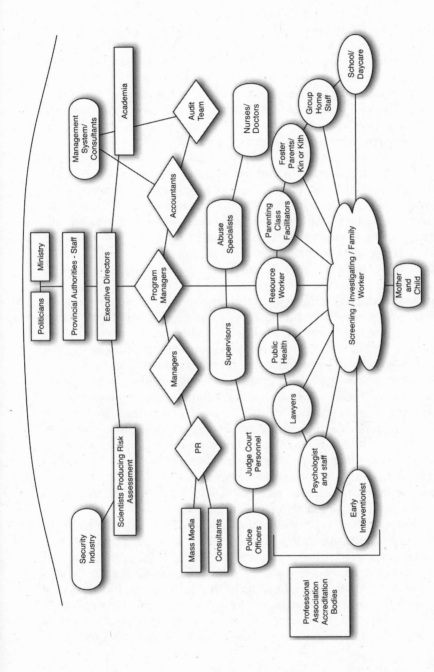

Figure 8.1: Job Creation in Child Welfare

discourses provide not only jobs but also an organizing principle for the work of many people. Management, professionals, politicians, scientists, contractors, and users of services all have a stake in the risk assessment process and its sequelae. One set of professionals is coordinated by risk in the investigation phase, and other actors are brought in for risk reduction. Still others attend to accounting procedures, interpretations of law, the development of risk tools, and so on. All 'relevant' people are then coordinating their activities, thoughts, and appearances to the goals of assessing and reducing risk.

Improving the coordination of professionals and services in order to avoid gaps and overlaps in services is generally viewed as an important professional goal, and risk technologies appear to assist in this process. They also work to smooth the management of complex courses of action. In the process, however, risk technologies can also serve to homogenize professional practice. To whatever extent risk acts as a fulcrum for coordination, numerous workers must adopt similar definitions and categories as points of reference. Risk assessments form basic professional understandings of the individual service user, and approved risk reduction strategies become a common pursuit, one that fuels growth in the human services sector. The unique knowledge and skills of the different professionals and contract service providers involved begin to dissolve in this process. In fact, it could be that risk and its standardizing practices are dissolving differences among professions. Ironically, while professionals consolidate some power through the coordination and consolidation of thought and practice, they simultaneously lose another form of power through homogenized definitions and prescriptions. In a rigid risk regime, professionals have reduced power to name problems, explore options, raise questions, create plans, and make relationships with clients. The use of standardized risk templates is not only a mechanism that coordinates but one that controls, functioning efficiently to narrow the theatres of professional decision making and judgment.

Risk is but one type of standardized practice that has entered the delivery of human services in recent years. Risk assessment, and no doubt other standardizing mechanisms, employs the use of computer technology that may provide the appearance of choice. In Keiler's view we live with a 'sleight of hand that bedevils us: the illusion of power and choice perpetuated to disguise a diminishing sphere of action' (2006: 11). To illustrate, Keiler uses the example of pointing a cursor: 'What precision, what access, what an array of options!'

Professionals often distance themselves from these standardizing and alienating work processes in an effort to maintain an image of themselves as having integrity as helpers. Workers in our study frequently described themselves as 'different' from other workers. Those 'others' were seen as rule followers, rigid, and often insensitive. Interviewees described themselves as more caring, as working more holistically, as able to limit the inhumanity that they perceived to be present in the organizational setting. We as researchers, reflecting back on ourselves as practitioners, realized that we, too, had engaged in this mental practice of feeling superior to others. Such beliefs help us to hide from ourselves the less seemly parts of our day and perhaps to forgive ourselves for our often dimly perceived part in the relations of ruling. We may also try create a sense that our helping practices are more effective than those of our colleagues. Of course, we distance ourselves from each other in this process. All the same, documents activated by professionals continue to legitimize and reproduce the system in place.

Individualizing Responsibility

As some commentators say, the 'right' has done a better job of employing and deploying risk than has the political left. The apparatus of individualizing risk has entered and facilitated the shaping of many 'helping' institutions. Risk assessments carried out by human service professionals virtually always focus on the person and not on the social context, thus reinforcing the individualizing of risk and the notion that risk resides in the person rather than in the social context. All helping professionals now practise in the context of a diminishing social welfare state in both its concrete and rhetorical forms. In their practice of risk, professionals unwittingly assist in this process of demise, and they elevate the project of encouraging 'people themselves [to] become small, private alternative experts' on risk (Beck, 1992).

Among the primary functions of risk assessment are the assignment of blame and the assessment of liability. As one child welfare worker said:

It's all about liability, who's to blame.

The assumed neutrality of risk assessment instruments glosses over the reality that blame is being assigned, generally to the individual client. As currently practised in many human services, risk assessment, in fact, helps to shift blame from decision makers to lower-level actors, especially to front-line professionals and to users of services. In the process neoliberal ideology is reinforced and legitimated, through identifying, blaming, and 'responsibilizing' particular individuals for their troubles. 'The social' is diminished. At the same time, the liability of decision makers for their policies is considerably reduced, since responsibility for assessing and reducing risk has been downloaded to the front line. Professionals themselves, recognizing the potential for their own liability, may attempt to shift responsibility further down the hierarchy by inflating risk assessment scores. The result of these methods is the intensification of processes that blame the victim, while dominant groups swim free, or at least can breathe more easily.

The individualized character and uncertain results of risk reduction exercises have received little attention in child welfare or in other fields of human service delivery to vulnerable populations. The common 'educational' approach, represented by the numerous versions of parenting classes, anger management, addictions programs, and so on, is supported by virtually no evidence of effectiveness. In fact, the plethora of individualized programs and prescriptions that are offered help to hide the socially structured nature of the many problems that clients face. Following the thinking of modernity, classes and programs call on a belief in rational approaches to problem solving: if we can just learn the *right things*, life will be better and safer. Sinking to the background are notions of bringing people together to advocate and organize for change. The educational approach individualizes problems and the required solutions to them, charges clients with the responsibility to help themselves through solutions that continually monitor their efforts and extend social control over them, while at the same time covering over the systemic issues that provide the context for the situations in which they find themselves in the first place. Meanwhile, professionals are losing touch with activism, political movements, and the ability to advocate on behalf of oppressed people (Harlow, 2004).

Many of our plans for service users are no doubt helpful, well-intentioned efforts, and they are often appreciated by the recipients themselves. But that should not prevent us from examining their effects. Among these is the dispersal of populations of poor and vulnerable people among time-limited programs and services that generally do not provide long-term associations, friendships, or supports, and that certainly provide no opportunity to organize themselves, find common purposes, identify solutions, or examine the roots of their problems. Recipients may inadvertently add to this effect by trying to differentiate themselves from others – 'I'm not like them' – for fear of guilt by association. This divisive effect prevents any organized support for people to challenge either the causes of or the required 'solutions' to their problems. This critique is not an argument for ghettoizing poor people, but rather it is intended to point out that apparently helpful solutions to social problems have other effects. Among these are barriers to serious community organizing and development by service users themselves. It's almost as though we fear they will discover the commonality of their experiences and problems and begin to demand change. However, at least one study of parents involved with child welfare services shows that 'mutual aid' approaches led to benefits for parents that the usual services did not, including increased levels of perceived social support, self-esteem, reduced stress, and improved attitudes towards parenting (Cameron and Birnie-Lefcovitch, 2000).

Risk practice is driven by fear and blame. As Tony Benn, Britain's former prime minister, remarks in Michael Moore's film *Sicko*, democratic practices and participation decline in an atmosphere of fear and demoralization. It is much more difficult to govern people who are confident, who challenge, and who are unafraid of the consequences of questioning authority.

Complying with Managerial Processes

Given that risk assessment has been subjected to substantial criticism, and given that the underlying idea of predicting human behaviour is deeply suspect, why do organizations continue to insist on the use of risk assessment instruments? Protection from liability, production of a more orderly work process, and increased accountability of employees to the institution form some compelling arguments for those who favour risk regimes. Risk and its technologies can act as a kind of Trojan horse, somewhat surreptitiously bringing neoliberal forms of managerialism into local sites. Under cover of risk, controls within organizations can be substantially tightened, without much fear of opposition. This is especially but not only the case where risk assessments are involuntary and where assessments are closely tied to budgets and cost-containment objectives. There has, of course, been some resistance to intensified workloads produced through risk management systems, as we saw in our case illustration. However, there has been little resistance and, in fact, surprisingly swift acceptance of much managerial practice based on the belief that order has been brought to chaos through these procedures. The 'doing' of risk appears to fit seamlessly with the goals of efficiency and accountability and to justify disciplinary practices. Since the goals of accountability and efficiency have already been introduced in most workplaces, professionals are accustomed to some of their demands, such as targeting resources, saving money, insistence on 'efficient' work practices, and the production of measurable outcomes. Frequently, these preoccupations have already taken precedence over professional ideals, codes of ethics, and goals in the workplace via management-imposed rules and regulations. In our case study, we see how management and professional ideas are merged within a single dictat:

> Picking a number ... that's in a sense your clinical judgment. (Social Worker)

This is an important development for human service professionals, because in these circumstances, 'the room for professional maneuver and creativity is severely limited' (Parton et al., 1997).

It is important to notice that it is not only risk and risk assessment that produce these increasingly controlled approaches to human services delivery that shift power from professionals to managers. Morgen (2001), for instance, examines the introduction of 'self-sufficiency' regimes in American welfare departments. She associates this innovation with neoliberal political forms and ideals of practice with welfare recipients. A process similar to the introduction of risk assessment was followed. First, a federal law dealing with welfare reform was passed, called the Family Support Act of 1998. This law and its accompanying apparatus espoused a new mission, that of self-sufficiency for clients of the welfare system. Instructions to workers were to wean clients from their dependency on public moneys and get them into the workforce. Clients were to be made 'accountable' to the system, and results were tied to budget targets. Workers were expected to monitor clients for compliance. Morgen shows how workers soon internalized the philosophy of the system, and some workers even felt 'empowered' by this new regime (2001: 755). The author, however, concludes that workers in effect became accomplices to neoliberal advocates of this belt-tightening approach to welfare. She also notes that even those who disliked and resisted the system could find no way to 'translate their own discontent' into a broader critique of the policy and its effects on clients.

It is well known that professional practice in many sites of helping is increasingly driven by numbers and calculations, which are determined and decided outside the site of actual practice and experience. Some of this has a basis in science and its research procedures. Numbers, determined through cost calculations drives some practices, perhaps the greatest share. In Ontario nursing homes, for instance, workers have to 'police the briefs.' Each resident adult requiring diapers is allowed $1.20 per day for this purpose. The diapers have a stripe that changes colour when it is 75 per cent wet, and it cannot be changed until it reaches that point. Even if the resident has just been bathed, a diaper with less than 75 per cent of moisture must be put back on the person (Welsh, 2007: A1 and A17).

Human service professionals have not accepted at all willingly the cost limits and accountability measures imposed on them in organizations. Many have waged fights against this 'money over people' mentality. They face a regular if not always clearly acknowledged struggle between professional values and skills versus the goals of corporate culture. They try, as our child welfare workers did, to slip between the cracks of managerial practices to form helping relationships with those they serve. Workers who do this successfully win the respect of service users. But in the process they do not always win the respect of their employers. We were told stories of workers being fired because they spent too much time with families and insufficient time on the computer files.

There is no question that a process of 'reskilling' helping professionals, especially those employed by the state, is in progress. This reskilling is in the direction of management practices; the more forms, and reliance on forms, the harder it is to squeeze in professional objectives and practices.

In addition to some reskilling, professionals are being conscripted into the process of extending managerial practices not only to their office procedures but directly into the lives and homes of the users of services, especially through gatekeeping and resource management procedures. In the American system of health management organizations (HMOs), which are insurance organizations that govern the resources for health care, physicians are sometimes employed and paid substantial benefits to identify 'reasonable' grounds for denying insurance claims. They may even be given targets for the numbers of claims they need to deny in order to remain in good standing with the employer (Moore, 2007). These practices operate entirely for purposes of increasing profits. Professionals employed or paid by government operate within an apparent logic of cost containment rather than profit. They would be unlikely to get bonuses for reducing costs, but their standing as professionals does rely on 'moving the case along' (Worker), on demonstrating their efficiency, and on a record of solid accountability to the organization employing them. Both private and public employers are supposed to be providing help to people who need it, but the logic in both cases is based on the managerial objectives of saving the employer money and on justifying money spent.

Summary: Risk as Ideology

Attention to risk and risk assessment is generally presented to the public and to the professionals who will administer it with a promise of prediction and prevention. The surface reality is that of a well-oiled machine, with guiding documents in place, individuals accountable for their own life projects and mistakes, professionals accountable for their decisions, and necessary help being provided. However, this presentation is ideological; that is, it hides and distorts an underlying reality, which is that risk practices as they are generally presented do not represent any such pure agenda. Rather, risk extends particular kinds of power relations into the workplace, largely unseen but nevertheless powerful.

These power relations are not wholly visible to actors on the scene, but are held in place by ideologically presented notions of improved safety. As seen in our case study, they present a microcosm of power relations at a more general level. We see the same kinds of relations of reliance on truths presented by authorities in the name of prevention at national levels, for instance, by the American government and its Department of Homeland Security. We see homogenizing practices extended into all aspects of the welfare state and its contracted programs. We see 'science' in the form of student testing as a gatekeeping and resource rationing method. We are exhorted to solve the problems of global capital by shopping rather than by questioning whether there are other ways to organize ourselves.

We have argued that fear helps to fuel these shifting and solidifying power relations. The vast and growing security industry justifies ceding power to those whose claims of knowledge are supported by science. Insecurity in this neoliberal era has come to mean personal fear. Our fears of bad people and 'evildoers' help to keep us from raising questions about the everyday work practices that we engage in. However, it might be to our own benefit to raise questions about the reality of these fears. We might ask who it is that is reminding us of all these supposed threats, and what might their motives be? Who is being blamed for what we fear? What can be justified in the name of risk? While we ponder these questions, we might also consider whether and how the ideology of risk reinforces the basic tenets of neoliberal policies and whether we want to assist in the success of that project. If we do not, read on.

Risk and Social Justice

The picture of risk assessment that we have painted in this book is rather bleak. It is a case study of extreme risk measures, in an era of shrinking social resources, applied to people who are considered to be among the least worthy of our citizens – 'bad mothers.' We recognize that it is problematic for professionals in such circumstances to work for change, and of course, not every instance of assessment for risk will present this level of difficulty. However, we see that many forms of risk and risk assessment can bring surveillance, intrusion, and control of particular individuals under the guise of prevention – 'so it never happens again.' Individual risk can obscure the value of social justice and, in fact, 'the social' itself.

What do we mean by social justice? The concept of social justice is poorly defined in the literature. Most definitions are abstract, referring generally to the just treatment of individuals in a society and the fair distribution of the benefits of society. Many articles, even books written on the subject, fail to provide a working definition of social justice. In general, following Leonard (1997: 163), we consider social justice to be an 'emancipatory idea' that allows us to move from acceptance to resistance and then to social change. Among Leonard's suggestions (1997: 164) are strategies to depathologize service users, strengthen discourses of 'interdependence,' struggle against the homogenization of people, and enhance our own reflexive capacities. The creation of alternate discourses that enter the public domain suffi- ciently to influence opinion and policy is critical. He suggests practices such as co-authored narratives (Krane and Davies, 1999) and the development of new forms of collectivity and collective resistance. For professionals this would mean challenging our own power to apply disciplinary measures to service users.

More specifically, we can try to define social justice in relation to our own experience and research. The abrogation of rights for some populations, rights that are assumed and accorded to others, often by law, constitutes social *in*justice. Chen (2003) points out the importance of creating space for challenging the rationalizations that are used to defend unequal treatment for particular groups. For example, former U.S. Secretary of Defense Rumsfeld famously defended torture and other unlawful tactics at internment camps on the basis that the torturers were dealing with 'terrorists.' Those people are different, he said, and so 'different rules apply.' We are among the many who beg to disagree that the rules ought to be changed or suspended for designated groups of 'different' people. Social justice, for us, means that the same basic rules protecting legal, social, and civil rights *do* apply to all, including access to information about what is being done, why it is being done, and rights of appeal for decisions considered to be unjust.

We recognize the 'modernist' flavour of this recommendation. Leonard (1997) has persuasively argued that there are features of the modernist project that should be retained and re-emphasized if a new kind of welfare is to be achieved. He references the work of Doyal and Gough, who argue for the recognition of universal human needs. Health and autonomy, they submit, are preconditions for any human action. People can be seriously harmed by alterable social circumstances that compromise health and autonomy. Social justice, they argue, 'exists in inverse proportion to serious harm and suffering' (1991: 2). Leonard's proposal recognizes that the postmodern emphasis on difference must also be accounted for. Social justice, we agree, also involves accounting for the social locations and special needs of particular groups and individuals.

We do not argue that individuals should be free of all responsibility for their problems. However, individual risk assessment can have the effect of assigning blame and responsibility for problems that individuals did not create and simply cannot address on their own. A social justice approach redeems 'the social,' ensuring an examination of and attempts to redress imbalances between individual and social capacities and responsibilities for problems.

Social justice also requires that all relevant groups, including service users, have an authentic role in the development of service strategies. Service users are the least powerful and most blamed of the 'stakeholders' in the arena of human services. People who use social services are the main repository of the 'bads' that are unequally distributed to social members, and they are almost always overlooked in planning efforts. The experience and knowledge of those whom we claim to be serving deserve our time and attention and our creativity to assist in the construction of pathways to genuine participation and social change.

Lewis et al. pointed out some years ago the inevitability that as time goes on 'only need defined as high risk will receive service' (1995: 91). In other words, sanctioned definitions of risk rather than need will act as the trigger for the flow of resources and the priorizing of work activities (Kemshall et al., 1997). A social justice approach, in contrast, assumes need as the basis for resource eligibility. In many risk assessment processes, the economic circumstances of the assessed individual are not part of the calculation of risk, even though economic issues are primary concerns for many of the people who use social services. Our examination of risk assessment places the technologies of individual risk in the social and economic contexts of global economic dynamics and change. A social justice approach requires this contextualizing of risk.

A just approach does not ignore the individual in favour of the social but rather involves practices of individualizing without homogenizing. Waerness (1996) argues that good work involves responding to clients as distinct persons. We remind ourselves of our Aboriginal respondents, who at best could provide an appearance of compliance with the prescribed risk regime because their circumstances were never envisioned by the undoubtedly white and probably male creators of the risk assessment instruments in use. The homogenization of whole populations is one of the more odious characteristics of modernist science, and it stands in direct contradiction to the ethics of most helping professions. Our study shows in detail how homogenizing processes of science not only exclude other knowledge and meanings but directly damage the lives of people. Social justice in this era recognizes that which is unique about individuals and groups.

Social justice is necessarily reflexive. Risk technology can produce a conceptual apparatus with the capacity to justify considerable intrusion into lives and prospects and to justify the withholding of actual help. The ongoing critique of what we are asked to do and what we *actually* do is absolutely necessary to just practice in a socially fluid context. In the course of our study, we met many workers who were actively engaged in 'praxis,' meaning the ongoing process of acting, reflecting, and acting on the basis of reflection. They are engaged in the ongoing debates, meanings, agendas, power relations, and implications of assessing for risk and social justice agendas. They raise questions about taken-for-granted truths, they are in a continual process of learning about their clients' lives, they challenge orthodoxy when necessary, they create new paths to follow in the service of clients' needs, and they see themselves as part of a profession and institution rather than as an exception. These workers are active agents who are realistic and who remain optimistic in tightly managed and often oppressive systems. They operate successfully on two parallel and often contradictory tracks, that of case manager and that of professional practitioner. They are key actors in the front line in any emancipation project.

Where Do Human Service Professionals Go from Here?

How is it that an idea, even one that many find counterintuitive, an idea that is costly and basically unmanageable, can be imposed on us, essentially unchallenged, be welcomed even, as a saving technology? The case of risk assessment in child welfare provides an exemplar. Even those who were its champions sooner or later came to question its usefulness and eventually whether it was even doable. Some of us also examined, as in this book, the hidden objectives, cruelty, and questionable ethics of risk assessment. We note that the New York risk assessment model adopted by many Canadian provinces, including Ontario and British Columbia, had long since been rejected and replaced in New York itself by the time of our study. Most Canadian provinces have either instituted substantial modifications or have replaced the original system and much of its apparatus with something at least slightly less intrusive and more flexible. But what has been learned? Without critical science, and its focus on understanding what is going on beneath the surface, we may learn little from this exercise. The skills of deconstructing and exploring received wisdom, and the confidence to challenge organizations and employers that ask us to engage in unethical or unprofessional behaviour, will be needed to subvert similar errors.

The first question to be asked is whether we really need risk assessment in the helping professions. There may be legitimate uses for these individualized instruments, but the arguments need to be made, and the science defended. In the child welfare field, there is sufficient concern about the viability of these instruments (e.g., Rycus and Hughes, 2003; Baumann et al., 2005) to raise serious questions about their continued use. Rather than viewing risk as 'real' and 'scientific,' a perspective on risk as a social construction allows some critical questions, such as the following:

- What are the assumptions and multiple purposes embedded in risk technologies?
- Whose risk becomes the focus?
- What will happen to those people labelled risky, and who will have to act on the labelling?
- Do reasonable plans for risk reduction follow from an assessment?
- How is the work of assessing risk accomplished?
- What does the assessment of 'risk' actually accomplish?

A professional and informed space for questioning, challenging, sharing, and deciding about the usefulness of tools is necessary to this endeavour. Space for people to identify what they consider to be their own relevant risks would need to be created. Some serious ethical issues ought to be raised especially about the justification for conducting any risk assessment. If there is no intention and plan to use the information to improve the situation for vulnerable people, the use of the technology is surely questionable.

This discussion has to acknowledge that not all dangers can be avoided. We cannot avoid uncertainty, and bad things will happen, no matter how much prediction we try to do (Parton, 1998); we're in denial if we think otherwise. The alternative is a kind of enforced cocooning, encouraging a psychology of fear and insecurity. At this point, we might even do well to encourage some kinds of risk taking. As one worker in our study noted, adolescents love risk, and we are generally powerless to stop them. Ungar's book *Too Safe for Their Own Good* (2007) argues that parents are 'bubble-wrapping' their children out of fear of every kind of injury and danger. Ungar suggests that if children aren't allowed to push some limits and experience some consequences they will not learn how to make good decisions. The author calls up research support for the idea that children who are allowed some freedom to experiment are actually injured less frequently than those whose limits of behaviour and risk are very closely monitored.

If we do want to integrate the idea of risk into professional practice, how can 'the social' be incorporated? If we are going to use risk assessment, why not look at the social conditions that create potential danger and 'risk' for particular groups, communities, or problems. It is, after all, illogical and ethically dubious to make individuals culpable for socially created problems.

Risk assessment instruments could identify specific socially and politically constructed risks facing vulnerable populations. Tools could score the accessibility of affordable housing, calculate the risks following from inadequate income, examine the risks of inadequate child care, and list the actual helping resources available for particular problems. Much if not all of this information is already available in the social policy literature and could be adapted to a scenario of calculating risk for specific groups or individuals. The risk reduction efforts logically following from this notion of risk would be community based and more democratic. Such efforts would return us to the idea of shared social responses to socially created risks like unemployment and the inevitable 'risks' of living such as accidents and illness. This is not utopian thinking. Experience in the use of Risk Assessment Monitoring System (PRAMS), outlined in Chapter 4, demonstrates the feasibility of developing social risk assessment and acting to reduce 'risk' at group and social levels.

This discussion is not meant to suggest that simply privileging professional autonomy over managerial practice is the answer to the problems of providing effective service. Indeed, those in the helping professions have played substantial roles in the work of controlling and 'normalizing' populations. However, there are some persuasive arguments for ensuring that helping professionals are active players in the plans and programs that they administer. Professionals are the people on the ground, dealing with the everyday problems of people and communities. To subjugate their discipline-based and experiential knowledge to sets of computations and factors determined well outside the local situation is surely counterproductive. In the child welfare arena, as Parada reports, people with ten or fifteen years of experience were being told that they were doing the work in the 'wrong' way and would have to be supervised and taught to do work differently (2004: 75). Yet in the face of criticisms of the new way, and in fact its replacement by yet another new way, we might want to raise questions about who really did/does know what was/is best. Teachers, nurses, and other professionals, especially at the lower end of the professional hierarchy, and of course, not only in Canada, are similarly excluded from providing their knowledge. As one very experienced British teacher said, 'in all my years of teaching no one has ever asked me what I thought was the best way to teach' (Forrester, 2000: 140).

Professionals, unlike management and markets, operate at least in theory under codes of ethics and conduct and have some professional accountability outside the organization that employs them. They have mission statements that generally include ideals of caring and doing 'no harm,' as the medical profession states. We could view the sentiment expressed by our study participants of being different from those 'other' workers as a significant point of departure. This feeling of wanting to do a different kind of work than what is asked of them flags a deep knowledge that something is wrong with what workers have been asked to do. A need to feel different, along with the knowledge that there are other ways of working, provides a beginning impetus for change. Rather than allowing this sentiment to divide them from others, professionals might investigate the nature of this feeling and find others who share these thoughts. Conscious reflection on how it is that they want to be different helps to establish new goals for working life. Efforts to develop 'subject to subject' relationships rather than expert-to-client connections alters feelings about the work for both people (Strega and Carriere, 2009).

Feminists have been particularly vocal and articulate in demonstrating what professions could do to improve human life experience. Parton (2003) cites feminist discourse on the ethics of care, especially emphasizing the importance of care work and emotional connectedness in helping relationships. We live in societies that value rational thinking, neutrality, and objectivity. In this context, the moral road involves identifying and respecting the 'right' rules. Feminism, on the other hand, involves a 'relational self,' for whom morality involves 'patterns of behaviour, perceptions and interpretations' (2003: 10). The 'ethics of care' involve openness to the other person and placing communication and responsiveness in the forefront of practice considerations. Tronto (1993) shows how care is not only a moral concept but has the potential to be both political and democratic.

Professionals also have an ethical obligation to challenge ideas imposed on them in the workplace. We recognize and have heard from many workers and students that such challenges can be intimidating and sometimes dangerous to themselves and even their clients. The spaces available for manoeuvre shrink with textually coordinated practices and managerialism, while blame for mistakes accumulates at the front line. Understanding this, we give no encouragement to precipitous and 'risky' activities. But regularly pushing the envelope in the direction of social justice is surely not beyond us. We do ask professionals to recognize that 'you are not different.' Owing to the coordination and homogenization of work practices, experiences of professionals in the same or similar settings are going to be remarkably similar to those of other workers. The formation of alliances within the profession and among other professions can lead to more socially just outcomes.

And Finally ...

On a northern reserve, we interviewed an experienced Aboriginal social worker about his attempts to apply the provincial risk assessment model to families on the reserve. He told us that Aboriginal peoples believe that different groups of people bring different gifts to the world. Aboriginal peoples, he said, are stewards of the land and nature, preserving resources for future generations. The gift white people bring is invention; they are always coming up with something new:

> And sometimes, when we see white folks coming, we think, 'What have they thought of now?' (Aboriginal Social Worker)

Our hope is that our research will help put professionals on critical alert for the next invention promising 'progress' they need not question.

Appendix: Some Notes on Methodology

The methodologies employed in our study included elements of case study and policy research. Social policy research draws on secondary sources to develop analysis of social policies and programs, as we did in Chapter 3. Case studies, as Yin (2003) points out, are useful in understanding how and why things happen. They are not generalizable to populations, but they do provide detailed examination, as we do, of specific sites of activity. Our primary methodology, however, is institutional ethnography, explained in more detail below.

In institutional ethnography, interview subjects are chosen for their expertise in navigating the local site(s) under investigation. For this study, we interviewed 46 people: 19 parents, 18 social workers, and 9 key informants. Approximately half of each sub-sample was interviewed in Ontario and half in British Columbia, our two study sites.

Parents, primarily mothers, were identified by staff in various support organizations to participate. We sought parents who had been assessed for risk and, where possible, who had significant experience in dealing with the child welfare system. Several of these parents were of Aboriginal background. Workers were located through snowball and convenience sampling techniques. Workers' willingness to talk about their work was a primary criterion for selection, but we also sought workers involved in different agencies, geographical locations, of a variety of racial and cultural backgrounds, and who were engaged in different stages of the work process in order to provide as complete a description of various aspects of work processes as possible. Key informants were selected on the basis of our knowledge that they had played key roles or had specific kinds of knowledge about the development and running of the risk assessment system. Interviewees were asked general questions about their knowledge of and experience with risk assessment. Workers were asked to describe specific tasks they do in the normal course of their work, how they know what to do, and with whom and how they coordinate their work. Parents were asked to describe their experiences with the risk assessment and risk reduction processes, while key informants were asked to describe and explore the development and uses of risk assessment processes and tools from their particular vantage points.

Our focus was on risk assessment processes in place from 1997 onward. Most interviews took place between 2002 and 2006, although one worker was interviewed in 2007. During this period the risk assessment process under study was at its most intense. We are careful to acknowledge some changes in the processes over the course of the study, but we also recognize that even with some changes in provincial directions, the kinds of work processes and ways of thinking introduced by risk assessment procedures continue on, and are recognizable to workers who remain in the system as of this time. This insight is confirmed and reconfirmed in conversation with people familiar with the workings of child protection systems and other human services, people who respond in classes, at conferences, and in other public situations with instant and insightful recognition of the generalized and generalizing processes that we describe.

The analysis of data employed the following approaches:

Institutional ethnography places local activities in their social and historical contexts. This task involves identification and exploration of relevant contexts and analysis of those contextual elements that reveal generalized and generalizing social, historical, and economic processes, that is, those that shape and affect people's lives at the level of 'the social.' In this study, notions of modernity and postmodernism provide broad theoretical influences for understanding our current social condition, while the welfare state and neoliberalism provide more concrete and institutionalized forms of social and economic arrangements to which we all attend and articulate certain decisions and activities.

Part I outlines contexts of generalized risk thinking, welfare state organization and reorganization, and their effects on the Canadian social context and on human service practice contexts relevant to risk assessment. Chapter 5 explores the historical context relevant to risk assessment in child protection. Engaging in this analysis, of course, involves an assumption that 'the social' exists and that we as individuals are part of a social context beyond our individual and family lives.

Typically, institutional ethnography researchers engage in mapping the local site under discussion in order to specify how work is ordered and coordinated. Texts of various kinds are central to this mapping process because texts coordinate activities across local sites and also coordinate local practices with generalizing social processes. We used maps to assist in developing accurate descriptions and analysis of our sites and relationships between context and practices. In this case, 'study sites' involve both a specific provincial work organization and a more general view of the organization of work processes involved in accomplishing risk assessment.

In institutional ethnography, researchers enter the field of study from an identified entry point. We entered our study from the perspective of the actual activities of parents and workers who carry out the work processes involved in accomplishing risk assessment in a child protection setting. In line with all critical approaches to research, the researchers make no pretense of neutrality and do not present themselves as 'objective observers.' Rather, researchers declare their interests and subject positions, as we did in the beginning part of this book. In institutional ethnography it is helpful if they enter the study site as knowledgeable observers, as this enables them to ask questions and follow leads that an inexperienced observer would not notice. This is seen as an advantage to the project rather than 'bias.' We identified ourselves in the opening pages of the book as experienced in the general field of endeavour we studied.

Researchers knowledgeable about study sites may have ideas at the outset of research about how activities are put together and coordinated, but as in other kinds of qualitative research they are obliged to continually test their ideas against the data that they collect. Truth tests involve accuracy of description of the site – do participants recognize the description provided? – and whether the analysis rings true for participants. As each interview leads to new insights, those are checked with later interviewees. All interviewees are not asked the same questions. Rather, interviews uncover information that leads to new questions, which may mean identifying respondents with particular kinds of knowledge or experience. In this way, researchers attempt to create a rich description of the site of study (Campbell and Gregor, 2002). These were the steps we followed in our interviewing process.

As the study proceeds, researchers select particular themes or 'threads' relevant to the study purposes for more scrutiny. Much might be said or uncovered that will not be focused on in the study at hand. Rather, researchers select certain ideas or activities that they wish to track through the various levels of social context, history, and current activity. The purpose of this strategy is to maintain a focus on examining how local sites of activity help to accomplish the 'relations of ruling.'

Institutional ethnography analysis involves creating a description of what people actually do in their work settings (Chapters 6 and 7). The idea of 'work' is broadly interpreted to include activities beyond job descriptions and paid labour. In our study, for instance, the work of parents caring for children and attempting to gear their activities to the goal of accomplishing risk assessment requirements is considered to be work, and in fact, work without which the system would not function. The personal characteristics of the participants are not an object of evaluation or analysis, although selected aspects of their social location may be. The actual work people do to accomplish a work process, the reasoning, intentions, and thought processes that they employ towards this goal and the ways in which they coordinate their activities with those of others, including those not present in the immediate site, are examined to create a full description of how things happen in the various ways that they do (Smith, 2005). These are the strategies we used in developing Chapters 6 and 7.

Special attention is paid in the analysis to how local activities are 'hooked up' (Smith, 1990) to ruling relations, that is, those relations through which social organization is accomplished. The idea of 'ruling' recognizes that the activities of people are regulated in specific ways and that 'individual will and judgment are systematically superseded' (Rankin and Campbell, 2006: 17) This form of analysis allows for a measure of generalization, since local sites, while unique in some ways, require people to engage in activities that articulate to overarching or 'generalizing' social processes, guiding documents, and dominant discourses. Thus, activities and reasoning processes in one site of work on risk assessment will be understandable to people doing similar work in other sites. The objective of analysis at this level is to provide an examination and analysis of how ruling relations are accomplished through the labour of people in their everyday worlds of action. We see this analysis as following Gramsci's idea of hegemony (1992), meaning ways that ruling relations are embedded in institutions and become internalized, through work and social processes, in individuals and their ways of thinking.

In this case, we argue that what may seem the minutia of identifying risky parenting practices and trying to reduce those risks works to serve larger social and neoliberal purposes of moral and conduct control, involving the compliance of both professional and client populations through textually mediated practices. A prominent and intended outcome, we argue, is the protection of those at the highest levels of relevant bureaucracies from social blame for catastrophes.

From this analysis, we move in Chapter 8 to place our conclusions about ruling relations, and especially relations of power, into a social justice framework. From this perspective, we explore how the social organization of producing risk assessment uncovered and examined in our previous analysis creates power imbalances and conditions of oppression and surveillance, and we comment on how we think this analysis could and should be addressed by human service professionals.

References

Abbott, P., and Meerabeau, L. (Eds.). (1998). *The Sociology of the Caring Professions*, 2nd ed. London: UCL Press.

Adam, B. (1996). Re-vision: The centrality of time for an ecological social science perspective. In S. Lash, B. Szerszynski, and B. Wynne (Eds.), *Risk, Environment and Modernity: Towards a New Ecology*, 84–103. London: Sage.

Adam, B., Beck, U., and Van Loon, J. (Eds.). (2000). *The Risk Society and Beyond: Critical Issues for Social Theory*. Thousand Oaks: Sage.

Adams, J. (2003). Risk and morality: Three framing devices. In R. Ericson and A. Doyle (Eds.), *Risk and Morality*, 87–103. Toronto: University of Toronto Press.

Adams, J. (1995). *Risk*. London: University College Press.

Amin, S. (1989). *Eurocentrism*. New York: Monthly Review Press.

Auden, W.H. (1948). *The Age of Anxiety: A Baroque Eclogue*. London: Faber and Faber.

Austin, M., and D'Andrade, A. (2005). Risk and safety assessments in child welfare: Instrument comparisons. *Evidence for Practice*, 1–13. Berkeley: University of California, School of Social Welfare, Center for Social Services Research.

Austin, R. (1983). The insurance classification controversy. *University of Pennsylvania Law Review* 131: 517–83.

Baher, E. (1976). *At Risk: An Account of the Battered Child*. NSPCC, Research Department. London: Routledge and Kegan Paul.

Baines D. (2004). Pro-market, non-market: The dual nature of organizational change in social services delivery. *Critical Social Policy* 24(1): 5–29.

Baker, T., and Simon, J. (Eds.). (2002). *Embracing Risk: The Changing Culture of Insurance and Responsibility*. Chicago and London: University of Chicago Press.

Barber, J., Trocmé, N., Goodman, D., Shlonsky, A., Black, T., and Leslie, B. (2007). *The Reliability and Predictive Validity of Consensus-Based Risk Assessment*. Toronto: Centre of Excellence for Child Welfare.

Barbaree, H., Seto, M., Langton, C., and Peacock, E. (2001). Evaluating the predictive accuracy of six risk assessment instruments for adult sex offenders. *Criminal Justice and Behavior* 28(4): 490–521.

Barn, R., and Mantovani, N. (2007). Young mothers and the care system: Contextualizing risk and vulnerability. *British Journal of Social Work* 37: 225–43.

Barry, A., Osborne, T., and Rose, N. (1996). *Foucault and Political Reason: Liberalism, Neo-liberalism and Rationalities of Government*. Chicago: University of Chicago Press.

Battle, K. (2006). *The Choice in Childcare Allowance: What You See Is Not What You Get*. Ottawa: Caledon Institute for Social Policy.

Battle, K. (2001). *Relentless Incrementalism: Deconstructing and Reconstructing Canadian Income Security Policy*. Ottawa: Caledon Institute for Social Policy.

Battle, K., and Torjman, S. (1995). *How Finance Re-formed Social Policy*. Ottawa: Caledon Institute for Social Policy.

Battle, K., Mendelson, M., and Torjman, S. (2006). *Towards a New Architecture for Canada's Adult Benefits*. Ottawa: Caledon Institute for Social Policy.

Baumann, D., Law, J., Sheets, J., Reid, G., and Graham, J. (2005). Evaluating the effectiveness of actuarial risk assessment models. *Child and Youth Services Review* 27: 465–90.

Baumann, Z. (2002). *Society under Siege*. Malden: Polity.

B.C. Handbook for Action on Child Abuse and Neglect. (2003). Compiled by the Ministry of the Attorney General, Ministry of Children and Family Development, Ministry of Community, Aboriginal and Women's Services, Ministry of Education, Ministry of Health Services, Ministry of Human Resources. Victoria: Ministry of Children and Family Development.

Beaumont, B. (1999). Risk assessment and prediction research. In P. Parsloe (Ed.), *Risk Assessment in Social Care and Social Work*, 69–106. London and Philadelphia: Jessica Kingsley.

Beck, U. (1992 [1986]). *The Risk Society: Towards a New Modernity*. Thousand Oaks: Sage.

Beck-Gernsheim, E. (1996). Life as a planning project. In S. Lash, B. Szerszynski, and B. Wynne (Eds.), *Risk, Environment and Modernity: Towards a New Ecology*, 140–53. London: Sage.

Beckstead, D., and Brown, W.M. (2005). *Provincial Income Disparities through an Urban-Rural Lens: Evidence from the 2001 Census*. Ottawa: Government of Canada, Micro-Economic Analysis Division.

References   243

Belanger, A., and Caron Malenfant, E. (2005). *Population Projections of Visible Minority Groups, Canada, Provinces and Regions, 2001–2017.* Cat. no. 91-541. Ottawa: Statistics Canada.

Bell, M. (1999). Working in partnership in child protection: The conflicts. *British Journal of Social Work* 29: 437–55.

Bernstein, P. (1996a). *Against the Gods: The Remarkable Story of Risk.* New York: Wiley.

Bernstein, P. (1996b). The new religion of risk management. *Harvard Business Review* (March/April): 47–51.

Beveridge, W. (1942). *Social Insurance and Allied Services.* Cmd. 6404. London: HMSO.

Blackstock, C. (2003). First Nations child and family services: Restoring peace and harmony in First Nations communities. In K. Kufeldt and B. McKenzie (Eds.), *Child Welfare: Connecting Research Policy and Practice*, 331–43. Waterloo: Wilfrid Laurier University Press.

Blackstock, C., Trocmé, N., and Bennett, M. (2004). Child welfare response to Aboriginal and non-Aboriginal children in Canada: A comparative analysis. *Violence against Women* 10(8): 901–16.

Bourgon, G., and Bonta, J. (2004). Risk assessment for general assault and partner abusers. Ottawa: Solicitor General of Canada, Ministry of Public Safety and Emergency Preparedness.

Boychuk, G. (2004). *The Canadian Social Model: The Logics of Policy Development.* Research Report F36. Ottawa: Canadian Policy Research Networks.

Bradshaw, P., Murray, V., and Wolpin, J. (1996). Women on boards of nonprofits: What difference do they make? *Nonprofit Management and Leadership* 6: 241–54.

Brearley, C. (1982). *Risk and Social Work.* London: Routledge and Kegan Paul.

Breines, W., and Gordon, L. (1983). The new scholarship on family violence. *Signs* 8: 491–531.

Brissett-Chapman, S. (1997). Child protection, risk assessment and African American children: Cultural ramifications for families and communities. *Child Welfare* 74(1): 45–63.

British Columbia Child, Family and Community Service Act. (1996). RSBC. Retrieved 27 Jan. 2009 from www.qp.gov.bc.ca.

British Columbia Ministry for Children and Families. (Undated). *Practice Standards for Child Protection.* Victoria: Author.

Broad, D., and Antony, W. (Eds.). (1999). *Citizens or Consumers? Social Policies in a Market Society.* Halifax: Fernwood.

Broadbent, E. (1999). Citizenship today: Is there a crisis? In D. Broad and W.

Antony (Eds.), *Citizens or Consumers? Social Policies in a Market Society*, 22–36. Halifax: Fernwood.

Brock, D. (Ed.). (2003). *Making Normal: Social Regulation in Canada*, 209–34. Scarborough: Thomson Nelson.

Brown, D. (2004). *Working the System: Rethinking the Role of Parents and the Reduction of 'Risk' in Child Protection Work.* Master's thesis, University of Victoria.

Brown, L., Haddock, L., and Kovach, M. (2002). Watching over our families and children: The Lalum'utul'smun'eem. In B.Wharf (Ed.), *Community Work Approaches to Child Welfare*, 131–51. Toronto: University of Toronto Press.

Bryant, T. (2004). Housing and health. In D. Raphael (Ed.), *Social Determinants of Health: Canadian Perspectives*, 217–31. Toronto: Canadian Scholar's Press.

Bunting, M. (2004, 25 Oct.). The age of anxiety. *Guardian.* Retrieved from http://www.guardian.co.uk/world/2004/oct/25/terrorism.comment.

Burchell, G. (1996). In A. Barry, T. Osborne, and N. Rose (Eds.), *Foucault and Political Reason: Liberalism, Neo-liberalism and Rationalities of Government*, 19–36. Chicago: University of Chicago Press.

Burchell, G., Gordon, C., and Miller, P. (Eds.). (1991*). The Foucault Effect: Studies in Governmentality.* Chicago: University of Chicago Press.

Burke, P. (1999). Social services staff: Risks they face and their dangerousness to others. In P. Parsloe (Ed.), *Risk Assessment in Social Care and Social Work,* . 107–18. London and Philadelphia: Jessica Kingsley.

Caldwell, M. (2002). What we do not know about juvenile sexual reoffense risk? *Child Maltreatment* 7(4): 291–302.

Callahan, M. (1993). Feminist approaches: Women recreate child welfare. In B. Wharf (Ed.), *Rethinking Child Welfare in Canada*, 172–209. Toronto: McClelland and Stewart.

Callahan, M., and Callahan, K. (1997). Victims and villains: The portrayal of child welfare in the press. In G. Ternowetsky and J. Pulkingham (Eds.), *Child and Family Policies: Struggles, Strategies and Options*, 40–56. Halifax: Fernwood.

Callahan, M., and Lumb, C. (1995). My cheque and my children: The long road to empowerment in child welfare. *Child Welfare* 74(3): 795–819.

Callahan, M., and Swift, K. (2007). Great expectations and unintended consequences: Risk assessment in child welfare in B.C. In L. Foster and B. Wharf (Eds.), *People, Politics and Child Welfare*, 158–83. Vancouver: UBC Press.

Callahan, M., Rutman, D., Strega, S., and Dominelli, L. (2005). Looking promising: Contradictions and challenges for young mothers in care. In D.
Gustafson (Ed.), *Unbecoming Mothers: Women Living Apart from Their Children*, 185–209. New York: Haworth.

Cameron, G., and Birnie-Lefcovitch, S. (2000). Parent mutual aid organizations
in child welfare demonstration project: A report of outcomes. *Children and
Youth Services Review* 22(6): 421–40.

Campaign 2000. (2006). *Oh Canada: Too Many Children in Poverty for Too Long*.
Ottawa: Author. Retreived 2 Aug. 2007 from www.campaign2000.ca/rc/
rc06/06_C2000NationalReportCard.pdf

Campaign 2000. (2008). *Family Security in Insecure Times: The Case for a Poverty
Reduction Strategy for Canada*. Retrieved 27 Jan. 2009 from
http://www.campaign2000.ca/rc/01bulletin/Nov01Bulletin4p.pdf.

Campbell, M., and Gregor, F. (2002). *Mapping Social Relations: A Primer in
Doing Institutional Ethnography*. Aurora: Garamond.

Canadian Broadcasting Corporation. (2007, 1 March). Wage gap widening
despite boom. Retrieved 24 Oct. 2007 from http://www.cbc.ca/canada/
story/2005/09/14/canada_poverty20050914.html.

Canadian Broadcasting Corporation. (2005, 14 Sept.). Canadian poverty
rising despite economic boom. Retrieved 24 Oct. 2007 from http://www
.cbc.ca/canada/story/2005/09/14/canada_poverty20050914.html.

Canadian Broadcasting Corporation. (2002, 13 Dec.). Canada's wealth disparity rivals third world. Retrieved 24 Oct. 2007 from
http://www.cbc.ca/canada/story/2002/12/13/disparity021213.html.

Canadian Centre for Policy Alternatives. (2006, 20 Nov.). *Growing
Gap,Growing Concerns: Canadian Attitudes towards Income Inequality*. Ottawa:
Author.

Canadian Council for Social Development. (2006). *The Progress of Canada's
Children and Youth*. Ottawa: Author. Retrieved 2 June 2007 from
http://www.ccsd.ca/pccy/2006/.

Carvel, J. (2007, 6 Sept.). Child binge drinkers at greater risk of alcoholism,
says study. *Guardian*, 16.

Cash, S. (2001). Risk assessment in child welfare: The art and science. *Children and Youth Services Review* 23(22): 811–30.

Castel, R. (1991). From dangerousness to risk. In G. Burchell, C. Gordon, and
P. Miller (Eds.), *The Foucault Effect: Studies in Governmentality*, 281–98.
Chicago: University of Chicago Press.

Casteneda, C. (2000). Child organ-stealing stories: Risk, rumour and reproductive technologies. In B. Adam, U. Beck, and J. Van Loon (Eds.),

The Risk Society and Beyond: Critical Issues for Social Theory, 136–54. London: Sage.

Centers for Disease Control. (2006). *List of Publications Using Multistate PRAMS Data*. Retrieved 4 April 2009 from: http://www.cdc.gov/prams/References/PublicationList052006.doc

Centre for Global Development. (2006). *Commitment to Development Index*. Retrieved 3 April 2007 from http://www.cgdev.org/section/initiatives/_active/cdi.

Chau, S., Fitzpatrick, A., Hulchanski, D., Leslie, B., and Schatia, D. (2001). *One in Five … Housing as a Factor in the Admission of Children to Care: New Survey of Children's Aid Society of Toronto Updates 1992 Study*. Toronto: University of Toronto, Centre for Urban and Community Studies.

Chen, X. (2005). *Tending the Gardens of Citizenship: Child Saving in Toronto, 1880s–1920s*. Toronto: University of Toronto Press.

Chen, X. (2003). Constituting 'dangerous parents' through the spectre of child death: A critique of child protection restructuring in Ontario. In D. Brock (Ed.), *Making Normal: Social Regulation in Canada*, 209–34. Toronto: Thomson Nelson.

Christie, A., and Mittler, H. (1999). Partnership and core groups in the risk society. *Child and Family Social Work* 4(3): 231–40.

Cicchinelli, L. (1989). Risk assessment models: CPS agencies and future directions. In *CPS Risk Assessment Conference: From Research to Practice – Designing the Future of Child Protective Services*, 7–22. Burlington, VT, and Washington, DC: American Public Welfare Association.

Clark, G. (2002). Embracing fatality through life insurance in eighteenth-century England. In T. Baker and J. Simon (Eds.), *Embracing Risk: The Changing Culture of Insurance and Responsibility*, 80–96. Chicago: University of Chicago Press.

Cohen-Schlanger, M., Fitzpatrick, A., Hulchanski, J.D., and Raphael, D. (1995). Housing as a factor in admissions of children to temporary care: A survey. *Child Welfare* 74(3): 547–62.

Colclough, L., Parton, N., and Anslow, M. (1999). Family support. In N. Parton and C. Wattam (Eds.), *Child Sexual Abuse: Responding to the Experiences of Children*, 159–80. Chichester and Toronto: Wiley.

Cooley, Mason. (1986). *City Aphorisms, Third Selection*. New York. Retrieved from http://www.bartelby.com/.

Cooper, M. (2001). *Housing Affordability: A Children's Issue*. CPRN Discussion Paper F/11. Ottawa: Canadian Policy Research Networks.

Cossman, B., and Fudge, J. (2002). *Privatization, Law and the Challenge to Feminism*. Toronto: University of Toronto Press.

Cradock, G. (2004). Risk, morality and child protection: Risk calculation as guides to practice. *Science, Technology and Human Values* 29(3): 314–31.

Crawford, T. (2007, 20 Jan.). Fear palpable for post-9/11 parents. *Toronto Star,* L2.

Culhane, D. (2003). Their spirits live within us: Aboriginal women in Downtown Eastside Vancouver emerging into visibility. *American Indian Quarterly* 27(3/4): 593–606.

Culpitt, I. (1999). *Social Policy and Risk.* London: Sage.

D'Andrade, A., Benton, A., and Austin, M. (2005). *Risk and Safety Assessment in Child Welfare: Instrument Comparisons.* Berkeley: University of California, School of Social Welfare, Center for Social Services Research.

Davies, C. (2000). Care and transformation of professionalism. In C. Davies, L. Finlay, and A. Bullman (Eds.), *Changing Practice in Health and Social Care,* 343–54. London: Sage.

Davies, C. (1995). *Gender and the Professional Predicament in Nursing.* Buckingham: Open University Press.

Dean, M. (1999). Risk, calculable and incalculable. In D. Lupton (Ed.), *Risk and Socioculural Theory: New Directions and Perspectives,* 131–59. Cambridge: Cambridge University Press.

Dean, M. (1995). Governing the unemployed self in an active society. *Economy and Society* 24: 559–83.

DePanfilis, D. (1996). Implementing child mistreatment risk assessment systems: Lesssons from theory. *Administration in Social Work* 20(2): 41–59.

Department of Human Resources and Social Development Canada. (2003). *Social Security Statistics, Canada and Provinces, 1978–79 to 2002–03.* Ottawa: Author.

DeVault, M. (1999). *Liberating Method: Feminism and Social Research.* Philadelphia: Temple University Press.

Dhalla, I., Kwong, J., Streiner, D., Baddour, R., Waddell, A., and Johnson, I. (2002). Characteristics of first-year students in Canadian medical schools. *Canadian Medical Association Journal* 166(8): 1029–35.

Di Manno, R. (2006, 6 Dec.). Minding the minders. *Toronto Star,* A7.

Doern, G., and Reed, T. (2000). *Risky Business: Canada's Changing Science-Based Policy and Regulatory Regime.* Toronto: University of Toronto Press.

Douglas, M. (1992). *Risk and Blame: Essays in Cultural Theory.* London: Routledge.

Douglas, M. (1990). Risk as a forensic resource. *Daedalus* 119: 1–14.

Douglas, M., and Wildavsky, A. (1982). *Risk and Culture: An Essay in the Selection and Interpretation of Technological and Environmental Dangers.* Berkeley: University of California Press.

Doyal, L., and Gough, I. (1991). *A Theory of Human Need*. London: Macmillan.

Drummond, D., and Tulk, D. (2006). *Lifestyles of the Rich and Unequal: An Investigation into Wealth Inequality in Canada*. Toronto: Toronto Dominion Bank Financial Group. Special Report. Retrieved 25 Oct. 2007 from http://www.td.com/economics/special/dt1206_wealth.pdf.

Drummond, D., Burleton, D., and Manning, G. (2004). Affordable housing in Canada: In search of a new paradigm. In D. Hulchanski and M. Shapcott (Eds.), *Finding Room: Policy Options for a Canadian Rental Housing Strategy*, 15–68. Toronto: University of Toronto, Centre for Urban and Community Studies.

Dumbrill, G. (2005). Ontario's child welfare transformation: Another swing of the pendulum? *Canadian Social Work Review* 23(1/2): 5–19.

Duxbury, L., and Higgins, C. (2002). *Work-Life Conflict in Canada in the New Millennium: A Status Report*. Ottawa: Canadian Policy Research Networks.

Ecumenical Coalition for Economic Justice. (1993). Beyond Adjustment: Emerging Alternatives to the Crisis in Africa. Paper presented at the ECEJ Workshop, 27–9 Sept., Toronto.

Ehrenreich, B. (1990). *Fear of Falling: The Inner Life of the Middle Class*. New York: Harper Collins.

English, D., and Pecora, P. (1994). Risk assessment as a practice method in child protective services. *Child Welfare* 73(5): 451–73.

English, J., and Young, W. (2006). The federal government and social policy at the turn of the 21st century: Reflections on change and continuity. In A. Westhues (Ed.), *Canadian Social Policy*, 47–68. Waterloo: Wilfrid Laurier University Press.

Ericson, R., and Doyle, A. (2004). *Uncertain Business: Risk, Insurance and the Limits of Knowledge*. Toronto: University of Toronto Press.

Etzioni, A. (1969). *The Semi-Professions and Their Organization: Teachers, Nurses, Social Workers*. New York: Free Press.

Evans, B.M., and Shields, J. (2000). *Neoliberal Restructuring and the Third Sector:*

Reshaping Governance, Civil Society and Local Relations. Working Paper 13. Toronto: Ryerson University School of Business, Center for Voluntary Sector Studies.

Evetts, J. (2006). Short note: The sociology of professional groups. *Current Sociology* 54(1): 133–43.

Evetts, J. (2003). The sociological analysis of professionalism: Occupational change in the modern world. *International Sociology* 18(2): 395–415.

Ewald, F. (1991). Insurance and risk. In G Burchell, C. Gordon, and P. Miller

(Eds.), *The Foucault Effect: Studies in Governmentality*, 197–210. Chicago: University of Chicago Press.

Falco, G., and Salovitz, B. (1997). Clinical versus actuarial risk assessment in child protective services: Results from recent research in New York. Paper presented at the 11th Annual CPS Roundtable on Risk Assessment, San Francisco.

Family and Children's Services of Elgin County. What Is the Ontario Risk Assessment Model? (2006). Retrieved 3 Oct. 2007 from http://www.caselgin.on.ca/html/abuse-riskmodel.html.

Farris-Manning, C., and Zandstra, M. (2003). *Children in Care in Canada: A Summary of Current Issues and Trends with Recommendations for Future Research*. Ottawa: Child Welfare League of Canada. Retrieved 25 Oct. 2007 from http://www.nationalchildrensalliance.com/nca/pubs/2003/Children_in_Care_March_2003

Ferguson, H. (1997). Protecting children in new times: Child protection and the risk society. *Child and Family Social Work* 2: 222–34.

Fetherstone, B. (2004). Why gender matters in child welfare and protection. *Critical Social Policy* 26(2): 294–314.

Fine, M. (2005). Individualization, risk and the body: Sociology and care. *Journal of Sociology* 41(3): 247–66.

Flynn, R.J., and Bouchard, D. (2005). Randomized and quasi-experimental evaluations of program impact in child welfare in Canada: A review. *Canadian Journal of Program Evaluation* 20(3): 65–100.

Forrester, G. (2000). Professional autonomy versus managerial control: The experience of teachers in an English primary school. *International Studies in Sociology of Education* 10(2): 133–51.

Foster, L. (2007). Trends in child welfare: What do the data show? In L. Foster and B. Wharf (Eds.), *People, Politics and Child Welfare in British Columbia*, 34–65. Vancouver: UBC Press.

Foster, L., and Wharf, B. (2007). *People, Politics and Child Welfare in British Columbia*. Vancouver: UBC Press

Foster, L., and Wright, M. (2002). Patterns and trends in children in the care of the province of British Columbia: Ecological, policy and cultural perspectives. *Too Small to See, Too Big to Ignore: Child Health and Well-Being in British Columbia*. In M. Hayes and L. Foster (Eds.), Canadian Western Geographical Series, vol. 35, 103–40. Victoria: Western Geographical Press.

Foucault, M. (1995). *Discipline and Punish: The Birth of the Prison*. New York: Vintage.

Foucault, M. (1981). Omnes et singulatim: Toward a criticism of political reason. In *The Tanner Lectures on Human Values*, part II, 223–54. Salt Lake City: University of Utah Press.

Foucault, M. (1980). *Power/Knowledge: Selected Interviews and Other Writings, 1972–1977*. New York: Pantheon.

Fournier, S., and Crey, E. (1997). *Stolen from Our Embrace: The Abduction of First Nations Children and the Restoration of Aboriginal Communities*. Vancouver: Douglas and McIntryre.

Fox, N. (1999). Postmodern reflections on risk, hazards and life choices. In D. Lupton (Ed.), *Risk and Sociocultural Theory: New Directions and Perspectives*,12–33. Cambridge: Cambridge University Press.

Franklin, B., and Parton, N. (2001). Press-ganged! Media reporting of social work and child abuse. In M. May, R. Page, and E. Brunsdon (Eds.), *Understanding Social Problems: Issues in Social Policy*, 233–47. Oxford: Blackwell.

Fraser, S. (2002, 26 Nov.). *Opening Statement to the Standing Committee on Public Accounts*. Retrieved 22 Sept. 2008 from http://www.oag-bvg.gc.ca/internet/English/osh_20021126_e_23354.html.

Freud, S. (1946). *Civilization and Its Discontents*, 3rd ed. London: Hogarth Press and Institute of Psycho-Analysis.

Frickel, S. (2006). Our toxic gumbo: Recipe for a politics of environmental knowledge. *Understanding Katrina: Perspectives from the Social Sciences*. Retrieved 2 Feb. 2007 from http://understandingkatrina.ssrc.org/.

Friendly, M., and Beach, J. (2005). *Early Childhood Education and Care in Canada 2004*. 6th ed. Toronto: University of Toronto, Childcare Resource and Research Unit.

Friendly, M., and Ferns, C. (2006, March). *The State of the National Child Care Program and Provincial/Territorial Contexts*. Toronto: University of Toronto, Childcare Resource and Research Unit.

Furedi, F. (2006). *The Culture of Fear Revisited: Risk Taking and the Morality of Low Expectation*. 4th ed. London: Continuum.

Furniss, E. (1995). *Victims of Benevolence: The Dark Legacy of the Williams Lake Residential School*. Vancouver: Arsenal Pulp Press.

Gambrill, E., and Shlonsky, A. (2001). The need for comprehensive risk management systems in child welfare. *Children and Youth Services Review* 23(1): 79–107.

Gambrill, E., and Shlonsky, A. (2000). Risk assessment in context. *Children and Youth Services Review* 22(11/12): 813–37.

Gandhi U. (2007, 30 Oct.). Autism groups support earlier screening. *Globe and Mail*. Retrieved 2 Nov. 2007 from http://www.theglobeandmail.com/servlet/story/LAC.20071030.AUTISM.30/PPVStoryU.

Garland, D. (1997). Governmentality and the problem of crime. *Theoretical Criminology* 1(2): 173–214.

Gendreau, P., Little, T., and Goggin, C. (1996). A meta-analysis of the predictors of adult offender recidivism: What works! *Criminology* 34: 575–607.

Giddens, A. (1999a). Risk and responsibility. *Modern Law Review* 62(1): 1–10.

Giddens, A. (1999b). Runaway world. *BBC Reith Lecture.* Retrieved 28 Jan. 2009 from http://news.bbc.co.uk/hi/english/static/events/reith_99.

Giddens, A. (1994). *Beyond Left and Right: The Future of Radical Politics.* Stanford: Stanford University Press.

Giddens, A. (1991). *Modernity and Self-Identity: Self and Society in the Late Modern Age.* Cambridge: Polity.

Giddens, A. (1990). *The Consequences of Modernity.* Cambridge: Polity.

Glassner, B. (1999). *The Culture of Fear: Why Americans Are Afraid of the Wrong Things.* New York: Basic Books.

Globe and Mail. (2007, 3 March). Laval officer shot dead one week into new job, A9.

Goddard, C., Saunders, B., Stanley, J., and Tucci, J. (1999). Structured risk assessment procedures: Instruments of abuse? *Child Abuse Review* 8(4): 251–63.

Goldberg, M. (2004). *Tracking Changes in the Community Social Services Sector: Impacts in British Columbia from 2001–2003.* Report prepared for Community Social Services Council of B.C. Vancouver: Social Planning and Research Council of British Columbia.

Gordon, L. (1988). *Heroes of Their Own Lives: The Politics and History of Family Violence – Boston, 1880–1960.* New York: Viking.

Gove, T. (1995). *Report of the Gove Inquiry into Child Protection,* vol. 1, *Matthew's Story,* and vol. 2, *Matthew's Legacy.* Victoria: Ministry of Social Services.

Government of British Columbia. (1998). *Report of the B.C. Children's Commission.* Victoria: Government of B.C.

Gramsci, A. (1992). *Prison Notebooks.* Editor and Translator J. Buttegieg New York: Columbia University Press.

Gray, J., Cutler, C., Dean, J. and Kempe, C. (1977). Prediction and prevention of child abuse and neglect. *Child Abuse and Neglect* 1: 45–58.

Hacking, I. (1990). *The Taming of Chance.* Cambridge: Cambridge University Press.

Hacking, I. (1975). *The Emergence of Probability.* Cambridge: Cambridge University Press.

Haines, T., Hill, K., Bennell, K., and Osborne, R. (2006). Recurrent events counted in evaluations of predictive accuracy. *Journal of Clinical Epidemiology* 59(11): 1155–61.

Hamilton, C., Adolphs, S., Nerlich, B. (2007). The meanings of risk: A view from corpus linguistics. *Discourse and Society* 18(2): 163–81.

Hannah-Moffat, K., and Maurutto, P. (2003). *Youth Risk/Need Assessment: An Overview of Issues and Practices*. Ottawa: Department of Justice.

Hannah-Moffat, K., and Shaw, M. (2001). *Taking Risks: Incorporating Gender and Culture into Classification and Assessment of Federally Sentenced Women*. Ottawa: Status of Women Canada.

Hanlon, G. (1998). Professionalism as enterprise: Service class politics and the redefinition of professionalism. *Sociology* 32(1): 43–63.

Hanlon, G., Goode, J., Gretbatch, D., Luff, D., O'Cathain, A., and Strangleman, T. (2006). Risk society and the NHS: From the traditional to the new citizen? *Critical Perspectives on Accounting* 17: 270–82.

Harlow, E. (2004). Why don't women want to be social workers any more? New managerialism, post-feminisim and the shortage of social workers in social service departments in England and Wales. *European Journal of Social Work* 7(2): 167–79.

Harnett, C. (2007, 1 June). Revamping of Laurel House traumatic for clients and staff: Second home to mentally ill closing doors to make way for more structured program. *Times Colonist*. Retrieved 1 Nov. 2007 from http://www.canada.com/victoriatimescolonist/news/story.html?id=5dd6a73a-b3e4-4082-adb9-6d51ee7631b5&k=55907.

Hasenfeld, Y. (1982). *Human Service Organizations*. Englewood Cliffs, NJ: Prentice-Hall.

Hay, D. (2005). A new social architecture for Canada's 21st century. In *Research Highlights*. Ottawa: Canadian Policy Review Networks. Retrieved 22 Oct. 2007 from http://www.cprn.org/documents/35088_en.pdf.

Health Canada. (2004). *Smog and Your Health*. Ottawa: Minister of Health.

Health Canada. (2002). *Canada's Aging Population*. Ottawa: Minister of Public Works and Government Services.

Heap, J. (1995). Constructionism in the rhetoric and practice of fourth-generation evaluation. *Evaluation and Program Planning* 18(1): 51–61.

Hearn, J. (1982). Patriarchy, professionalization and the semi-professions. *Sociology* 16(2): 184–202.

Heimer, C. (2002). Insuring more, ensuring less: The costs and benefits of private regulation through insurance. In T. Baker and J. Simon (Eds.), *Embracing Risk: The Changing Culture of Insurance and Responsibility*, 116–45. Chicago: University of Chicago Press.

Hendryx, M., and Rohland, B. (1997). Psychiatric hospitalization decision making by CMHC staff. *Community Mental Health Journal* 33(1): 63–73.

Hill, R. (2006). *Disproportionality in Child Welfare: An Update.* Baltimore: Annie E. Casey Foundation.

Hilton, Z., and Simmons, J. (2001). The influence of actuarial risk assessment in clinical judgments and tribunal decisions about mentally disordered offenders in maximum security. *Law and Human Behaviour* 25(4): 393–408.

Hoge, R.D. (2002). Standardized instruments for assessing risk and need in youthful offenders. *Criminal Justice and Behaviour* 29(4): 380–96.

Hoggett, P. (1990). *Modernisation, Political Strategy and the Welfare State: An Organizational Perspective.* Studies in Decentralisation and Quasi-Markets, no. 2. Bristol: University of Bristol, School of Advanced Urban Studies.

Hornby, H. (1989). *Risk Assessment in Child Protective Services: Issues in Field Implementation.* Portland, ME: National Child Welfare Resource Center for Management and Administration.

Houston, S., and Griffiths, H. (2000). Reflections on risk in child protection: Is it time for a shift in paradigms? *Child and Family Social Work* 5(1): 1–10.

Howe, D. (1996). Client experiences of counselling and treatment interventions: A qualitative study of family views of family therapy. *British Journal of Guidance and Counselling* 24(3): 367–75.

Hulchanski, D., and Shapcott, M. (2004). *Finding Room: Options for a Canadian Rental Housing Strategy.* Toronto: University of Toronto, Centre for Urban and Community Studies.

Human Resource and Skills Development Canada. (2008). *Child and Family Services Statistical Report 1996–97 to 1998–99, March 2001.* Ottawa: Government of Canada. Retrieved 27 Jan. 2009 from http://ww.hrsdc.gc.ca/eng/cs/sp/sdc/socpol/publications/reports/2001-001347/page08.shtml.

Human Resources and Social Development Canada. (2006). *Social Security Statistics Canada and Provinces 1978–79 to 2002–03.* Ottawa: Author. Retrieved 20 July 2007 from http://www.hrsdc.gc.ca/en/cs/sp/sdc/socpol/tables/pre/tab421.shtml.

Human Resources and Social Development Canada. (2006, 26 June). *Achieving Coherence in Government of Canada Funding Practice in Communities: The Community Non-profit Sector in Canada.* Ottawa: Author. Retrieved 24 June 2007 from http://www.hrsdc.gc.ca/en/cs/sp/sdc/task_force/tfci/page03.shtml.

Human Resources Development Canada and the Canada Employment Insurance Commission. (2001, Dec.). Clarity and improved transparency needed to demonstrate compliance with the Employment Insurance Act in setting premium rates. *Report of the Auditor General*. Ottawa: Auditor General of Canada. Retrieved 15 Oct. 2008 from http://www.oag-bvg.gc.ca/internet/English/osh_20020319_e_23339.html.

Hume, M. (2006, 5 Dec.). A very filthy room of one's own. *Globe and Mail*. Retrieved 24 Oct. 2007 from http://www.theglobeandmail.com/servlet/story/RTGAM.20061205.wxbchomeless05/BNStor y/National.

Ismael, J., and Vaillancourt, Y. (Eds.). 1988. *Privatization and Provincial Social Services in Canada: Policy, Administration and Delivery*. Edmonton: University of Alberta Press.

Ives, P. (2004). *Language and Hegemony in Gramsci*. London: Pluto Press.

Jackson, A., and Robinson, D. (with Bob Baldwin and Cindy Wiggins). (2000). *Falling Behind: The State of Working Canada, 2000*. Ottawa: Canadian Centre for Policy Alternatives.

Jagannathan, R., and Camasso, M. (1996). Risk assessment in child protective services: A canonical analysis of the case management function. *Child Abuse and Neglect* 20(7): 599–612.

Jenson, J. (2004). *Catching Up to Reality: Building the Case for a New Social Model*. Research Report F35. Ottawa: Canadian Policy Research Networks.

Johnston, P. (1983). *Native Children and the Child Welfare System*. Toronto: Canadian Council on Social Development, in association with James Lorimer Publishers.

Jones, C. (1979). Social work education, 1900–1977. In N. Parry et al. (Eds.), *Social Work, Welfare and the State*, 72–88. London: Edward Arnold.

Jones, R. (1996). Decision-making in child welfare. *British Journal of Social Work* 26: 509–22.

Kasperson, J., and Kasperson, R. (2005). *The Social Contours of Risk: Publics, Risk Communication and the Social Amplification of Risk*. London, and Sterling, VA: Earthscan.

Kasperson, R., and Kasperson, J. (1996). The social amplification and attenuation of risk. *Annals of the American Academy of Political and Social Science* 54(5): 95–105.

Keay, D. (1987, 31 Oct.). AIDS, Education and the Year 2000. *Woman's Own*, 8–10.

Keiler, G. (2006, Dec.). Notebook: Loaded. *Harper's*, 11.

Kelly, T., Simmons, W., and Gregory, E. (2002). Risk assessment and management: A community forensic mental health practice model. *International Journal of Mental Health Nursing* 11: 206–13.

Kemshall, H. (2002). *Risk, Social Policy and Welfare*. Buckingham: Open University Press.

Kemshall, H., and Maguire, M. (2001). Public protection, partnership and risk penalty: The multi-agency risk management of sexual and violent offenders. *Punishment and Society* 3(2): 237–64.

Kemshall, H., Parton, N., Walsh, M., and Waterson, J. (1997). Concepts of risk in relation to organizational structure and functioning within the personal social services and probation. *Social Policy and Administration* 31(3): 213–32.

Kemshall, H., and Pritchard, J. (Eds). (1996). *Good Practice in Risk Assessment and Risk Management*, vol. 2, *Key Themes for Protection, Rights and Responsibilities*. London: Jessica Kingsley.

Kerr, D., and Joseph Michalski, H. (2005). *Income Poverty in Canada: Recent Trends among Canadian Families 1981–2002*. Discussion Paper 05-02. London: University of Western Ontario, Population Studies Centre.

Kerstetter, S. (2002). *Rags and Riches: Wealth Inequality in Canada*. Ottawa: Centre for Policy Alternatives.

Krane, J., and Davies, L. (2000). Mothering and child protection practice: Rethinking risk assessment. *Child and Family Social Work* 5: 35–45.

Kropp, P., and Hart, S. (2004). *The Development of the Brief Spousal Assault Form for the Evaluation of Risk (B-SAFER): A Tool for Criminal Justice Professionals – Research Reports*. Ottawa: Department of Justice Canada. Retrieved 18 March 2007 from http://www.justice.gc.ca/en/ps/rs/rep/2005/rr05fv-1/index.html.

Kropp, P., Hart, S., and Lyon, D. (2002). Risk assessment of stalkers: Some problems and possible solutions. *Criminal Justice Behavior* 29(5): 590–600.

Krysik, J., and Lecroy, C. (2002). The empirical validation of an instrument to predict risk of recidivism among juvenile offenders. *Research on Social Work Practice* 12(1): 71–81.

Laird, G. (2007). *Shelter: Homelessness in a Growth Economy – Canada's 21st Century Paradox*. Calgary: Sheldon Chumir Foundation for Ethics in Leadership.

Langan, J. (1999). Assessing risk in mental health. In P. Parsloe (Ed.), *Risk Assessment in Social Care and Social Work*, 153–78. London: Jessica Kingsley.

Lash, S. (1994). Reflexivity and its doubles: Structure, aesthetics, community. In U. Beck, A. Giddens, and S. Lash (Eds.), *Reflexive Modernization*, 110–73. Stanford: Stanford University Press.

LeDoux, J. (1998). *The Emotional Brain: The Mysterious Underpinnings of Emotional Life*. New York: Simon and Schuster.

Lee, K. (2000). *Urban Poverty in Canada: A Statistical Profile*. Ottawa: Canadian Council on Social Development.

Leiss, W. (2000). Between expertise and bureaucracy: Risk management trapped at the science-policy interface. In G. Doern and T. Reed (Eds.), *Risky Business: Canada's Changing Science-Based Policy and Regulatory Regime*, 49–74. Toronto: University of Toronto Press.

Leonard, P. (1997). *Postmodern Welfare: Reconstructing an Emancipatory Project.* London: Sage.

Leslie, B., and O'Connor, B. (2002). What are the products of the Ontario Risk Assessment Tool? *Journal of Ontario Association of Children's Aid Societies* 46(4): 2–9.

Levanthal, J. (1988). Can child maltreatment be predicted during the perinatal period? Evidence from longitudinal cohort studies. *Journal of Reproductive and Infant Psychology* 6: 139–61.

Lewis, J., Bernstock, P., and Bovell, V. (1995). The community care changes: Unresolved tensions and policy issues in implementation. *Journal of Social Policy* 24(1): 73–94.

Lindsay, D. (2003). *The Welfare of Children.* 2nd ed. New York: Oxford University Press.

Lipsky, M. (1980). *Street Level Bureaucracy: Dilemmas of the Individual in Public Services.* New York: Russell Sage.

Little, J., and Rixon, A. (1998). Computer learning and risk assessment in child protection. *Child Abuse Review* 7(3): 165–77.

Lodomel, I., and Trickey, H. (2001). *An Offer You Can't Refuse: Workfare in International Perspective.* Bristol: Policy.

Loury, G. (2007, July/Aug.). Why are so many Americans in prison? Race and the transformation of criminal justice. *Boston Review: A Political and Literary Forum.* Retrieved from http://bostonreview.net/BR32.4/article_loury.php: 1-13.

Lupton, D. (1999). *Risk and Sociocultural Theory: New Directions and Perspectives.* Cambridge: Cambridge University Press.

Lyle, C., and Graham, E. (2000). Looks can be deceiving: Using a risk assessment instrument to evaluate the outcomes of child protection services. *Children and Youth Services Review* 22(11/12): 935–49.

Mackenzie, H. (2007). Raising the minimum wage in Ontario: Behind the numbers. *Economic Facts, Figures and Analysis* 8(1): 1–3. Retrieved 26 Oct. 2007 from http://www.growinggap.ca/files/Raising%20Ontario's%20minimum%20wage.pdf.

MacMillan, M., Thomas, B., Walsh, C, Boyle, M., and Shannon, H. (2005). Effectiveness of home visitations of public-health nurses in prevention of the recurrence of child physical abuse and neglect: A randomized controlled trial. *Lancet* 365: 1786–96.

McNally, D. (2006). *Another World Is Possible: Globalization and Anti-Capitalism.* Winnipeg: Arbeiter Ring Publishing.

MacNicol, J. (1987). In pursuit of the underclass. *Journal of Social Policy* 16(3): 293–318.

Magura, S., and Moses, B. (2001). *Outcome Measures for Child Welfare Services: Theory and Applications.* Washington: Child Welfare League of America.

Marshall, T.H. (1992). Citizenship and social class. Part I of T.H. Marshall and T. Bottomore (Eds.), *Citizenship and Social Class*, 1–51. London: Pluto Press.

Marteau, T., and Dormandy, E. (2001). Facilitating informed choice in prenatal testing: How well are we doing? *American Journal of Medical Genetics* 106(3): 185–90.

Marx, K., and Engels, F. (1947 [1846]). *The German Ideology*, parts 1 and 3. New York: International Publishers.

Meinhard, A., and Foster, M. (1996). *Women's Voluntary Organzations and the Restructuring of Canada's Voluntary Sector: A Theoretical Perspective.* Working Paper Series, no. 6. Toronto: Ryerson University School of Business, Centre for Voluntary Sector Studies. Retrieved 26 Oct. 2007 from http://www.ryerson.ca/cvss/work.html.

Michalski, J., Alaggia, R., and Trocmé, N. (1996). *A Literature Review of Risk Assessment Models.* Toronto: University of Toronto, Faculty of Social Work,Centre for Applied Social Research.

Mills, C. Wright. (1959). *The Sociological Imagination.* New York: Oxford University Press.

Monahan, J., Steadman, H., Silver, E., Appelbaum, P., Robbins, P., Mulvey, E., Roth, L., Grisso, T., and Banks, S. (2001). *Rethinking Risk Assessment: The MacArthur Study of Mental Disorder and Violence.* New York: Oxford University Press.

Monahan, J., Steadman, H., Appelbaum, P., Robbins, P., Mulvey, E., Silver, E., Roth, L., and Grisso, T. (2000). Developing a clinically useful actuarial tool for assessing violence risk. *British Journal of Psychiatry* 176: 312–19.

Monahan, J., and Steadman, H. J. (Eds.). (1994). *Violence and Mental Disorder: Developments in Risk Assessment.* Chicago: University of Chicago Press.

Monbiot, G. (2007, 28 Aug.). How the neoliberals stitched up the wealth of nations for themselves. *Guardian*, 27.

Moore, M. (2007). *Sicko.* A film directed by Michael Moore.

Morgen, S. (2001). The agency of welfare workers: Negotiating devolution, privatization, and the meaning of self-sufficiency. *American Anthropologist* 103(3): 747–60.

Mulvale, J. (2001). *Reimagining Social Welfare: Beyond the Keynesian Welfare State.* Aurora: Garamond.

Munro, E., and Rumgay, J. (2000). Role of risk assessment in reducing homicides by people with mental illness. *British Journal of Psychiatry* 176: 116–20.

Mwarigha, M.S. (2002). *Towards a Framework for Local Responsibility: Taking Action to End the Current Limbo in Immigrant Settlement – Toronto*. Toronto: Maytree Foundation.

National Council of Welfare. (2006). *Welfare Incomes 2005*. Ottawa: Author.

National Council of Welfare. (1979). *In the Best Interests of the Child*. Ottawa: Author.

Neumann, W. (1991). *Social Research Methods*. Boston: Allyn and Bacon.

New York Department of Social Services. (1992 and 1994). *The New York State Risk Assessment and Services Planning Model*. Publication 1160. New York: State of New York.

Neysmith, S. (Ed.). (2000). *Restructuring Caring Labour: Discourse, State Practice and Everyday Life*. Toronto: Oxford University Press.

Novak, M. (2007). Summoned to stewardship: Make poverty reduction a collective legacy. Toronto: Campaign 2000. Retrieved 26 Oct. 2008 from www.campaign2000.ca.

OECD Social Indicators, Society at a glance: 2006 edition. (2007). Retrieved 30 Oct. 2008 from http://fiordiliji.sourceoecd.org/pdf/society_glance/10.pdf.

Oldershaw, L. (2002). *A National Survey of Parents of Young Children*. Ottawa: Invest in Kids Foundation.

O'Malley, P. (2004). *Risk, Uncertainty and Government*. London: Glasshouse.

O'Malley, P. (1999). Governmentality and the risk society. *Economy and Society* 28(1): 138–48.

Omidvar, R., and Richmond, T. (2003). *Settlement and Social Inclusion in Canada*. Working Paper Series: Perspectives on Social Inclusion. Toronto: Laidlaw Foundation.

O'Neil, P. (2007, 28 June). Vancouver a scarred paradise, U.N. says. *Vancouver Sun*. Retrieved 24 Oct. 2007 from http://www.canada.com/vancouver-sun/story.html?id=2acd99cd-3017-47ce-8e49-437d83bd7411&k=61909.

Ontario Association of Children's Aid Societies. (2008, 1 Oct.). *Report on Children in Care across Ontario*. Retrieved 27 Jan. 2009 from http://www.cashn.on.ca/index.php/2008/10/14/report-on-children-in-care-across-ontario/

Ontario Association of Children's Aid Societies. (2007). Personal communication.

Ontario Association of Children's Aid Societies. (2000*). Ontario Child Welfare Eligibility Spectrum*. Toronto: Author.

Ontario Association of Children's Aid Societies. (1998). *Inquest Recommendations by Topic*. Toronto: Author.

Ontario Child Welfare Secretariat. (2006). *Child Protection Standards in Ontario. Toronto: Ministry of Children and Youth Services.* Toronto: Author.

Ontario Ministry of Children and Youth Services. (2007). *Ontario Child Protection Tools Manual.* Retrieved 9 Jan. 2009 from http://www.gov.on.ca/children/graphics/stel02_179888.pdf.

Ontario Risk Assessment Model (ORAM). (1998, 2000). Toronto: Ontario Ministry of Community and Social Services.

Ornstein, M. (2000). *Ethno-Racial Inequality in the City of Toronto: An Analysis of the 1996 Census.* Toronto: City of Toronto.

Papaioannou, A., Parkinson, W., Cook, R., Ferko, N., Coker, E., and Adachi, J. (2004, 21 Jan.). Prediction of falls using a risk assessment tool in the acute care setting. *BMC Med* 2: 1. Published online. Retrieved 22 Jan. 2008 from http://www.pubmedcentral.nih.gov/articlerender.fcgi?artid=333435.

Parada, H. (2004). Social work practices within the restructured child welfare system in Ontario. *Canadian Social Work Review* 21(1): 67–85.

Parsloe, P. (1999). *Risk Assessment in Social Care and Social Work.* London: Jessica Kingsley.

Parton, N. (2008). The change for children program in England: Towards the preventive-surveillance state. *Journal of Law and Society* 35(1): 166–87.

Parton, N. (2006). Every child matters: The shift to prevention whilst strengthening protection in children's services in England. *Children and Youth Services Review* 28(8): 976–92.

Parton, N. (2005). Protecting children in time: Child abuse, child protection and the consequences of modernity. *Sociological Review* 53(3): 579–80.

Parton, N. (2003). Rethinking professional practice: The contributions of social constructionism and the feminist ethics of care. *British Journal of Social Work* 33(1): 1–16.

Parton, N. (1998). Risk, advanced liberalism and child welfare: The need to rediscover uncertainty and ambiguity. *British Journal of Social Work* 28: 5–27.

Parton, N., Thorpe, D., and Wattam, C. (1997). *Child Protection: Risk and the Moral Order.* London: Macmillan.

Pecora, P. (1991). Investigating allegation of child maltreatment: The strengths and limitations of current risk assessment systems. In M. Robin (Ed.), *Assessing Child Maltreatment Reports: The Problems of False Allegations,* 73–92. New York: Haworth.

Pelton, L. (1994). The role of material factors in child abuse and neglect. In G. Melton and D. Barry (Eds.), *Protecting Children from Abuse and Neglect: Foundations for a New National Strategy,* 131–81. London: Guilford.

Pendakur, R. (2000). *Immigrants and the Labour Force: Policy, Regulation and Impact.* Montreal: McGill-Queen's University Press.

Perell, K., Nelson, A., Goldman, R., Luther, S., Prieto-Lewis, N., and Ruben-
stein, L. (2001). Fall risk assessment measures: An analytic review. *Journals
of Gerontology Series A: Biological Sciences and Medical Sciences* 56:
M761–M766.

Petersen, A.R. (1996). Risk and the regulated self: The discourse of health
promotion as politics of uncertainty. *Australia and New Zealand Journal of
Sociology* 32(1): 44–57.

Piven, F., and Cloward, R. (1993). *Regulating the Poor: The Functions of Public
Welfare*, updated ed. New York: Vintage.

Popper, K. (1969). *The Positivist Dispute in German Sociology*. Translated by F.
Adey and D. Frisby. NewYork: Harper and Row.

Powell, J., Geddes, J., Hawton, K., Deeks, J., and Goldacre, M. (2000). Suicide
in psychiatric hospital in-patients: Risk factors and their predictive power.
British Journal of Psychiatry 176: 266–72.

Pressman, S. (2007). The decline of the middle class: An international perspective. *Journal of Economic Issues* 41: 181–201.

Rankin, J., and Campbell, M. (2006). *Managing to Nurse: Inside Canada's Health
Care Reform.* Toronto: University of Toronto Press.

Reality. A publication of the Real Women of Canada. (2005, Sept./Oct.).
Increased Government Funding for Feminist Only Organization. Retrieved 22
Oct. 2007 from http://www.realwomenca.com/archives/newsletter/2005
_sept_oct/article_6.html.

Regehr, C., Chau, S., Leslie, B., and Howe, P. (2002). Inquiries into deaths of
children in care: The impact on child welfare workers and their organization. *Children and Youth Services Review* 24(12): 885–902.

Regehr, C., Chau, S., Leslie, B., and Howe, P. (2002). An exploration of supervisors' and managers' responses to child welfare reform. *Administration in
Social Work* 26(3): 17–36.

Reitz, J.G. (2001). Immigrant skill utilization in the Canadian labour market:
Implications of human capital research. *Journal of International Migration
and Integration* 2(3): 347–78.

Rigakos, G. (2002). *The New Parapolice: Risk Markets and Commodified Social
Control.* Toronto: University of Toronto Press.

Rigakos, G. (1999). Hyperpanoptics as commodity: The case of the parapolice. *Canadian Journal of Sociology* 24(3): 381.

Rigakos, G., and Hadden, R. (2001). Crime, capitalism and the risk society.
Theoretical Criminology 5(1): 61–84.

Risley-Curtiss, C., and Heffernan, K. (2003). Gender biases in child welfare.
Affilia 8(4): 395–410.

Roberts, D. (2000). Race and the politics of child welfare. *Institute for Policy Research News* 21(1). Retreived 26 Oct. 2007 from www.northwestern.edu /ipr/publications/newsletter/iprn0006/roberts.html.

Robertson, S. (1999). Risky business: Market provision, community governance and the individualization of risk in New Zealand education. *International Studies in Sociology of Education* 9(2): 171–91.

Romaniuk, T. (2008, 11 Dec.) *Supreme Court Strikes Down Portions of Employment Insurance Act.* Centre for Constitutional Studies. Retrieved 5 Jan 2009 from http://www.law.ualberta.ca/centres/ccs/news/?id=216.

Rosanvallon, P. (2000). *The New Social Question: Rethinking the Welfare State.* Princeton: Princeton University Press.

Rose, N. (1998). Governing risky individuals: The role of psychiatry in new regimes of control. *Psychiatry, Psychology and Law* 5(2): 177–99.

Rose, N. (1996a). Governing 'advanced' liberal democracies. In A. Barry, T. Osborne, and N. Rose (Eds.), *Foucault and Political Reason: Liberalism, Neoliberalism and Rationalities of Government*, 37–64. Chicago: University of Chicago Press.

Rose, N. (1996b). The death of the social? Re-figuring the territory of government. *Economy and Society* 25(3): 327–56.

Rose, N. (1996c). Psychiatry as a political science: Advanced liberalism and the administration of risk. *History of the Human Sciences* 9(2): 1–23.

Royal Society of Britain. (1992). *Risk: Analysis, Perception and Management.* London: Author.

Rutman, D., Callahan, M., Lundquist, A., Jackson, S., and Field, B. (2000). *Substance Use and Pregnancy: Conceiving Women in the Policy Making Process.* Ottawa: Status of Women Canada.

Rutman, D., Strega, S., Callahan, M., and Dominelli, L. (2002). 'Undeserving' mothers? Practitioners' experiences working with young mothers in/from care. *Child and Family Social Work* 7(3): 149–59.

Rycus, J.S., and Hughes, R.C. (2003). *Issues in Risk Assessment in Child Protective Services.* Columbus,OH: North American Resource Center for Child Welfare.

Saint-Martin, D. (2004). *Coordinating Interdependence: Governance and Social Policy Redesign in Britain, the European Union and Canada.* Ottawa: Canadian Policy Review Networks.

Salamon, M., Anheier, H., and Associates. (1999). Civil society in comparative perspective. In *Global Civil Society: Dimension of the Nonprofit Sector*, 1–40. Baltimore: Johns Hopkins Center for Civil Society Studies.

Saunders, D. (2007, 4 Aug.) The secrets of Canada's world-leading middle-class success. *Globe and Mail*, F4.

Savoie, D. (Ed.). (1993). *Taking power. Managing government transitions.* Toronto: Institute of Public Administration.

Scanlon, E., and Devine, K. (2001). Residential mobility and youth well-being: Research, policy and practice issues. *Journal of Sociology and Social Welfare* 28(1):119–38.

Scott, A. (2000). Risk society or angst society? Two views of risk, consciousness and community. In B. Adam, U. Beck, and J. Van Loon (Eds.), *The Risk Society and Beyond: Critical Issues for Social Theory*, 33–46. London: Sage.

Scott, J. (1995). Some thoughts on theory development in the voluntary and nonprofit sector. *Nonprofit and Voluntary Sector Quarterly* 24: 31–40.

Scott, K. (2003). *Funding Matters: The Impact of Canada's New Funding Regime on the Nonprofit and Voluntary Sector.* Ottawa: Canadian Council on Social Development.

Serin, R., Mailloux, C., and Hucker, S. (2001). The utility of clinical and actuarial assessments of offenders in pre-release psychiatric decision-making. *Forum on Corrections Research* 13(2): 36.

Shapcott, M. (2001). *The Ontario Alternative Budget 2001.* Technical Paper 12. Ottawa: Canadian Centre for Policy Alternatives.

Shortt, A.L., Fealy, S., and Toumbourou, J.W. (2006). The mental health Risk Assessment and Management Process (RAMP) for schools, II: Process evaluation. *Australian Journal for the Advancement of Mental Health* 5(3). Retrieved 3 Oct. 2007 from www.auseinet.com/journal/vol5iss3/shortt.pdf.

Simon, J. (2005). Reversal of fortune: The resurgence of individual risk assessment in criminal justice. *Annual Review of Law and Social Science* 1: 397–421.

Simon, J. (1998). Managing the monstrous: Sex offenders and the new penology. *Psychology, Public Policy and Law* 4(1/2): 452–67.

Simon, J. (1988). The ideological effects of actuarial practices. *Law and Society Review* 22(4): 771–800.

Simon, J. (1987). The emergence of a risk society: Insurance, law, and the state. *Socialist Review* 95: 61–89.

Smith, B., and Donovan, S. (2003). Child welfare practice in organizational and institutional context. *Social Service Review* 77(4): 541–63.

Smith, D.E. (2005). *Institutional Ethnography: A Sociology for People.* Toronto: Altamira Press.

Smith, D. (1990). *The Conceptual Practices of Power: A Feminist Sociology of Knowledge.* Toronto: University of Toronto Press.

Smith, J., Forster, A., and Young, J. (2006). Use of the STRATIFY falls risk assessment in patients recovering from acute stroke. *Age and Ageing* 35(2): 138–43.

Soros, G. (1998). *The Crisis of Capitalism*. New York: Public Affairs.

Splane, R. (1965). *Social Welfare in Ontario, 1791–1893: A Study of Public Welfare Administration*. Toronto: University of Toronto Press.

Starr, R., DePanfilis, D., and Hyde, M. (1994). Current issues in risk assessment. In T. Tatara (Ed.), *Seventh National Roundtable on CPS Risk Assessment*, 183–98.Washington: American Public Welfare Association.

Statistics Canada. (2007, 12 June). Women hold more degrees, but still earn lower wages. *CBC News*.

Statistics Canada. (2003). *Canada's Ethnocultural Portrait: The Changing Mosaic*. Ottawa: Minister of Industry.

Statistics Canada. (2001). *Aboriginal Peoples of Canada*. Ottawa: Author. Retrieved 4 June 2008 from http://www12.statcan.ca/english/census01/Products/Analytic/companion/abor/canada.cfm#2.

Stone, D. (1989). At risk in the welfare state. *Social Research* 56(5): 591–623.

Strega, S., and Carriere, J. (2009). *Walking This Path Together: Anti-Racist and Anti-Oppressive Child Welfare Practice*. Halifax: Fernwood.

Strega, S., Fleet, C., Brown, L. Dominelli, L., Callahan, M., and Walmsley, C. (2008). Connecting father absence and mother blame in child welfare policies and practices. *Children and Youth Services Review* 30(7): 705–16

Svensson, L. (2006). New professionalism, trust and competence: Some conceptual remarks and empirical data. *Current Sociology* 54(4): 579–93.

Swift, K. (In press). Risky women: The role of 'risk' in the construction of the single mother. In S. Gavigan and D. Chunn (Eds.), *The Legal Tender of Gender: Historical and Contemporary Perspectives on Welfare Law, State Policies and the Regulation of Women's Poverty*. Oxford: Hart Publishing.

Swift, K. (2001). The case for opposition: An examination of contemporary child welfare policy directions. *Canadian Review of Social Policy* 47 (Spring): 59–76.

Swift, K. (1995a). *Manufacturing 'Bad Mothers': Critical Perspectives on Child Neglect*. Toronto: University of Toronto Press.

Swift, K. (1995b). An outrage to common decency: Historical perspectives on child neglect. *Child Welfare* 74(1): 71–91.

Swift, K. (1995c). Missing Persons: Women in Child Welfare. *Child Welfare* 74(2): 486–502.

Swift, K., and Parada, H. (2004). Child welfare reform: Protecting children or policing the poor? *Journal of Law and Social Policy* 19: 1–17.

Tator, C., and Henry, F. (2006). *Racial Profiling in Canada: Challenging the Myth of a Few Bad Apples*. Toronto: University of Toronto Press.

Taylor-Gooby, P., and Zinn, J. (2005). *Current Directions in Risk Research: Rein-*

vigorating the Social? Economic and Social Research Council, Social Contexts and Responses to Risk Network, Working Paper 2005/8. Canterbury: University of Kent at Canterbury, School of Social Policy.

Taylor-Gooby, P., Dean, H., Munro, M., and Parker, G. (1999). Risk and the welfare state. *British Journal of Sociology* 50(2): 177–94.

Teeple, G. (2004). *The Riddle of Human Rights*. Aurora: Garamond.

Tierney, K. (1999). Toward a critical sociology of risk. *Sociological Forum* 14(2): 215–42.

Torjman, S. (2000). *Employment Insurance: Small Bang for Big Bucks*. Ottawa: Caledon Institute of Social Policy. Retrieved 18 Oct. 2008 from http://www.caledoninst.org/Publications/PDF/1-894159-89-6.pdf.

Tremper, C., and Kostin, G. (1997). *No Surprises: Controlling Risk in Volunteer Programs*. Washington: Non-Profit Risk Management Center.

Trocmé, N., and Lindsey, D. (1996). What can child homicide rates tell us about the effectiveness of child welfare services? *Child Abuse and Neglect* 20(3): 171–84.

Trocmé, N., Fallon, B., MacLaurin, B., Daciuk, J., Felstiner, C., Black, T., et al. (2005). *Canadian Incidence Study of Reported Child Abuse and Neglect – 2003: Major Findings*. Ottawa: Minister of Public Works and Government Services Canada.

Tronto, J. (1993). *Moral Boundaries: A Political Argument for an Ethic of Care*. New York: Routledge.

Tsui, M., and Cheung, F. (2004). Gone with the wind: The impacts of managerialism on human services. *British Journal of Social Work* 34: 437–42.

Ungar, M. (2007). *Too Safe for Their Own Good*. Toronto: McClelland and Stewart.

United Nations Population Fund (UNFPA). (2006). *Annual Report*. New York: United Nations. Retrieved 22 Oct. 2008 from http://67.205.103.77/about/reoprt/2006/poverty.html.

United States Department of Health and Human Services, Department of Children and Families. (2005, April). *National Survey of Children and Adolescent Well-Being (NSCAW): CPS Sample Component Wave 1 Data Analysis Report*. Retrieved 23 Aug. 2008 from http://www.acf.hhs.gov/programs/opre/abuse_neglect/nscaw/reports/cps_sample/cps_toc.ht ml.

United States Department of Homeland Security. (2006). *Automated Targeting System*. Retrieved 24 May 2007 from http://www.dhs.gov/xlibrary/assets/privacy/privacy_pia_cbp_ats.pdf.

Useem, M. (1987). Corporate philanthropy. In W.W. Powell (Ed.), *The Nonprofit Sector: A Research Handbook*, 340–59. New Haven: Yale University Press.

Victoria Cool Aid Society. (2007). *Housing First – Plus Supports: Summarizing the Results of the 2007 Homeless Needs Survey Conducted from February 5 to 9, 2007, in the Capital Regional District of British Columbia, Canada.* Victoria: Author.

Viner, R., and Taylor, B. (2005). Adult health and social outcomes of children who have been in public care: Population-based study. *Pediatrics* 115(4): 894–9.

Waerness, K. (1996). On the rationality of caring. In S. Gordon, P. Benner, and N. Noddings (Eds.), *Caregiving: Readings in Knowledge, Practice, Ethics and Politics,* 231–55. Philadelphia: University of Pennsylvania Press.

Wald, M., and Woolverton, M. (1990). Risk assessment: The emperor's new clothes? *Child Welfare* 69(6): 483–511.

Webb, S. (2006). *Social Work in a Risk Society.* Houndmills, U.K., and New York: Palgrave Macmillian.

Weber, M. (1970 [1946]). Science as a vocation. In H.H. Gerth and C. Wright Mills (Eds.), *From Max Weber: Essays in Sociology,* 129–58. London: Routledge and Kegan Paul.

Weller, F., and Wharf, B. (1997). *From Risk Assessment to Family Action Planning.* Victoria: University of Victoria, School of Social Work, Child, Family and Community Research Program.

Welsh, M. (2007, 30 July). Senior care 'revolution' faltering. *Toronto Star,* A1 and A17.

Welsh, M. (2007, 20 April). Stopping a killer is not that easy. *Toronto Star,* A6.

Welsh, M. (2006, 6 Dec.). Agencies slow to track at-risk kids: Auditor. *Toronto Star,* A4 and A7.

Wilensky, H. (1964). The professionalization of everyone. *American Journal of Sociology* 70(2): 137–59.

Wilkinson, I. (2001a). *Anxiety in a Risk Society.* London: Routledge.

Wilkinson, I. (2001b). Social theories of risk perception: At once indispensable and insufficient. *Current Sociology* 49(1): 1–22.

Wolfe, J. (2006). Risk, fear, blame shame and the regulation of public safety. *Economics and Philosophy* 22(3): 409–27.

Wong-Yim, P., Sarmiento, L., Wade, M., Davis, B., Anderson, M. (2006). A Decision Tree Incorporating Vapor Intrusion into Screening Risk Assessments of Hazardous Waste Sites. Presented at the 45th Annual Meeting of the Society of Toxicology, 7 March, San Diego, California.

Wood, E. (2003). *Empire of Capital.* London: Verso.

World Bank. (2006). *Global Economic Prospects 2006.* Washington: Author.

Yalnizyan, A. (2005). Canada's commitment to equality: A gender analysis of the last ten budgets, and will community voices shape public choices? *Perception* 27(3/4): 3.

Yin, R. (2003). *Case Study Research*. Thousand Oaks: Sage.

Young, P.C., and Tomski, M. (2002). An introduction to risk management. *Physical Medicine and Rehabilitation Clinics of North America* 13(2): 225–46.

Index

success of, 48–9; and surveillance,
46; universalization of, 212;
waning of, 9–10. *See also* social
programs
Welsh, M., 157
Wildavsky, A., 30, 36–7
Wilkinson, I., 33, 35, 50, 51
women: and Employment Insurance,
73; employment of, 82; organizations, 79–80; and semi-professions,
92. *See also* gender; mothers
Wood, E., 34

work. *See* employment
work practices. *See* social work
practices
workers. *See* child welfare workers; front-line workers; social
workers
workfare, 46, 72
workload: case closures and, 157;
documentation and, 146; risk
management and, 224

Yin, R., 235